Hitchcock as Activist
Politics and the War Films

Studies in Cinema, No. 36

Diane M. Kirkpatrick, Series Editor

Professor, History of Art
The University of Michigan

Other Titles in This Series

Hitchcock as Activist
Politics and the War Films

by
Sam P. Simone

UMI RESEARCH PRESS
Ann Arbor, Michigan

Produced and distributed by
UMI Research Press
an imprint of
University Microfilms International
A Xerox Information Resources Company
Ann Arbor, Michigan 48106

Library of Congress Cataloging in Publication Data

Simone, Sam P., 1945-
  Hitchcock as activist.

    (Studies in cinema ; no. 36)
    Revision of thesis (Ph.D.)—Brigham Young
University, 1982.
    Bibliography: p.
    Includes index.
    1. Hitchcock, Alfred, 1899-   2. World War,
1939-1945—Motion pictures and the war.   I. Title.
II. Series.
PN1998.A3H558   1985   791.43'0233'0924   85-1035
ISBN 0-8357-1654-6 (alk. paper)

To my best friend and loving wife, Linda.
No one did more in helping me
toward the successful completion
of this work than she.

(Courtesy Stanley Caidin, Caidin Film Company)

Contents

Acknowledgments

I am grateful for the sponsorship of the Department of Theatre and Cinematic Arts at Brigham Young University which made the publication of this book possible. I wish to thank Harold Oaks, Charles Metten, Tad Danielewski, Marion Bentley and Robert Nelson, faculty members of the Department, whose encouragement and assistance greatly facilitated this project. I am grateful to Don Norton of the English Department at B.Y.U. and his student assistants, whose keen intellects and editorial skills made easier the editing of this book. I wish to thank Linda Mortensen and C. J. Cheney, who typed the original manuscript. Finally, I am grateful to Woodie and George, teachers at Mesa College, San Diego, who encouraged my academic career in theatre and cinematic arts.

Preface

Film critics, historians, and biographers extol Alfred Hitchcock as the cinematic master of suspense and the psychological drama. However, Alfred Hitchcock is more than a mere showman in his film art. I will show him to be a staunch activist in his support of freedom and liberty. His films champion the United States, whose government personifies and extends national and international democracy as the basic political form of the free-world ethic.

This book parallels selected films of Alfred Hitchcock with political history to ascertain his political ideology concerning World War II. His feature films, as ideological and historical documents, manifest the conflict between democracy and Nazism in the classical dramatic form of the conflict between protagonist and antagonist. Hitchcock's heroes and their associates are mainly protagonists who support democracy, while his villains and their associates are the antagonists who support Nazism. The dramatic forms of melodrama and suspense are the primary structural components of these films. They contain a definite propaganda level, well integrated yet discernible at the entertainment level. Although Hitchcock's films do not relate to specific historical events in macrocosm, they do relate directly and in creative microcosmic representation to historical events of World War II.

The following three questions are explored and answered in this book: how World War II espionage and sabotage are made evident in Hitchcock's films of that period; what political ideology is advocated in selected Hitchcock films of World War II and how it parallels the ideology of the United States; and how Alfred Hitchcock creates and resolves suspense in his political films.

Chapters are organized as follows: Chapter 1 describes Alfred Hitchcock's background, emphasizing his desire for personal, professional, and political freedom. In the four chapters that follow, four Hitchcock films are paralleled with political history: *Foreign Correspondent* (1940), with the progressive deterioration and termination of the United States isolation policy and entrance into World War II; *Saboteur* (1942), with the threat and reality of sabotage in the United States; *Lifeboat* (1944), with national and international dissension concerning World War II; and *Notorious* (1946), with espionage and the development of the atomic bomb. Chapter 6 answers the three questions raised in this preface. These four films were selected for this book because their plots show major concern for the historical and political realities of World War II.

1

The Background Years: 1899–1939

The Early Years

Alfred Hitchcock was born in London on August 13, 1899. Although his early life was filled with happy experiences and memories, two incidents stood out as psychological traumas.

When Hitchcock was small, he woke up one Sunday evening to find his parents gone and a maid waiting over him. Such parental abandonment terrified him. He retained this incident in his conscious mind through his adult life, and after the birth of his daughter, Patricia, it caused him to decree to his wife, Alma Reville, that there would always be hot Sunday dinners, and that they as parents would always be in calling distance of Patricia during her childhood.[1]

The second traumatic incident in Hitchcock's early life is the now famous story of his police station experience.

> I suppose the earliest thing I can think of is when my father . . . sent me with a note to the local chief of police, who glanced at the little piece of paper and then led me along a corridor and I was locked in a cell for five minutes. Then he let me out and said, "That's what we do to naughty boys." I always think it was the clang of the door which was the potent thing—the sound and the solidity of that closing door and the bolt. But it hasn't altered the fact, even though I can trace that episode so many years ago, that I'm still scared of policemen. In fact, I don't drive a car on the simple fact that if you don't drive a car you can't get a ticket. I mean, the getting of a ticket, to me, is a rather suspenseful matter.[2]

The trauma of these two experiences inclined Hitchcock to create a visual form of anxiety in the film world: suspense. The twentieth century has been appropriately called the "age of anxiety"; in Richard Schickel's judgment the films of Hitchcock would permit vicarious cathartic release for his audiences from at least some of the anxieties of the time.[3]

Hitchcock's youthful hobbies centered around the freedom afforded through real and imagined travel. "As a young boy he was possessed by wanderlust, and by the time he was eight he had ridden every bus line in London and explored all its docks and shipping terminals." A second hobby involved imaginary journeys of adventure through "keeping tabs on the British merchant fleet by purchasing 'Lloyd's Bulletin,' a shipping newspaper, and then scurrying home to plot the ships' positions on a huge wall chart.''[4] A third hobby concerned his fascination with New York City. Hitchcock recounts, "I used to send for train schedules . . . and I knew many of the timetables by heart. Years before I ever came here, I could describe New York, tell you where the theatres and stores were located.''[5] These hobbies were Hitchcock's ways to explore freely the environment of London and vicariously, the world. Journeys on buses all over London gave him great knowledge of the physical city and confidence to do on-location shooting when his film career began.

Alfred Hitchcock's parents were devout Catholics, and the young boy was sent to St. Ignatius College, a Jesuit institution. In recalling his school days, Hitchcock talked about the Jesuits and how they implemented a strict order of punishment that created a situation of prolonged fear in him:

> It was probably during this period with the Jesuits that a strong sense of fear developed—moral fear—the fear of being involved in anything evil. I always tried to avoid it. Why? Perhaps out of physical fear. I was terrified of physical punishment. In those days they used a cane made of very hard rubber. I believe the Jesuits still use it. It wasn't done casually, you know; it was rather like the execution of a sentence. They would tell you to step in to see the father when classes were over. He would then solemnly inscribe your name in the register, together with the indication of the punishment to be inflicted, and you spent the whole day waiting for the sentence to be carried out.[6]

In the leisure time of his middle and late teenage years, Hitchcock independently pursued his growing interest in cinema through attending film screenings and reading cinema trade magazines. He became aware of films in production throughout the world and determined he would one day be part of the production world of film. American and German films influenced Hitchcock more than British films. These two sources gave Hitchcock the works of "Chaplin, Griffith, all the Paramount Famous Players pictures, Buster Keaton, Douglas Fairbanks, Mary Pickford, as well as the German films of Delca-Bioscop, the company that preceded UFA.''[7]

From St. Ignatius College, Hitchcock matriculated to the University of London, where he entered a course to prepare him for work as an electrical engineer. He studied acoustics, electricity, mechanics, and navigation.[8] But the matter of making a living forced him to leave school to find a job.

W. T. Henley Telegraph Company, a firm engaged in the manufacture of electric cables, provided the eighteen-year-old Hitchcock with a job as a technical clerk. In a matter of weeks, he advanced from technical clerk to estimator clerk. Even this work, however, was no challenge to him.

> As an estimator he would constantly have requests for estimates arrive on his desk, would let them pile up, and then deal with them all in a brief frenzy of activity which impressed his superiors with the extraordinary amount of work he had done that particular day. Until, that is, complaints started to come in about the inordinate delays certain customers were experiencing in receiving their estimates.[9]

The management personnel at Henley's liked the bright young Hitchcock. They knew he was taking a night class in graphic arts—drawing and illustration—at London University under E. J. Sullivan.[10] Furthermore, Hitchcock delighted his fellow workers when he drew humorous caricatures of them, which appeared in the firm's house magazine. He was also to contribute articles and suspense stories. One example of such talent appeared in June, 1919, in Henley's Social Club magazine. It was entitled "Gas," and signed "Hitch."

> She had never been in this part of Paris before . . . So this was the Montmartre? That horror where danger lurked under cover of night, where innocent souls perished without warning—where doom confronted the unwary—where the Apache revelled.
>
> She moved cautiously in the shadow of the high wall, looking furtively backward for the hidden menace that might be dogging her steps. Suddenly she darted into an alley way, little heeding where it led—groping her way on in the inky blackness, the one thought of eluding the pursuit firmly fixed in her mind—on she went——Oh! when would it end?——Then a doorway from which a light streamed lent itself to her vision——In here——anywhere, she thought.
>
> The door stood at the head of a flight of stairs——stairs that creaked with age, as she endeavoured to creep down——then she heard the sound of drunken laughter and shuddered—surely this was—No, not that! Anything but that! She reached the foot of the stairs and saw an evil-smelling wine bar, with wrecks of what were once men and women indulging in a drunken orgy—— then they saw her, a vision of affrighted purity. Half a dozen men rushed towards her amid the encouraging shouts of the rest. She was seized. She screamed with terror—better had she been caught by her pursuer, was her one fleeting thought, as they dragged her roughly across the room. The fiends lost no time in settling her fate. They would share her belongings—and she—the rats should feast. Then they bound her and carried her down the dark passage. Up a flight of stairs to the riverside. The water rats should feast, they said. And then——then swinging her bound body to and fro, dropped her with a splash into the dark swirling waters. Down she went, down, down; conscious only of a choking sensation, this was death——then—
> —"It's out, Madam," said the dentist. "Half a crown please."[11]

After Hitchcock was promoted to Henley's advertising department, in charge of writing and editing copy for newspapers and advertisements, he loved his work. Illustrations and layouts were also his responsibility. Friends and fellow workers were amazed at Hitchcock's willingness to remain late at night because of the esthetic pleasure he derived from checking late arrivals of proofs of future advertisements. "For the first time some call was being made on his imagination and powers of invention; for the first time he was in the business of directing the public's responses through practical psychology."[12]

The Formative Years in Filmmaking: 1920–1929

Although Hitchcock found his new job enjoyable and challenging, it was only a forerunner of professional artistic development for his entrance into film. One day in 1920, Hitchcock read in a cinema trade magazine that Paramount's Famous Players-Lasky was going to open a studio in London. He had always been intrigued by the technical excellence and superiority of American films. Hitchcock related what went through his mind at this time. "It never occurred to me to go and offer my services to a British company; yet, as soon as I read that an American company was going to open a studio, I said to myself, 'I want to do their titles.'"[13]

Walter Wanger, a prominent American producer, explains how Hitchcock landed his first job in film.

> [Hitchcock] felt that film title cards were atrocious and decided to design some to present to the new producers. He worked for five days and nights, carefully lettering art title cards using the names of the first announced production, *The Sorrows of Satan*, to fill out the list of credits.
>
> After battling past the army of secretaries to the assistants, he somehow managed to wrangle his way to the top man, who looked at Hitchcock's work and informed him that he was in England to make not *The Sorrows of Satan* but another film altogether. Persistent as ever, Hitchcock created a whole new batch of title cards for the right film, *The Great Day*, which the producer saw and liked.
>
> In his new job as a title writer for Famous Players-Lasky, Hitchcock added symbolic drawings to the otherwise unadorned titles. This was something novel and attracted attention.[14]

Alfred Hitchcock, by the age of twenty, had taken the initiative to develop his drawing, illustrating, and writing talents. Now he had acquired a new job in the world of film as a film title designer. The next ten years of his life in film would give him exposure to American, German, Russian, and English cinema. His formative years of developing filmmaking techniques (1920–1925), and four films he directed (1925–1929), foreshadow his years of fruition in the 1930s.

Multiple artistic talents permitted Hitchcock many experiences in the collective art form of film. The 1920s were the beginning of Hitchcock's eclectic film education in the predominantly silent cinema. From 1920 to 1922, Hitchcock wrote and designed the title cards for four films: *Call of Youth*, *The Great Day*, *Princess of New York*, and *Tell Your Children*.[15]

Paramount abandoned the Islington Studios in 1922 because its films were not making money. Hitchcock was left without a job. When Sir Seymour Hicks asked Hitchcock if he would like to help him finish a film, the title card designer became the assistant director on *Always Tell Your Wife* (1922).

The void created by Paramount was to be filled by a new English film company, Gainsborough, with Michael Balcon, Victor Saville, and John Freedman as the main founders and producers. Hitchcock helped them move in and promptly received a job as assistant director to Graham Cutts. The job lasted for three years (1922–1925). He also wrote scripts and designed sets for *Woman to Woman*, *The White Shadow*, *The Passionate Adventure*, *The Blackguard*, and *The Prude's Fall*. John Russell Taylor explains how Hitchcock became an auspicious jack-of-all-trades for Gainsborough:

> When they needed someone to write a script for *Woman to Woman* based on the play they had bought, [Hitchcock] volunteered to do that, too. They asked what evidence he could produce that he was capable of doing such a job; he brought out the practice script, they were impressed and

he got that job, too, working in collaboration with the director, Graham Cutts. But that was not all. During his earlier time at Islington he had become friendly with an art director who had originally been slated to work on *Woman to Woman* and who had recommended him to the company. But then it turned out that the art director could not design the film after all, and so Hitchcock, with his background in design and draughtsmanship, volunteered to do that, too. All he needed, he said, was a draughtsman, some carpenters and a bit of other practical help. And so, to his great pleasure, he was able to hire back nearly all the people he knew who had been thrown out of work with the closing down of Famous Players-Lasky [16]

The Blackguard (1924) was shot at the UFA studios in Germany. Hitchcock, a teenage admirer of German film, worked as a writer, designer, and assistant director on this joint English-German venture. The year 1924 was the apex of the German expressionistic movement. Hitchcock was very much interested in the German methods of art design and direction. The production of the film *Sunrise*, directed by F. W. Murnau, was especially captivating for Hitchcock.

> Hitch watched fascinated whenever he had the chance, and was particularly impressed by the art of Robert Herlth and Walter Rohrig, Murnau's art directors. There seemed to be no trick in the book that they did not know and exploit. One day Hitch watched Murnau setting up and shooting a short scene on the platform of a railway station where a train had just come in. The carriage nearest the camera was the real thing, with passengers getting on and off. Then the next few carriages were constructed in forced perspective to give the impression of receding into the distance in a very small space. But such was Murnau's concern for detail that to give life to the background he had placed another full-size railway carriage in the far distance across the lot, with passengers getting in and out of it, in such a way that when photographed the foreshortened fake carriages would neatly join up the two far-separated real carriages. What you can see on the set is what you see on the screen. It was a lesson Hitch was never to forget.[16]

After finishing *The Blackguard* and *The Prude's Fall*, Graham Cutts, the director of these films, went to Michael Balcon and told him he no longer wanted to use Hitchcock as an assistant director. Cutts was jealous of Hitchcock's "boy wonder" status and felt he was getting too much credit. Hal Young, Cutts' cameraman, disliked Hitchcock for no apparent reason and poisoned Cutts' mind against his assistant director. Michael Balcon decided it was time for Hitchcock to become a director. When asked by Balcon whether he would like to direct a picture, Hitchcock replied, "I've never thought about it."[18] Balcon asked him to think about it. Hitchcock did and responded "Alright, when do we start?"[19]

Hitchcock had progressed from title card writer and designer to director in five years. He was now ready to take on a job that allowed him creative freedom and production responsibility. The four films that helped Hitchcock find and free his esthetic and dramatic form, and became the foundation for his work in the 1930s, were *The Pleasure Garden* (1925), *The Lodger* (1926), *The Farmer's Daughter* (1928), and *Blackmail* (1929).

The Pleasure Garden was memorable to Hitchcock because it was the first film he directed. Also, the numerous problems involved helped Hitchcock to develop perseverance and tenacity—traits of character essential for success in film. The main actors, crew, and Hitchcock were involved in considerable on-location shooting in continental Europe. The customs inspectors at the Italian border would prove to be a minor nemesis to the novice director. Because of the limited budget, the cameraman informed Hitchcock that they did not have the money to pay the customs duty on the camera and unexposed film. The cameraman told him not to worry, remarking to Hitchcock, who was in bed in the sleeper, that the camera and film were under his bed. The director, a man terrified of policemen and authority, broke out in a cold sweat. The customs inspectors failed to find the camera, but they did find 10,000 feet of film and confiscated it. Hitchcock and his crew arrived in Genoa, Italy on a Sunday with no film. Tuesday was the first day of shooting. The police authorities presented them with the confiscated film on Monday, Hitchcock paid the duty, and the on-location shooting for Tuesday was set.[20]

The second incident occurred on Tuesday. Hitchcock reached into his wallet to pay a debt incurred while shooting and found his wallet empty. He had been robbed of 10,000 lira while asleep in his hotel room the night before. A shudder ran through his body as he realized he could have been murdered had he awakened while the theft was taking place.

The third incident happened a few days later. Inadvertently, Hitchcock broke a window getting off a train in Zurich, Switzerland. He was charged 35 francs. Hitchcock arrived in Munich with only one pfennig in his pocket.[21]

For all the mishaps and added expense for the on-location shooting of *The Pleasure Garden*, Michael Balcon was glad to have the film completed. He remarked to Hitchcock that the lighting and cutting style was American. This comment pleased Hitchcock more than the London *Daily Express* praise of him as a "young man with a master mind."[22]

The Lodger (1926) was the third film Hitchcock directed. *The Mountain Eagle*, his second commercial film, had been shelved because the producers felt its sale value would be of no financial consequence at the box office. Today only six frames remain of this film. According to Hitchcock, *The Lodger* was his first genuine film: "*The Lodger* is the first picture possibly influenced by my period in Germany. The whole approach to this film was instinctive with me. It was the first time I exercised my style. In truth, you might almost say that *The Lodger* was my first picture."[23]

The story of Jack the Ripper serves as the basis for the film's plot. Ivor Novello, a matinée idol of the silent screen, plays a tense boarder who is suspected of committing multiple murders in London. This is the first appearance of a theme which would become prevalent in subsequent Hitchcock films: an innocent man accused of a crime and his escape from the police who continue in pursuit.

The Lodger is filled with innovations. For example, Hitchcock has members of a family look up toward the ceiling as they listen to the boarder pacing back and forth in his room. Then the audience sees him pacing back and forth, because Hitchcock has placed Ivor Novello on a thick plate of glass and shot the movement of his feet. This shot actualizes the omnipresent freedom of the camera. Such a subjective shot makes the audience a part of the family and also puts them in a psychologically preyed-upon position by the supposed murderer above them.

Other innovations resulted directly from Hitchcock's exposure in Germany to expressionistic filmmaking techniques.

If the two films Hitch had directed in Germany were very American in style, *The Lodger*, "A Story of the London Fog," was very German: dark shadows, strange angles and disconcerting compositions in order to convey an atmosphere of neurosis and ambiguity. The German cinema at this time had a special corner in atmosphere, and had built up a repertory of visual language— mirrors and reflections, for example, are usually deceiving; stairs are inescapable, the movement of characters on them creating a feeling of elation or dejection, their spiralling up into the shadows strangely unsettling the spectator, he cannot quite say why. All these elements had cropped up in connection with the character of Jack the Ripper two years before in the third episode of Paul Leni's *Waxworks*, a picture which Hitch had certainly seen, either in Germany or at the showings of the new Film Society, which Hitch had joined shortly after its foundation in London in 1925. They crop up again in *The Lodger*, but in almost all respects Hitch's treatment is otherwise very different: Leni's account of Jack the Ripper is all hallucinatory expressionistic fantasy, while Hitch's is clearly rooted, like all his later work, in everyday reality.[24]

A number of people in the front office wondered what Hitchcock was up to in the making of *The Lodger*. On completion of the film, C. M. Woolf, a producer, was scheduled to view it and make a decision on its release. Alfred Hitchcock and his close friend and associate, Alma Reville, spent the afternoon walking from Tower Bridge to the Islington studios in an attempt to lessen their anxiety. They hoped Woolf would like the film and release it. Their hope was in vain. Woolf disliked the film, failed to understand it, and had it shelved. Hitchcock had now made two back-to-back flops.

Two months later, Michael Balcon decided to show *The Lodger* to Ivor Montagu. Montagu was aware of the avant-garde advances of the German and Russian cinema and, like Hitchcock, was a member of the London Film Society, a body established for the serious study of films of both national and international interest and merit. Montagu viewed the film and was stunned by the beautiful balance of realism and expressionism. Moreover, the overall power of the visual story made this film the vanguard in British expressionistic cinema. He worked with Balcon and Hitchcock to promote clarity, so the audience would more readily accept this novel British film. In his study of Hitchcock's British films, Maurice Yacowar notes that:

Montagu recut some sequences . . . had Hitchcock reshoot others, commissioned poster artist E. McKnight Kauffer to design the titles, and trimmed the volume of titles down to a total of eighty, remarkably low for the time. Particularly in light of Hitchcock's later development, however, one still must consider *The Lodger* a Hitchcock film. Happily, neither the critics nor the paying public shared the reservations which the distributor had about the film. *The Lodger* was Hitchcock's first booming success. "It is possible that this film is the finest British production ever made," enthused *Bioscope* (Sept. 16, 1926) in a typical reaction.[25]

The success of *The Lodger* was to cause the producers at Gainsborough to release *The Mountain Eagle*, in an attempt to cash in on the growing popularity of the Hitchcock name and mystique. He had managed the rare achievement of succeeding with the general public and critics alike. *The Lodger* was "an unusually vivid, atmospheric thriller with a comforting happy ending."[26]

The happy ending of this film also led to a happy beginning. Alma Reville and Alfred Hitchcock were married on December 2, 1926. Their life together was to be one of mutual love and respect as they faced the challenges and problems of the cinema world—it was a perfect match.

The Farmer's Wife (1928) is a noteworthy film because it motivated in Hitchcock the desire to use montage. Hitchcock had to work out the camera set-ups himself, because his cameraman fell ill. A definition of montage follows in an excerpt from a conversation between Hitchcock and François Truffaut:

> F. T.: Just the same, the way in which you handled the adaptation from stage to screen reflects a tenacious effort to create pure cinema. At no time, for instance, is the camera placed where the audience would be if the shooting had been done from the stage, but rather as if the camera had been set up in the wings. The characters never move sideways; they move straight toward the camera, more systematically than in your other pictures. It's filmed like a thriller.
>
> A. H.: What you mean is that the camera is inside the action. Well, the idea of photographing actions and stories came about with the development of techniques proper to film. The most significant of these, you know, occurred when D. W. Griffith, improving on the earlier efforts of the British G. A. Smith and the American Edwin S. Porter, began to set the strips of film together in sequence. This was the beginning of cinematographic rhythm through the use of montage.
>
> I don't remember too much about *The Farmer's Wife*, but I know that filming that play stimulated my wish to express myself in purely cinematic terms.[27]

Not only does Hitchcock give a historical review of the prominent men who used montage, he presents a lucid and clear definition of the nebulous term: "the camera is inside the action." The Russian Lev Kuleshov was to demonstrate the montage technique, which Hitchcock had the good fortune to view and, later, abstract.

> And in [Hitchcock's] early days as a director he sees a short film demonstration by the Soviet theorist, Lev Kuleshov. A close-up of the actor Ivan Mosjoukine is followed by a shot of a dead child. Kuleshov cuts back to the same close-up, and Mosjoukine's face appears to be expressing compassion. Then he substitutes a bowl of soup for the dead child and cuts back to the same close-up again. Mosjoukine no longer looks compassionate, but hungry.[28]

According to Hitchcock, pure cinema is complementary pieces of film put together, like notes of music make a melody. "There are two primary uses of cutting or montage in film: montage to create ideas—and montage to create violence and emotions."[29]

The first example given by Kuleshov shows the montage of emotion (death); the second shows the montage of idea (hunger). This type of juxtapositioning of shots was to gain great currency among the Russian filmmakers of the 1920s— chief among them Sergei Eisenstein, whose films were screened by the London Film Society.

The Farmer's Wife, even though it motivated in Hitchcock the desire to create montage, was not the first film in which he used it. *The Lodger*, his silent suspense thriller, was praised by Truffaut because it showed "great visual inventiveness."[30] Hitchcock's own words present a narrative description of a sequence in which a montage of ideas is created visually:

> We took fifteen minutes of a winter afternoon in London, starting about five-twenty. We opened with the head of a blond girl who is screaming. I remember the way I photographed it. I took a sheet of glass and spread her hair around until it filled the frame. Then we lit the glass from behind so that one would be struck by her light hair. Then we cut to show an electric sign advertising a musical play, *Tonight, Golden Curls*, with the reflection flickering in the water. The girl has drowned. She's hauled out of the water and pulled ashore. The consternation of the bystanders suggests that a murder has been committed. The police arrive on the scene, and then the press. The camera follows one of the newsmen as he moved toward a telephone. He isn't a local reporter, but a wire-service man who is calling his office. And now I proceed to show everything that happens as the news spreads around.
>
> First, the item is typed out on the wire-service machine so that we are able to read a few sentences. Then it is forwarded on the teletypes. People in clubs learn the news. Then there is a radio announcement, with people tuned in to the broadcast. Finally, it is flashed on an electric news sign—you know, like on Times Square. And each time, we give additional information, so that you learn more about the crime. The man murders only women. Always blondes. He invariably strikes on a Tuesday. How many he has killed to date. Speculations on his motives. He goes around dressed in a black cloak and carries a black bag.[31]

With the juxtapositioning of shots, a story may be created through the power of progressive visual imagery. Hitchcock's background in art, plus budget considerations, led him to create a storyboard of visuals before the title cards and, later, the dialogue were written. Fort Buckle, a contemporary of Hitchcock, was to advance in theory what Hitchcock advanced in practice:

> I believe that balance and continuity and all other merits of a motion picture should be determined before the studio floor is reached. Only when our producers can visualize their pictures from scenarios shall we be really applying the Mind to the Film; unless we apply the Mind to the Film in the making there is little hope of its being worth while to apply the Mind to the Film after it is made.[32]

The primary concern of the artistic director is to paint the scene through a visually logical succession of pictures. Through visual analysis of cinema we come to agree with Hitchcock that "cinema is a succession of images put together like a sentence."[33] Montage becomes a visual syntax with infinite possibilities:

> You have a man look, you show what he sees, you go back to the man. You can make him react in various ways. You see, you can make him look at one thing, look at another . . . you can show his mind at work, comparing things—any way you run there's complete freedom. It's limitless, I would say, the power of cutting and the assembly of the images.[34]

Montage gave unique visual excitement and interest to Hitchcock's silent films of the 1920s. Influenced by American excellence in film production, German expressionism, and Russian montage, Hitchcock synthesized these methods in films such as *The Farmer's Wife* and *The Lodger*.

However, there was to be yet another innovation, one that would revolutionize the film industry: sound. On October 6, 1927, *The Jazz Singer* opened on Broadway in New York City. Al Jolson, the star of the film, said, "You ain't heard nothin' yet," then broke into song. Dialogue and song ushered in the "talkies," and the silent cinema was suddenly obsolete.[35]

The first commercial sound picture made in England was *Blackmail* (1929), a suspense film directed by Hitchcock. Kenneth MacPherson concluded his adulatory review of *Blackmail* with these words: "Some of us are beginning to say that talkies are an art."[36] Moreover, *Bioscope*, a cinema trade magazine, lavishly praised the film:

> By this masterly production Alfred Hitchcock amply fulfills the promise shown in his earlier efforts. He has given us a story of vital interest, played and directed in a manner which is convincing proof that the talking film affords opportunities to British producers which cannot be equalled in any other country.[37]

Blackmail is memorable on three counts. Hitchcock employed a unique use of sound to heighten the guilty conscience of the heroine; he used the Schufftan process, a combination of a slide and set, to give a more impressive visual reality; and Hitchcock's personal appearance in the film, sitting in a train car reading a book, created a visual ritual.

The use of sound in what is known as the knife scene is unique. The guilty conscience of the heroine, Alice, is transposed to the conscience of the audience through repetition of the word "knife" in the dialogue. Alice returns home in time to slip into her room undetected by her family. The evening before, she had stabbed a painter who had tried to rape her. She is called downstairs, where a breakfast scene follows. The news of the murder has already spread throughout the city, and a neighbor continues to talk about it at the breakfast table as Alice listens in fearful silence. "'What a terrible way to kill a man, with a knife in his back. If I had killed him, I might have struck him over the head with a brick, but I wouldn't use a knife.'"[38] Alice no longer listens, and the word "knife" is repeated again and again, becoming fainter and fainter at each repetition. Hitchcock thus forces the audience to share the aural subjective reality of the heroine's experience through tuning out, as does Alice, the impact of the

guilt-laden word "knife." Just when the audience and heroine alike have found
sanctuary from spoken words, "She hears her father's normal, loud voice:
'Alice, please pass the bread knife.' And Alice has to pick up a knife similar to
the one she used for the killing, while the others go on chattering about the
crime."[39] Sound bridges the guilt of the heroine to the audience's empathetic
identification with her character. We have judged her crime as a matter of self-
preservation and defense of her virtue. She is innocent. The subjective use of
dialogue, sounds, and images, along with the repetition of "knife," creates
anxiety and suspense. We suffer the anxiety that Alice will break, confess, and
be judged guilty of a crime of which we have found her, and ourselves, innocent.

The Schufftan process is used in *Blackmail* because a major chase sequence
in the British Museum could not be shot for lack of sufficient light. This process
involved the use of mirrors set at forty-five degrees to reflect a visually interesting
picture of the Museum.[40] Taylor explains in greater detail how

> Hitch had long-exposure photographs taken from the nine viewpoints from which he would have
> chosen to shoot in the Museum, made transparencies of them so that they could be back-lit to
> give the desired clarity and luminosity, then had the parts of the slides corresponding to the
> places where he wanted to put the live actors scraped away. The slide was then placed close to
> the camera and only the parts of the original setting immediately surrounding the actors built
> full-size so that when photographed the slide and the set fused together. All one might see,
> therefore, on the stage was a man by a door frame looking intently at nothing: the rooms on either
> side of the door frame and the cases of exhibits into which he appeared to be gazing were all on
> the slide.[41]

Hitchcock adds a final signature, as it were, to his films through a brief
personal appearance. This practice, which began with *The Lodger*, continued
through his career. Hitchcock first began appearing in his own films to fill the
screen. However, a problem developed. Audiences became more interested in
seeing Hitchcock than in attending to the story line. Subsequently, Hitchcock
decided to make his appearance in the first five minutes of his later films to avoid
distraction for the audience. His presence in *Blackmail* evoked humor and helped
to add variety to the suspense.

> There he sits on the London Underground, a portly figure in a pork-pie hat, quietly reading a
> book, while a horrible little boy leans over the back of the next seat to torment him and receives
> a sharp but ineffectual jab for his pains. It is the precursor of and model for many other such
> moments, and it somehow symbolizes Hitch's emergence as a public figure—a position unique
> among British filmmakers and ultimately to make him one of the most familiar faces and figures
> in the world.[42]

The 1920s were a formative period for Alfred Hitchcock. He spent those
years developing and realizing his potential and augmenting knowledge through
cinematic jobs such as title card designer, script writer, art director, cameraman,
assistant director, and director. The latter years of the decade he spent absorbing
and incorporating the style and methods of the Americans, Germans, Russians,
and English in his film art. When sound films became a necessity for economic

survival in the film world, Hitchcock was given the assignment to direct England's first sound film, *Blackmail*. These significant achievements are now history.

Master of Suspense in the 1930s

The 1930s closed with Alfred Hitchcock designated as film's Master of Suspense—a title he well deserved, as we shall see. According to Lawrence Hammond, "the story of British suspense films of the late Twenties and the Thirties is really the story of the young Alfred Hitchcock, and his films include some of the few made in London in that decade which stand the test of time and could be seen again by later generations without risibility or stagey embarrassment."[43]

Hitchcock's films have stood the test of time partly because they are readily identifiable within the genre of suspense. In his book *Image and Influence: Studies in the Sociology of Film*, Andrew Tudor defines genre and explains how different genres form vicarious worlds of experience for the viewing public:

> Film makers have genre conceptions; audiences become "subcultures of taste" focused on particular genres; the genre-world is one important element in film language. So though not all film realities derive from genre, some of the best established and most popular are genre-realities. That is, they are realities which we recognize and "understand" because a long series of movies (and other elements in our culture) have prepared us for them. For most of the time films offer us worlds outside our direct field of experience. They may make sense to us because we have read about them or seen photographs (outer space), because they live up to the images we have built up over the years (films set in historical eras); because we have seen many other films set in the same world (westerns, gangster movies, other genres); basically, because they are recognizable in some perspective or other that we bring to the cinema with us. Genre is thus the special case where a body of film is the prime source of definition of the specific film's reality.[44]

The suspense film has ten specific elements, of which all or some may be used by the filmmaker within a scene or sequence. The combination and duration of these elements in a sequence are the stylistic choices of the director. Hitchcock's pertinent comments are related to elements identified and defined by Wells Root in *Writing the Script* and Gordon Gow in *Suspense in Cinema*.

Conflict. This is the primary method of creating suspense. Conflict usually occurs during the exposition of a film where the basic contention between the antagonist/protagonist is established.[45]

A master antagonist. The hero is to be pitted against a superior or master antagonist. This alleged dooming of the hero is, in actuality, the dooming of the audience through identification with the protagonist. The audience is always the hero. Whenever possible, Hitchcock cast a star as the hero because he knew future audiences would care deeply about the hero's fate; unwittingly, the audience would experience another dimension of anxiety in an already suspenseful film.[46]

Compounding suspense. The mortal dangers the hero and heroine face are progressively increased until the climax.[47]

The dreadful alternative. A horrible fate awaits the hero if he fails to achieve his major objective. This might be "life or death, riches or ruin, love or loneliness." Established early in the film, the dreadful alternative adds another constant level of suspense.[48]

Audience in the superior position. The audience has information, or knowledge, which the characters in the film do not have, such as a five-minute time bomb previously placed under a sofa upon which the hero and heroine now sit.[49] Hitchcock once said, "A suspense [film] is not simply a Who-done-it. . . . It might better be called a When's-he-gonna-do-it."[50] In a conversation with Pete Martin, Hitchcock elaborated on this technique of suspense:

> The point is to let the audience know where the bomb is, but not let the characters in my story know. . . . For example, you and I are sitting here chatting. We needn't talk about death or anything of serious consequence, but if the audience knows that there's a bomb under my desk, set to go off, the suspense will be harrowing to them. But if we don't tell our audience about the bomb ticking away under my desk, and it goes off and blows us to smithereens, the only thing the audience will get is a shock, and a one-second shock at that, as opposed to sixty to ninety minutes of breath-holding waiting.[51]

The unexpected complication. This occurs when something totally unforeseen goes wrong to complicate the life of the hero and to increase his troubles. For example, the hero is tied up and placed in a boat, which is set adrift. The boat is then caught up in the progressively quickening current of the river and heads for a waterfall. Subsequent dialogue informs us that no one has survived going over the precipice.[52]

The subjective camera. The camera becomes the eyes of one of the characters, and the audience is forced momentarily to share the reality of the character's experience. This technique permitted Hitchcock to direct the audience. "Hitchcock has always been more the director of audiences than of films; his films being only the means through which that other end might be achieved."[53] Hitchcock himself explains the use of the subjective camera shot to draw the audience into the character's mind:

> The objective treatment, however, is also used when necessary; but for me, the objective is merely an extension of the theater because you are a viewer of the events that take place in front of you, but you are not necessarily in the mind of the person. Subjective shooting puts the audience in the mind of the character.[54]

Isolation. The hero in a film is often isolated from and unsuspecting of, or defenseless against, the antagonist's motives. Location may be used to pronounce the isolation of, and menace to, the potential victim.[55]

Claustrophobia.

> A representation of claustrophobia works by rule of contrast in the film medium, which has accustomed us to open spaces and freedom of action. To deprive us of these things, suddenly, is to gain the emotional advantage: an instant brainwash, as it were. Again, isolation is of the essence and the setting is vital. Cellars and sewers are apt. So are mirrored walls, with their heartless illusion of depth and space, and their taunting multiple reflections of the person confined within them.[56]

The much broader word, fear, will be used when applicable.

Mind of the murderer. The audience is made aware that the master antagonist has a deranged mind, which results in an incapacity to restrain himself from murder. Such awareness leads to suspense for the audience when a person we care about is, or will be, in the presence of the murderer.[57]

Hitchcock artfully combines these ten elements of suspense to lead his audience into internal states of cathartic response. The universal reality that Hitchcock shares with his audience is a fear of death. Hitchcock hopes the hero and heroine on the screen will represent the cultural ideal of the audience; this will help character identification as the audience takes a cinematic journey into the unknown. The longer the audience moves through a suspense situation in which the protagonists' lives are placed in progressive jeopardy, the more intense becomes the fear of death and the desire to preserve their lives, and, more important, our ideal lives.

The films of the 1930s established Alfred Hitchcock as the Master of Suspense in the eyes of the cinema world. I now focus on three of the best films of this period, *The Man Who Knew Too Much* (1934), *The Thirty-nine Steps* (1935), and *The Lady Vanishes* (1938). As a major sequence from each of these films is retold in story form, the specific elements of suspense are placed in brackets in this chapter only so that the reader may clearly perceive how Hitchcock used them repeatedly as internal structure for the narrative film.

The Man Who Knew Too Much has an obligatory scene prior to the main suspense scene at London's Royal Albert Hall. Located in his hideout with his friends, master antagonist Abbott (Peter Lorre) plays a record that will be part of the musical program at the Albert Hall that evening. He tells the gunman, Ramon (Frank Vosper), to kill the foreign ambassador, who will be attending the symphony, when the music reaches the apex of the crescendo at the clash of the cymbals [audience in superior position; mind of the murderer].

Bob and Jill Lawrence (Leslie Banks and Edna Best), British citizens who have learned of the assassination plan while on vacation in Switzerland, have returned to England but fear to go to the police with the information because the would-be assassins have kidnapped their daughter, Betty (Nova Pilbeam), and threaten to kill her if their plan is disclosed [conflict; mind of the murderer]. Bob Lawrence makes his way to the assassin's hideout and is incarcerated with his daughter [unexpected complication]. This leaves only Jill Lawrence free; she goes to the Royal Albert Hall [isolation].

Jill Lawrence stands in the foyer of the Albert Hall, hoping that her husband will appear. Ramon, the assassin, walks up to her, gives her a pendant belonging to Betty, then goes to his upper box seat and sits down, concealed by a curtain. The young mother goes to her seat on the main floor. She has a clear view of the orchestra, the ambassador, and the box seat area above. In Hitchcockian thematic terms this is the recurrent love-versus-duty conflict; in a psychological sense, it is the classical approach-approach conflict. The heroine is confronted with equally unfavorable alternatives: If she warns the diplomat, her daughter will be killed, and if she remains silent, the diplomat will be murdered [double dreadful alternative].

The orchestra begins to play and the audience becomes attentively silent. There are shots of the orchestra, Jill, the ambassador, the audience, and the upper box area where Ramon is concealed. This sequence is one of Hitchcock's master strokes as a filmmaker. The visual rhythm of the editing is in harmony with the sound rhythm of the orchestra. The shots are three to four seconds in length to match the aural rhythm of the orchestra. Hitchcock gives us an objective shot of Jill, followed by another shot of the orchestra from Jill's eyes and takes the shot out of focus [subjective camera]. He then cuts back to Jill, who is crying. When the orchestra enters the crescendo segment of the movement, Hitchcock deletes random shots of the audience and orchestra. The shots are now only slightly more than two seconds in duration: a triangular cutting from Jill to Ramon to the ambassador. This visual triangle is broken to intensify the suspense when Hitchcock cuts away to the tense hands of the musician who is prepared to strike the cymbals. Hitchcock then cuts back to the alternating triangular-three-shot. Each time we come to the shot of Ramon's upper box seat we see a gun slowly being extended through a curtain. Simultaneously, Jill jumps up and screams and the cymbals are struck [compounded suspense; fear].

At this point, Hitchcock cuts back to the hideout where Abbott and his associates are listening to the radio broadcast of the concert. We hear a gunshot. Hitchcock does not cut back to the Albert Hall but prolongs the suspense by letting the audience wonder if Ramon was successful. Shortly thereafter, Ramon returns and informs Abbot and the others that Jill's scream caused him to miss a direct hit of the ambassador who, consequently, only suffered a minor flesh wound.

Hitchcock managed to include all ten elements of suspense in the obligatory scene and major sequence of the film. John Taylor comments on the influence of this film on Hitchcock's career: "From *The Man Who Knew Too Much* onwards, the pattern was finally set, and the association of Hitchcock with the thriller was confirmed forever in the public mind."[58] And from then on film audiences eagerly awaited Hitchcock's next suspense film. He would not disappoint them.

Like its successful predecessor *The Man Who Knew Too Much*, *The Thirty-nine Steps* has excellent exposition in two sequences—one introductory and the other an inciting incident that starts the action and the main suspense. Richard Hannay (Robert Donat), on vacation from his home in Canada, is spending the evening at a London music hall. Shots are fired in the hall, and a mysterious lady, Annabelle Smith (Lucie Mannheim), asks Hannay to take her home. At his apartment, she informs him that she is a spy and intimates that they may have been followed. Peering through the window, Hannay sees two men waiting in the street below [conflict]. The woman warns him that the leader of the spies, who is trying to kill her, is a dangerous man with a dozen names, who can disguise himself to look like a hundred different people [master antagonist]. However, there is one thing he cannot disguise: half of the little finger is missing on his right hand. Annabelle then asks Hannay for a map of Scotland. He complies, and she goes to bed in his bedroom while Hannay sleeps on the couch. During the night, Annabelle stumbles into the living room and says, "Clear out quick or they'll get you next!"[59] She falls across Hannay's lap and, simultaneously, the knife in her back becomes visible to Hannay and the audience. Hannay finds the map of Scotland and notices that one of the houses in a hamlet has been circled.

Hannay's next move is to take a train to Scotland. Meanwhile, the dead body of Annabelle is discovered in Hannay's apartment by the landlady, and the police and the spies begin their search for him [dreadful alternative; compounding suspense; audience in a superior position]. The hero leaves the train and travels across the Scottish Highlands on foot in search of the hamlet circled by Annabelle on the map [isolation]. After an episode at a farm house where Hannay receives a coat which, unknown to him, contains a hymnal, he continues his journey and arrives at the home of Professor Jordan. At this point we arrive at one of the major sequences in the film.

Hannay introduces himself as Mr. Hammond to Jordan and his house guests, who have just returned from church. Jordan and Hannay leave the others and enter a private drawing room. Professor Jordan begins the conversation and sequence with these words: "Now, Mr. Hannay, I suppose it is safe to call you by your real name now?"[60] Hannay unequivocally states his innocence and Jordan supports his plea. The fugitive explains that Annabelle Smith was murdered by a foreign agent, because he wanted to "prevent her from telling the authorities a secret message vital to England's air defense."[61] Annabelle told

Hannay this information before her murder in his apartment. The following dialogue in the film shocks the audience:

JORDAN
Did she tell you what the foreign agent looked like?

HANNAY
There wasn't time. There was one thing. Part of his little finger was missing.

JORDAN
Which one?

HANNAY
(*Holding up his hand*) This one, I think.

JORDAN
(*The camera is placed behind Jordan with Hannay facing the camera in the background*) You're sure. (*Raises hand*) It wasn't this one [unexpected complication—the tip of Jordan's small finger is missing]?[62]

Jordan cannot let Hannay go, because his whole existence would be jeopardized, as Jordan explains, "If it became known that I'm not, er, what shall we say, not what I seem."[63] This fragment of dialogue exposes a prominent theme in this and subsequent films: appearance versus reality. Mr. Hammond is really Hannay, and the apparently respectable Professor Jordan is really the spy chief. Jordan suggests that he will leave Hannay his revolver so he may commit suicide. Hannay starts moving toward the door during the latter part of this dialogue. Hitchcock cuts to a moving subjective shot to force the audience to become the character of Hannay and accept his anxiety as their own [subjective camera; claustrophobia]. Jordan shoots Hannay, who falls to the floor [mind of the murderer]. Hannay is next seen talking with a police inspector. The hymnal in his borrowed coat had stopped the bullet, and Hannay, of course, allowed Jordan to think he was dead until he could escape and report the incident to the nearest police station.

Hitchcock has managed to include the ten basic elements in these selected sequences of *The Thirty-nine Steps*. The film has been, and is, a four-star success with critics and audiences of yesterday and today. Taylor comments on the director, who was elevated to international fame: "The film had a sensational success in the States as well as in Britain, and Hitch was truly an international figure."[64] *The Thirty-nine Steps* was one of Hitchcock's favorite films in his creative canon.

A third film of the 1930s period is *The Lady Vanishes*, an English film that won unprecedented international acclaim. It won the New York Critics' Award for best film of the year (1938), and Alfred Hitchcock won their best director award. Critics and creative people alike were charmed and captivated by the film.

Howard Barnes of the *New York Herald Tribune* summed up how the critics and audiences felt about Hitchcock upon the release of *The Lady Vanishes*: "Even in so synthetic a medium as the screen, it is possible to recognize the work of a master craftsman. *The Lady Vanishes* is a product of individual imagination and artistry quite as much as a Cézanne canvas or a Stravinsky score." Orson Welles reportedly saw the film eleven times and James Thurber twice more than that.[65]

A famous segment of *The Lady Vanishes* is the brandy glasses sequence. However, there is also a relevant obligatory scene in which Iris and Gilbert (Margaret Lockwood and Michael Redgrave) enter a train compartment to check on the identity of a passenger whose face is masked in bandages. A nun attends the patient. Gilbert begins to remove the bandages when Dr. Hartz (Paul Lukas), a brain surgeon, enters the cabin and stops Gilbert [conflict] from completing his task. Iris explains that they think it is Miss Froy, an elderly lady who has vanished from the train. Dr. Hartz requests that the two intruders meet him in the dining car. He wishes to momentarily remain behind to check on his patient. The hero and heroine leave the comparment. Hartz reprimands the nun.

NUN

You never said the old girl was English.

HARTZ

What difference does that make? In a few moments I shall order three drinks in the dining car; mine will be Sauterne. Now, one of the stewards is working for us. Listen carefully [master antagonist; audience in superior position; unexpected complication].[66]

This scene is an obligatory or revelatory one which serves to polarize the audience in choosing which characters to support. We now know Dr. Hartz is a ruthless spy who has kidnapped Miss Froy. The true character of Dr. Hartz, known to us but not to Iris and Gilbert, who are waiting in the dining car, renders the two romantic leads vulnerable to treachery.

Dr. Hartz joins the unsuspecting travelers. He orders three drinks from the steward, who is working for the spy ring. Iris and Gilbert voice their suspicions and knowledge of people who are guilty of subversive activities. Dr. Hartz patronizes them and intimates doubt when he hears their accusations. The drinks are brought to the table. Dr. Hartz receives a knowing and ominous glance from the steward. The audience is aware of the subterfuge because of the obligatory scene [fear]. They know that Dr. Hartz is not above kidnapping and murder, and thus the glasses contain either strong sedative or poison [mind of the murderer].

HARTZ

Well, what I cannot understand is why anyone should want to dispose of the old lady [subjective camera from Gilbert's position].

GILBERT

But that's just what sums up! All we know is that she was here on this train and now she is (*swallows drink*) gone.[67]

The last word spoken by Gilbert, "gone," has three meanings: Miss Froy, the drugged drink, and the astute Gilbert as a possible threat to Dr. Hartz are "gone" [compounding suspense]. A few lines later, Dr. Hartz offers this foreshadowing toast: "To our health, and may our enemies, if they exist, be unconscious of our purposes."[68] Iris does not take her drink until the end of the scene. Maurice Yacowar is perceptive in his understanding of Dr. Hartz's corrupt character. "For a brain surgeon to wish anyone unconscious seems perverse; for someone active in politics, it is a confession of treachery and covertness."[69]

The trio leave the dining car and enter a private compartment. Dr. Hartz informs them the person wrapped in bandages is indeed Miss Froy. Moreover, he tells them that he had a drug placed in their drinks which "paralyzes the brain and renders the victim unconscious."[70] Iris, followed by Gilbert, loses consciousness, and Dr. Hartz leaves the compartment [double isolation]. He intends to remove Miss Froy from the train and perform an operation on her that will not be successful [dreadful alternative]. As soon as Dr. Hartz leaves the car, Gilbert gets up and gently shakes the girl. Iris had fainted, and Gilbert had pretended to lose consciousness. The nun did not pass the information on to the steward and, consequently, Iris and Gilbert had not been drugged. In the above three sequences, the ten elements of suspense are present.

The sequential analysis of these films exposes the political areas of espionage and sabotage. The political realm is important for one specific reason: an awareness of the political level of Hitchcock's British films facilitates understanding the political level of his American films made or conceived during the World War II period. Of immediate concern are *The Man Who Knew Too Much* (1934), *The Thirty-nine Steps* (1935), *The Secret Agent* (1936), *Sabotage* (1936), and *The Lady Vanishes* (1938). A quotation from Furhammar and Isaksson's *Politics and Film* affirms the political focus of Hitchcock's films:

> From *The Man Who Knew Too Much* (1934) to *Lifeboat* (1943), Hitchcock's films seemed to be greatly concerned with politics, even if the particular demands of the thriller pattern into which political situations were skillfully woven meant that a great deal remained obscure or only partially stated. These films were nevertheless quite clearly about Nazism and the cold shivers that ran through Europe when political criminals became heads of state, when terror established its ministries in one country after another and some people adjusted themselves to the rule of force while others united to resist it.[71]

One objection may be raised against this statement. *The Man Who Knew Too Much* contains no evidence that the film was "quite clearly about Nazism." Authoritative books by authors Spoto, Taylor, Yacowar, Harris and Lasky, LaValley, and Durgnat do not state or imply that the espionage agents in *The Man Who Knew Too Much* are Nazis. Hitchcock himself points to a Russian influence rather than Nazi Germany. The ending of the film was taken from an actual occurrence in London, which Hitchcock recounts:

The incident took place around 1920, I think, and was known as the Sidney Street siege. Some Russian anarchists were holed up in a house and were shooting while the police were trying to get them out of there. It was a very difficult operation so they called out the soldiers. Churchill came down to supervise the operation. . . . They were even about to call on the artillery when the house caught fire and the anarchists came out.[72]

Despite some disagreement over political implications in *The Man Who Knew Too Much*, critics of Hitchcock's films from *The Thirty-nine Steps* (1935) to *The Lady Vanishes* (1938) all point to the Anglo-German relationship. In his review of *The Thirty-nine Steps*, Yacowar states,

Hannay is accompanied home by a strange German lady who claims to have fired the shots in order to escape two men who are trying to prevent her from telling the authorities a secret message vital to England's air defense.[73]

Donald Spoto sums up the irony of this situation. In an "inversion of ordinary plotting, Hitchcock has the German born spy working for England, and the Englishman (Professor Jordan) working for the enemy."[74] Although never explicit, the implication is that Professor Jordan is working for the Germans— Annabelle Smith is German-born, speaks German, and would be involved in espionage work in Germany and counterespionage work in England. We may reasonably assume she would be involved with an English-born German spy, Professor Jordan.

The historical setting of *The Secret Agent* (1935) is World War I. Richard Ashenden (John Gielgud) is sent by England's Foreign Office to Switzerland to locate and kill a German agent. The successful completion of this mission will greatly aid Britain's interests in the Middle East. One critic suggests the relevance of *The Secret Agent* to 1936:

The fact that the film takes place in 1916 does not lessen its significance for the international situation of 1936, nor, indeed, for any era in which politics and the waging of war exact such a terrible price from humanity. To have accomplished the statement of this theme without propaganda and without arch moralism is rare and admirable. To have accomplished it with such wit and style is the sign of genius.[75]

1916 was a year of aggression and war in Europe. Twenty years later, the realities of political upheaval are parallel. Writes the historian Roger Manvell,

The 1930s were, therefore, a melancholy period in world history, with the map both in central Europe and Asia constantly reflecting the changes taking place in the balance of power—Italy annexing Abyssinia (Ethiopia) in May 1936, the year in which Hitler marched into the demilitarized Rhineland and established formal relations with Italy and Japan through the foundation of the Rome-Berlin-Tokyo axis. It was the year too for the signing of the anti-Comintern pact between Berlin and Tokyo.[76]

Sabotage (1936) is an overt indictment of saboteurs who want to destory the City of London. Ted (John Loder), an undercover agent, tries to acquire legal evidence of sabotage "on a band of German and English spies who use a movie theatre as a 'front' to cover their activities."[77] Mr. Verloc (Oscar Homolka) is the saboteur and owner of the theatre. During the film, the camera enters the cinema theatre in the film to allow the audience watching Hitchcock's film to watch Sylvia Sidney, the heroine, become a member of the audience and watch a film within the film. Hitchcock will use the same method in *Saboteur* (1942). In this strong technique, the real audience and reel audience become one, the former brought to wonder if such incidents of sabotage could occur in their lives. However, no reported acts of German sabotage were perpetrated against England at this time. Hitler had a high regard for the English people and considered them an uncontaminated race. We will see that he did not have the same perspective of the non-German inhabitants of the United States.

The Lady Vanishes (1938) involves Nazi German espionage work in the form of mental manipulation by Dr. Hartz of Iris Henderson and the kidnapping of Miss Froy.

> Iris has been growing out of self-concern into a concern for a stranger (Miss Froy). Her moral awakening is leading her from her own comfort to concern for someone else. By arguing that her problem is a hallucination or a subjective projection, Hartz is forcing her into a regression, into her own mind instead of into the outside world for the object of her concern. She has gone from worrying about herself to worrying about someone else. He wants to make her think that that someone is still in her own mind, that she has not grown out.[78]

Gilbert, a young student of musical folklore, "intervenes" to personally and politically support Iris. However, the other English people on the train who had seen Miss Froy fail to support Iris's testimony for selfish reasons that are indicative of isolationism. Quoting Gavin Lambert, Maurice Yacowar holds this view:

> A few months after Chamberlain came to terms with Hitler at Munich, the British passengers still cling to an obstinate isolationism, reluctant to take the enemy seriously. . . . The conservative lawyer dies fluttering a white handkerchief.[79]

Raymond Durgnat also perceives subliminal political statements in Hitchcock's films. Durgnat's view complements Lambert's:

> It certainly mirrors a British mood immediately after Munich, but that mood isn't one simple thought. It's probably fair to say that if the scenery has shifted from England in *Sabotage* to Mittle Europ it's because the fear of internal disorder has given place to the question of English intervention on behalf of Czechoslovakia and Poland.[80]

In 1938, Neville Chamberlain received great support from his political cronies when he announced he would attend a Munich conference to be held on September 29. Italy, France, and Germany were the other countries invited. Hitler wanted the Sudetenland of Czechoslovakia, which was inhabited by almost three million Germans. Chamberlain was to invoke a policy of appeasement by giving Hitler the land and people he requested.

> The Munich conference phased the German occupation of the Sudeten areas from October 1st to October 10th. The Czech representatives were not even allowed to attend the discussions—

izing the unusual and achieving freshness and variety,'' this film was like the American films Hitchcock praised.[93] Unfortunately, C. M. Woolf was waiting in the wings to play his role as the master antagonist. Taking charge of the studio, he told Hitchcock and Ivo Montagu, a producer and scenario writer, that they would be fired if they rejected the assignment of doing a musical. Annoyed, Hitchcock wanted to throw in the towel with Gaumont British Films due to the absurd behavior of Woolf, and especially because Hitchcock considered *Waltzes from Vienna*, a musical, to be a bad film:

> I want to make a point. And that is that whatever happens in the course of your career, your talent is always there. To all appearances, I seemed to have gone into a creative decline in 1933 when I made *Waltzes from Vienna*, which was very bad. And yet the talent must have been there all along since I had already conceived the project for *The Man Who Knew Too Much*, the picture that reestablished my creative prestige.[94]

Ivor Montagu and Hitchcock knew that Woolf had purposefully sabotaged *The Man Who Knew Too Much* at the box office because he disliked Hitchcock and his new suspense genre. Hitchcock found Woolf's behavior a paradox of contradictions to which he did not wish to be subjected anymore. Ivor Montagu was more the mediator. He told Hitchcock that they should work on the musical until Michael Balcon returned from America. They did, and when Balcon returned he quickly cancelled the film and put his co-producer, Montagu, and best director, Hitchcock, to work on *The Secret Agent* (1936).[95]

Emigration to the United States

It was only a matter of time before Hitchcock would sign a contract to work in America. The shabby treatment he experienced at the hands of the producer C. M. Woolf had planted the seeds of discontent. His article on ''stodgy'' British films was a positive assessment of American films for their unusual setting and variety in combining ''the grave and gay'' in film drama.

In 1937, Hitchcock wrote the article, ''Directing,'' which he ended with an expression of desire for more freedom in his films:

> In a film you keep your whole action flowing; you can have comedy and drama running together and weave them in and out. Audiences are much readier now than they used to be for sudden changes of mood; and this means more freedom for a director. The art of directing for the commercial market is to know just how far you can go. In many ways I am freer now to do what I want to do than I was a few years ago. I hope in time to have more freedom still— if audiences will give it to me.[96]

Hitchcock began to believe that American audiences would permit him more freedom in his films. It will be remembered that Hitchcock's desire to enter the film industry was inspired by the technical excellence of the American cinema; his first two years of professional training and work were with an American company, Paramount's Famous Players-Lasky.

The German expressionist films Hitchcock had enjoyed in the early 1920s had ceased to be produced. According to Paul Rotha, "the German film died quietly."[97] Siegfried Kracauer understood why the German expressionist film had become extinct:

> One explanation offered is the exodus of many prominent German film artists and technicians about the middle of the twenties. Hollywood bought them up, as it did other foreign talents. Among the first to answer the call were Lubitsch, Pola Negri, Hans Kraly and Buchowetski. In 1925 and 1926 they were joined by a whole crowd, including the star directors E. A. Dupont, Ludwig Berger, Lupu Pick, Paul Leni and Murnau, and such actors as Veidt and Jannings. Erich Pommer (producer), too, could not resist the temptation. There is no doubt that Hollywood effected this wholesale importation not solely to heighten its own standards; the main idea was to eliminate a competitor extremely dangerous at the time.[98]

Although Fritz Lang was one exception to this mass migration, most prominent German filmmakers at the UFA studio were now residents of the film capital of the world, Hollywood. In 1939, Alfred Hitchcock and his family also emigrated from England to the United States. Hitchcock recounts his experiences with American producers in the United States and his decision to sign a contract with David O. Selznick:

> I first came to the U.S. in June 1938 to sign a contract with David O. Selznick. There had been American approaches in previous years by Universal and Sam Goldwyn, but I was always under contract to either Gaumont-British or ABC in England. In those days I was called England's "ace" director, and it was through David Selznick's brother, the agent Myron Selznick, with whom I'd been acquainted over many years, that I received an offer from David Selznick to come out to Hollywood and do the story of the *Titanic*; that was the original intention. . . . Just before I left England—where I'd returned after signing the contract—I got a message saying that he would like to change from the *Titanic* to *Rebecca*. So when I arrived here to start work in April 1939 it was on *Rebecca*.[99]

The Hollywood producer in the 1930s and 1940s was the "auteur" of the American film. David O. Selznick was no exception. In making *Rebecca* (1940), Hitchcock received the freedom afforded by large budgets, talented actors and actresses, and great technicians; but he had to pay the price exacted by the American film system of a producer who was totally autonomous in his authority. "In those days the individual producer was the man who made the pictures. He was king. The director, the writers, actors, designers, and the like were all subject to his taste and approval."[100]

Selznick was famous for the memos he sent to those who worked for him. He would vehemently state his approval or disapproval of anyone under contract to him. For Selznick, the successful novel was an object of sanctity, and film treatment must closely follow the plot of the novel itself. Hitchcock's common practice was to add scenes to a novel that would facilitate a variety of heavy drama and light comedy. Moreover, the visual story in *Rebecca* was achieved through montage, and was more important to Hitchcock than the pure reproduction of the novel. The following memo from Selznick caused Hitchcock to alter his treatment, in accordance with Selznick's wishes:

> Dear Hitch:
>
> It is my unfortunate and distressing task to tell you that I am shocked and disappointed beyond words by the treatment of *Rebecca*. I regard it as a distorted and vulgarized version of a provenly successful work, in which, for no reason that I can discern, old-fashioned movie scenes have been substituted for the captivatingly charming du Maurier scenes. This is particularly true in the Riviera sequence.
>
> I don't hold at all with the theory that the difference in medium necessitates a difference in storytelling, or even a difference in scenes. In my opinion, the only thing that is justified by the difference in medium is a difference in the manner in which a scene is told; and the only omissions from a successful work that are justified are omissions necessitated by length, censorship, or other practical considerations. Readers of a dearly loved book will forgive omissions if there is an obvious reason for them; but very properly they will not forgive substitutions.[101]

The film *Rebecca* was shot with the usual meticulous care and consideration which Hitchcock gave to his films. Selznick sent a number of memos to Hitchcock to complain of his working methods, as well as about internal problems with the film itself. Consider these examples of his complaints.

> [Tempo]: I personally don't think there is any danger of this picture being played too fast, and I think that if you speed the pace a little more even than you think is right we will be a lot better off, and in any event I would rather err on the side of too fast a tempo than on the slow side.[102]

> [Slow shooting]: Actually the script of each scene on this picture has in every case been out very much earlier than on almost any picture we have ever made, including *Gone With the Wind, A Star Is Born, The Prisoner of Zenda*, etc. And there are some good directors in this town who, for some reason unknown to me, persist in having each scene rewritten after it is rehearsed on the stage, and who still manage to make infinitely better time than we are making on *Rebecca*.[103]

> [Director's studio management]: There are various things about your methods of shooting which I think you simply must correct, because even if we permitted you to follow them on *Rebecca*, you would have to cure them on your next picture and succeeding pictures because nobody in Hollywood would stand for them, so we might as well clamp down on you for this picture. I refer to such things as letting the actors remain idle while the camera crew lines up, and the camera crew remain idle while actors are being rehearsed. It is just infantile not to realize that these two processes must go through simultaneously, and if the noise disturbs you, then rehearse them on the sidelines or somewhere.[104]

Hitchcock, however, did not change his directing style to placate Selznick as he did with the script treatment of *Rebecca*. *Gone With the Wind*, produced by Selznick, was absorbing his time and prevented him from reinforcing his criticisms through a conference with Hitchcock or extended presence on the *Rebecca* set. Hitchcock took advantage of Selznick's preoccupation with the premiere of *Gone With the Wind* on December 15, 1939, in Atlanta, and proceeded with the completion of his first American film.[105] Hitchcock was bold and successful in this matter:

It was a gamble on Hitch's part that *Rebecca* would turn out all right and thus all such irritations would be forgotten. And so it proved—the first preview, even very roughly assembled, was sensational, audiences loved the film, it won the Oscar for "Best Film of the Year," and it presented Selznick with an important new star in Joan Fontaine. Hitch was vindicated, and in after years Selznick would say that Hitch was the only director, absolutely the only director, whom he would trust completely with a picture.[106]

The Second World War

While Hitchcock worked on the early shooting of *Rebecca*, World War II began on September 1, 1939. Nazi Germany invaded Poland on that day and England gave Germany forty-eight hours to withdraw all troops. Germany's failure to respond resulted in a state of war between these two countries. Hitchcock, not eligible for military service because of his age (40) and excess weight, was to remain in the United States and finish *Rebecca*. Furthermore, the British Government had closed down all theatres, cinemas, and film studios in England, so there was nothing Hitchcock could do in England to aid the war effort through the propaganda power of film. Yet a number of Londoners at the beginning of the war accused their countrymen of failing to help protect the homeland.

Naturally, in all this flurry of accusation Hitch came in for his share. The most hurtful was from his old friend and associate Michael Balcon, who made an ill-considered statement to the press naming Hitch as one of those who had deserted Britain when she needed them most. Hitch and Alma were deeply upset that he of all people, who should have known better, had taken this line; and he himself soon regretted it, since he was unofficially informed that Hitch . . . was continuing film-making in America at the express request of the British Government.[107]

If one is to understand Hitchcock's political ideology, it is of paramount importance to review Hitchcock's reflection on film content. For the most part, he refused to talk about the content of his films; he was even more adamant to avoid discussion of the political content of his films. He said,

Where sometimes one gets a little into difficulties with the American people is that they want everything spelled out; and they worry about content. I don't care about content at all. The film can be about anything you like, so long as I'm making that audience react in a certain way to whatever I put on the screen.[108]

However, film historians and critics have made comments on the political orientation of Hitchcock's films. For example, Philip Dynia commented on the political message in Hitchcock's works: "Certain political activities are perfectly suited to the thriller genre in which Hitchcock's artistry thrives. These films refer, sometimes obliquely, to contemporary political events; in a few the political message becomes more overt."[109] James Monaco pinpointed Hitchcock's technique: "He has devised for his characters a response to disorder and oppression which is political."[110] Monaco meant that the protagonists seek to awaken and win support of the individual authorities and community. John

Russell Taylor would not differentiate between Hitchcock and his work: "For Hitchcock is not so much in his films; he *is* his films."[111] Hitchcock himself claimed that the message of the film is found in the picture. In other words, the message of the film is found in the sequential pictures he paints through his artistic control of script, storyboarding, set design, acting, directing, and editing:

> I'm like, let's say, a painter who paints flowers. It's the method of treating things that interests me. But on the other hand, if I were a painter, I would say: "I can't paint anything that doesn't contain a message."
>
> Method and message, that's the remarkable conflation that makes Alfred Joseph Hitchcock one of the greatest directors of the first century of film.[112]

The methods and messages of *Foreign Correspondent*, *Saboteur*, *Lifeboat*, and *Notorious*, films made by Alfred Hitchcock during the World War II period, certainly smack of political intent. The historical events of the day are implicit throughout them. We shall see that the unifying theme of these World War II films is the perpetuation of freedom framed in the political ideology of democracy.

2

Foreign Correspondent

Production: Walter Wanger, United Artists, 1940. *Director:* Alfred Hitchcock. *Scenario.* Charles Bennett and Joan Harrison. *Dialogues:* James Hilton and Robert Benchley. *Director of Photography:* Rudolph Mate. *Special Effects:* Lee Zavitz. *Sets:* William Cameron Menzies and Alexander Golitzen. *Music:* Alfred Newman. *Editing:* Otto Lovering and Dorothy Spencer. *Assistant Director:* Edmond Bernoudy. *Studio:* United Artists, at Hollywood. *Distributor:* United Artists, 1940, 120 minutes. *Principal Actors:* Joel McCrea (Johnny Jones, reporter), Laraine Day (Carol Fisher), Herbert Marshall (Stephen Fisher, her father), George Sanders (Herbert Folliott, reporter), Albert Bassermann (Van Meer), Robert Benchley (Stebbins), Eduardo Cianelli (Krug), Edmund Gwenn (Rowley), Harry Davenport (Mr. Powers), and Martin Kosleck, Eddie Conrad, Gertrude W. Hoffman, Jane Novak, Ken Christy, Crawford Kent, Joan Brodel-Leslie, Louis Borell.[1]

Foreign Correspondent, released in 1940, is the first politically-oriented suspense film Hitchcock made in the United States. In this film, he tries to make United States citizens aware of the dangers of the European war and the futility of isolationism. Joel McCrea plays Johnny Jones, an American newspaperman who is sent to Europe to report on the escalating internal conflicts of the nations that threaten world peace. In London, he meets a Dutch diplomat, Van Meer (Albert Basserman), who is carrying a secret treaty back to his country. Van Meer is kidnapped by the Nazis, and Johnny goes to Amsterdam to find him. Laraine Day plays Carol Fisher, an English girl who is romantically attracted to Johnny and who tries to help him rescue Van Meer. Herbert Marshall plays Stephen Fisher, Carol's father, who, though a nobleman and leader of an international peace party, is really a Nazi agent.

Johnny and an English reporter, Herbert Folliott (George Sanders), eventually rescue Van Meer but must hurry off to catch a plane to Washington, D.C., on which Fisher and his daughter are travelling. The plane is attacked by a German ship and crashes into the ocean. Fisher sacrifices his life for the sake of his daughter and the other survivors, who are picked up by an American ship en route to London. The hero and heroine conclude the film with a news broadcast to the United States informing listeners of the real danger of Nazi aggression in Europe.

Foreign Correspondent and the United States Foreign Policy of Isolationism

The second scene of the exposition opens with dialogue between Powers (Harry Davenport), editor of the *New York Globe*, and Brandon, a Globe reporter. Powers is irritated because his foreign correspondents have failed to send valid news of the real situation in Europe. Reel time is August 19, 1939. Powers remarks that he could get more "news out of Europe looking in a crystal ball."[2] Brandon thinks it might be advisable to send over Johnny Jones, a reporter who recently roughed up a policeman in the line of duty. Powers quips, "Beat up a policeman, eh, sounds ideal for Europe."[3] This line is an example of subtle and humorous political commentary, because Nazi Germany had literally become a police state from 1934 to 1939.

> When the Nazis came to power, there were 138,000 police in Germany. A year and a half later—by the end of 1934—there were 437,000, including 250,000 SS men. By the beginnings of the war there were 372,000 SS men within the German police system.[4]

Following is part of the dialogue between Johnny Jones and Mr. Powers. In this part of the exposition, Jones comes across as self-confident, unpretentious, politically innocent, and strongly individualistic. In short, he is Hitchcock's ideal of the American democratic man. The dialogue begins when Jones walks into Powers' office. Powers asks some general questions, and then comes to the point:

POWERS

What is your opinion of the present European crisis, Mr. Jones?

JONES

What crisis?

POWERS

I'm referring to the impending war, Mr. Jones.

JONES

Oh, that! Well, to tell you the truth, Mr. Powers, I haven't given it much thought.

POWERS

You don't keep up with our foreign news, do you, Mr. Jones?

JONES

Now look, Mr. Powers! If you're going to fire me you can scrap the intelligence test. It's perfectly okay with me. I can get a job on any other newspaper in town within the hour. So long.

POWERS

Wait a minute! Nobody fired you.[5]

Jones refuses to sit down because he thinks Powers is going to fire him. He does not want to place himself in an inferior position that would make it possible for Powers to intimidate him. He believes that Powers' questions on the European crisis are a ruse to get him fired because of his fight with the policeman.

However, Jones' political innocence, as well as his present boldness and previous aggressive behavior, have unwittingly won for him a new job. Powers offers Jones an expense account and the biggest story in the world—Europe. Jones' ignorance of the European situation is stressed as he responds:

JONES

Well, I'm afraid I'm not, er, exactly equipped, but I can do some reading up.

POWERS

No. No reading up. I like you just the way you are, Mr. Jones. What Europe needs is a fresh, unused mind.

JONES

A foreign correspondent, eh?

POWERS

No. A reporter. I don't want correspondence! I want news. Do you think you could dig up news in Europe?

JONES

I would be very happy to try, sir.[6]

Powers warns Jones against what he calls "paper bilging" and demands specifics rather than vague generalities concerning the "great Van Meer." Jones, who has no knowledge of Van Meer, is informed swiftly that he is one of the two signers of the Dutch Treaty with Belgium and his continued leadership in Holland could mean peace in Europe. It is, therefore, vital that America knows what Van Meer is thinking. This, then, is Johnny Jones' first assignment from Powers: "I want you to talk with him. Find out what's in that treaty and what he thinks is going to happen. Facts!"[7]

Jones, though courageous, is unaware of the political implications of what is taking place between European countries. Moreover, the foreboding conditions which will lead to war have not yet interested him. The situation is paradoxical—indicative of America's policy of isolationism at that time.

Although the policy of political non-involvement with the powers of Europe prevailed in the United States between World Wars I and II, its origin reached back to the period of the United States' birth as a nation, and to the foreign policy philosophies of George Washington, Thomas Jefferson, and James Monroe. Between the wars, those who favored isolationism as a foreign policy never tired of quoting these presidents. George Washington warned against political involvement by the United States in Europe:

The great rule of conduct for us in regard to foreign nations is, in extending our commercial relations to have as little *political* connection as possible. So far as we have already formed engagements let them be fulfilled with perfect good faith. Here let us stop.

It is our true policy to *steer clear of permanent alliances* with any portion of the foreign world, *so far, I mean, as we are now at liberty to do it . . . .*

> Taking care always to keep ourselves by *suitable* establishments on a respectable defensive posture, *we may safely trust to temporary alliances for extraordinary* emergencies . . . .[8]

Thomas Jefferson's message was similar:

> I have ever deemed it fundamental for the United States, never to take active part in the quarrels of Europe. Their political interests are entirely distinct from ours. Their mutual jealousies, their balance of power, their complicated alliances, their forms and principles of government, are all foreign to us. They are nations of eternal war. All their energies are expended in the destruction of the labor, property and lives of their people. On our part, never had a people so favorable a chance of trying the opposite system, of peace and fraternity with mankind, and the direction of all our means and faculties to the purposes of improvement instead of destruction.[9]

James Monroe's message, though aimed specifically at Russia, warned all foreign powers not to become politically involved with the American continents:

> In the discussions to which this interest has given rise and in the arrangements by which they may terminate the occasion has been judged proper for asserting, as a principle in which the rights and interests of the United States are involved, that the American continents, by the free and independent condition which they have assumed and maintain, are henceforth not to be considered as subjects for future colonization by any European powers.[10]

However, both Washington and Jefferson qualified their reservations about alliances. Washington's Farewell Address, the foundation of the United States foreign policy of isolationism, called for "temporary alliances for extraordinary emergencies" when expedient to our national and international interests. Thomas Jefferson, the father of United States democracy, had a strong allegiance to Britain:

> Great Britain . . . is the nation which can do us the most harm of any one, or all on earth; and with her on our side we need not fear the whole world. With her then, we should most sedulously cherish a cordial friendship; and nothing would tend more to knit our affections than to be fighting once more, side by side, in the same cause.[11]

A majority of Americans polled in the 1930s agreed with Jefferson's favoring of England. The poll, conducted in April 1938 by the American Institute of Public Opinion, recorded that 55 percent chose England as the European country they like best and another 11 percent chose France. Only 8 percent expressed a preference for Germany and 4 percent for Ireland.[12] In other words, 66 percent of the people polled in the United States "liked best" the prominent democracies of Europe. And it was presidential policy, especially under Franklin D. Roosevelt, incumbent from 1933–1945, to study what the people liked best before making decisions of national or international scope. I will show, as we progress through *Foreign Correspondent*, that President Roosevelt strongly supported a policy of progressive intervention in favor of the Allied Powers. However, he was a wise politician in international matters who avoided going beyond the wishes of the majority of his constituency. Carleton Allen, a political scientist, states how important it is for the politician to lead public opinion slowly and that Roosevelt's capacity in this area was exceptional.

The representative is always in the difficulty that if he is too far in advance of public opinion, and if he administers too many shocks, he may lose all further opportunities of "educating" his public, for the excellent reason that his public will throw him out of office. It may be heroic to become a voice crying in the wilderness, but it is not practically effective. It is not, therefore, always mere cowardice which prevents the politician from announcing, in blunt terms, what he really believes if he knows that it will be unpopular; he often has to consider how he can lead public opinion without letting it become aware that it is being led. The process is not only exceedingly delicate, but often painfully slow and to a statesman of strong judgment it must often tax patience almost beyond endurance. In modern times there is no more remarkable example of it than Mr. Roosevelt's handling of public opinion before America's entry into the war.[13]

Because the office of the President of the United States is an elected one, the incumbent must be sensitive to public opinion if he is to maintain the majority support of Congress and the voting public. From the results of a poll taken by the American Institute of Public Opinion between March 1939 and October 1941, it is apparent that Congress would have been forced to impeach President Roosevelt had he used his power as Commander in Chief of the Armed Forces to engage in offensive warfare against the Axis powers without a declaration of war by Congress. He would have been impeached because such action would not have been in keeping with the collective will of a democratic republic. The poll centered around the question of whether the United States Army and Navy should be sent abroad to fight Germany and Italy. Between May 1940 and October 1941, the question became more urgent. Americans were asked whether, if they were given a two-week deadline, they would vote to stay out of the war or to go into the war. In March 1939, 83 percent said they would vote to stay out of the war; in September 1939, 84 percent. In May 1940, the poll showed 86 percent opposed to war, and in January 1941, 88 percent. By October 1941, the percentage had dropped to 79.[14] Simon summarizes the statistics:

Two months before Pearl Harbor (in October 1941), 79 percent said that if given the opportunity they would vote to stay out of the war. Between March 1939, which was six months before the German invasion of Poland, and October 1941—in other words, after Britain and France had entered the war and Germany had invaded the Soviet Union and conquered almost all of Western Europe—there was no significant alteration in the public's desire not to become involved again.[15]

President Roosevelt had to state his intentions cautiously, especially when they concerned foreign policy. He, like the people he governed, became more and more alarmed at the aggressive behavior of the Axis powers (Germany, Italy, and Japan) as they denied other countries territorial rights and freedom of the seas. The mass media served to inform the United States and the world of Axis aggression. In this sense, *Foreign Correspondent* engages its world audience on two coexistent levels. Robert A. Harris and Michael S. Lasky have commented on these levels:

The obvious one is the entertaining chase—the cloak-and-dagger work of the New York crime reporter. The second is the flag-waving propaganda calling for an end of American isolationism in World War II.[16]

Let us return now to the dialogue of the first sequence of *Foreign Correspondent* and examine the entertainment and political propaganda levels along with a third level—suspense. The dialogue is between Jones, Powers, and Stephen Fisher.

JONES

Well, how about Hitler? Don't you think it would be a good idea to pump him? He must have something on his mind. (*Powers' secretary breaks in on the intercom to inform him that Mr. Stephen Fisher wants to see him.*)

POWERS

Did you ever hear of Stephen Fisher?

JONES

No. I'm afraid he is not on my beat.

POWERS

Well, he is from now on. He is head of the Universal Peace Party and very close to Van Meer. They're both working to keep Europe from going up in flames. (*Fisher comes in and Powers introduces him to Jones.*) Jones—I don't like that name. It's going to handicap you, young man. Now wait a minute. I have some sort of name here. Yes, Haverstock—Huntley Haverstock. Sounds a little more important, don't you think, Mr. Fisher?

FISHER

Quite. It's very dashing.

POWERS

It's better than Mr. Harvey Davis.

FISHER

Mr. Harvey Davis? What's the matter with that?

POWERS

We can't use that. That's the name of one of our greatest war correspondents twenty years ago. (*To Jones*) Well, speak up young man. You don't mind being Huntley Haverstock, do you?

JONES

A rose by any name, sir.

FISHER

Isn't it exciting being present at the christening of an American newspaper correspondent. Shouldn't we break a bottle of champagne or something over him?

JONES

You should break one over my head and see if I'm still awake. Huntley Haverstock?[17]

This part of the exposition is important for three reasons: the scene creates suspense that depends on the audience's knowledge of Hitler as a political force, the structure of the dialogue is subtly foreshadowing and the dialogue introduces the film's main theme of appearance versus reality. Jones' question about Hitler combines drama with a real political person, and Hitler's political ambitions had put the remaining free world in a state of suspense.

The structure of the dialogue subtly foreshadows the major conflict of the film and two other developments of the plot, but it makes a point on the political level, too. As Jones is asking the question about Hitler, Powers' secretary interrupts on the intercom system to inform her boss that Mr. Fisher wishes to see him. Fisher's introduction at this moment records the Hitler-Fisher union in the mind of the audience. This second point foreshadows the revelation of Fisher as a Nazi spy. Moreover, though Jones is not allowed to take on the name of the greatest war correspondent of the *New York Globe*, Harvey Davis, the mention of Davis indicates what Jones will become as the plot progresses. Finally, a third example of foreshadowing is Stephen Fisher's suggestion to break a bottle of champagne over the head of Johnny Jones, the origin of their hostile relationship, which is the major conflict in the plot. However, at the political level of the film, Hitchcock is telling the American people that this is, and will be, the attitude of Hitler toward any American who tries to uncover the truth of Third Reich spy activities in other European nations.

Appearance versus reality is the major theme of *Foreign Correspondent* and is carefully and closely linked to the conflicting ideologies of Nazism and democracy inherent in the respective characters of Stephen Fisher and Johnny Jones. As one of the leaders of the Universal Peace Party, Fisher appears sincerely dedicated to world peace. However, he is really a Nazi spy whose integrity and allegiance to England have been lost to Nazi totalitarian ideology. Johnny Jones is given the pseudonym of Huntley Haverstock by Mr. Powers, who believes it will be more acceptable to the Europeans. Jones also acquires an English hat and umbrella, accoutrements of the well-dressed London gentleman, for his odyssey to England and Europe. As his outward appearance deteriorates throughout the film, we discover his inner self, a real hero who is willing to fight and to sacrifice his life to discover and print the truth. Jones is a prime example of Hitchcock's ideal man, a representative of the United States democratic ideology and free press ethic. I will analyze the characters of Fisher and Haverstock (Jones) later, when they have been sufficiently developed to show their conflicting Nazi and democratic ideologies.

The next sequence takes place between Huntley Haverstock and Mr. Stebbins (Robert Benchley), another correspondent, at a London railway station. Stebbins provides comic relief. He gives Haverstock a number of cables, one of which is an invitation to the Universal Peace Party's upcoming luncheon, with Van Meer as the main speaker. The following dialogue highlights Stebbins' incompetence:

HAVERSTOCK
Oh, this is dealing with the Universal Peace Party. That's Fisher's organization, isn't it?

STEBBINS

I don't know. I don't follow those things very much. New York wants it, I send it. That's the secret of being a correspondent. I've been doing it for twenty-five years.[18]

Paradoxically, Stebbins is a newspaper correspondent who is not concerned with news or correspondence. This and subsequent scenes show us that he is more interested in liquor, his girlfriend Miss Clark, and betting on horses. His antics are humorous, but his intemperate life has created a void of valid news. Stebbins' character is basically isolationist when he says, referring to the Van Meer luncheon, "I don't follow those things very much." This lackadaisical attitude had caused Powers to exclaim,

POWERS

Stebbins makes me sick! They all make me sick! Europe about to blow up and all I can get out of my foreign staff is a daily guessing game. I want some facts . . . I want a reporter. Someone who doesn't know the difference between an ism and a kangaroo. A good honest crime reporter. That's what the *Globe* needs! That's what Europe needs! There's a crime hatching on that bedeviled continent![19]

The crime hatching on that "bedeviled continent" of Europe was World War II. Of course the war had already begun by the time *Foreign Correspondent* was released, but partially through the character of Stebbins, the film was definitely a persuasive document for the United States to abandon its attitude of isolationism and to want to join Britain in actually routing the German menace in Europe.

We may compare Stebbins with the United States isolationist Senator William E. Borah. I do not imply that Senator Borah was either debauched or an alcoholic, as Hitchcock portrayed the character of Stebbins, but both men failed to weigh all the political facts available to them. There is no evidence that Hitchcock meant personal reference.

The case with Senator Borah was as follows. President Roosevelt and Secretary Hull warned a group of senators that war in Europe was imminent. However, Senator Borah was the main opposition to a repeal of the arms embargo, which would have given ominous power to Roosevelt in his negotiations abroad to avert war. At one point, Secretary Hull told the group,

"I wish the Senator [Borah] would come down to my office and read the cables. . . . I'm sure he would come to the conclusion that there's far more danger of war than he thinks." To this Senator Borah petulantly replied: "So far as the reports in your Department are concerned, I wouldn't be bound by them. I have my own sources of information . . . and on several occasions I've found them more reliable than the State Department." Shortly after this dogmatic statement, the meeting adjourned. Some six weeks later Germany invaded Poland.[20]

The next significant sequence in *Foreign Correspondent* is between Haverstock and Van Meer. The morning after Haverstock encounters Stebbins, he has the good fortune to meet Mr. Van Meer, who is on his way to the luncheon.

As they take a cab through London, Haverstock tries to direct the conversation into political matters, but Van Meer carefully avoids making any statements about world affairs, especially the European war situation.

HAVERSTOCK

It's very kind of you, Mr. Van Meer.

VAN MEER

It's a pleasure, my boy. I dislike riding alone. One thinks too much while riding alone.

HAVERSTOCK

Yes, exactly. The Polish situation and the Dutch treaty with the Belgians must be on your mind quite a lot these days. What do you feel, Mr. Van Meer, England will do in case the Nazis . . .

VAN MEER

England is so beautiful.[71]

Van Meer sidesteps the question about England and Nazi Germany and neutralizes the conversation by talking about the commonplace. Interestingly, there is another level even more politically potent than the probing questions of Haverstock. The actor playing Van Meer, Albert Basserman, was an actor with Max Reinhardt's German theatre for many years. According to Donald Spoto,

> Albert Basserman, the most honored man in German theatre in this century, fled to freedom just before the war and, at seventy-three, was cast by Hitchcock in this heroic role. Basserman was to appear in several more American films before his death at eighty-five in 1952. His presence in *Foreign Correspondent* not only adds a real depth and dignity to the story, but also— like the director's use of Lucie Mannheim in *The Thirty-nine Steps* (as the mysterious Miss Smith, the German spy working for England)—shows us Hitchcock's compassion and humanity toward the German refugee. When many regarded these refugees with scorn and suspicion, a few men like Alfred Hitchcock not only gave them work, but with understanding insight cast them in *anti-Nazi* roles and made them sympathetic characters most representative of the forces of freedom. This element alone makes *Foreign Correspondent* a film whose message lies as much in one pre-production detail as in what we finally see on the screen.[22]

At the luncheon, Huntley Haverstock meets Stephen Fisher's daughter, Carol (Laraine Day), who is genuinely concerned with finding a peaceful solution to the growing threat of war in Europe. Huntley talks with her because she is in charge of publicity for the Universal Peace Party and, equally important, because he finds her attractive. To have an American reporter become romantically involved with an English girl was clever scripting on the part of Hitchcock, who had been commissioned by the British government to build American sympathy for Britain's war cause.

But like their respective countries, Haverstock and Carol don't see eye to eye on political matters.

HAVERSTOCK

Since you're handling the publicity for this outfit, you might give me a line on what it is all about.

CAROL

Well, just what is it you would like to know?

HAVERSTOCK

Well, in the first place, is this Mr. Fisher entirely on the level?

CAROL

Very much so.

HAVERSTOCK

He seems like a very nice guy.

CAROL

He is, I assure you.

HAVERSTOCK

Well, what is it that makes him or you think that an organization like this, made up of well-meaning amateurs, backed up against those tough military boys of Europe . . .

CAROL

Well, it's those well-meaning amateurs as you call them who go out and do the fighting when the war comes, isn't it?[23]

Carol Fisher is then called away to the head table for the luncheon. Haverstock tries to get her to sit at his table, but she declines because she has been called "a well-meaning amateur."

Van Meer was supposed to give a speech but, according to Stephen Fisher, he has been unexpectedly called away. Fisher calls on his daughter, Carol, to speak on what the Party stands for and why the audience has been requested to attend. She begins,

CAROL

Ladies and gentlemen: I trust, even making allowances for a father's exuberance, you do not think that I am in any way being put forward today as a substitute for Mr. Van Meer and, happily for us, no one can take Mr. Van Meer's place. What I can do, possibly, is clear up a few misapprehensions that seem to have crept into the public discussion of this movement and advise some of the epithets that have been applied to us by some who have not gone as deeply into the matter as they might. Now, I'm sure that there are some of you here today who think of us as such. And I should like to ask anyone who has called us well-meaning amateurs to stand up by his chair and tell me just why a well-meaning amateur is any less reliable than a well-meaning professional at a moment like this, but I'll not take the time. I think the world has been run long enough by the well-meaning professionals. We might give the amateurs a chance now. (*She stares at Haverstock.*) But what I really want to do is to give you a very brief idea (*she pauses*) of just . . . of just how far-reaching our amateur plans are. . . . (*Her father tries to help her in whispering a few words of direction.*) And just . . . er . . . what I mean to say, however much one may . . . I mean we should both . . . both of us. . . . (*Haverstock ends the scene with singular applause.*)[24]

The implication of this monologue is alliance through romance, and through this romance a new political identity is conceived for the United States. Huntley Haverstock, the American, is single—an isolationist. His budding romance with Carol Fisher promises to end his personal isolationism through union with an

English girl who, like her country, is struggling for world peace but is willing to
fight the war if it comes.

Hitchcock wanted his audience to identify first with the hero and heroine so
the audience would later accept the military alliance between the United States
and England that the film proposes. But before this proposal can be justified, the
hero, his friends and associates must suffer violations of international law and
common human rights. As Hitchcock continues to entertain his audience in the
next three sequences, he also portrays formidable international Nazi aggression.
The first sequence is obligatory and leads into a chase scene, followed by the
famous windmill sequence.

Amsterdam is the location of the first sequence. A short montage of shots
visually introduces the city and its environs to the audience. It is raining, and the
establishing shot is of numerous steps leading up to a large building. A large
crowd on the steps creates a corridor where the main action is played, first
between Stephen Fisher and Haverstock. Fisher explains he will be going back
to London and regrets he will be unable to attend the peace conference. He
introduces an acquaintance of his to Haverstock and exits the scene. Haverstock
sees Mr. Van Meer coming up the steps and breaks away to greet him.

HAVERSTOCK

Mr. Van Meer, how are you? We somehow seemed to lose each other the day before yesterday.
So sorry you were called away. (*A puzzled expression is seen on Van Meer's face.*) Don't you
remember me? We shared the same cab together on the way to the luncheon.

REPORTER

May I have your picture, Mr. Van Meer? Thank you.[25]

The photographer shoots Van Meer, pulling the trigger when the flash bulb
ignites. In an interview, Hitchcock commented on how real life copied the reel
life of this assassination incident:

> Things have reached a point where those who live a life of wild and improbable adventure are
> copying devices from my movies . . . such as my picture *Foreign Correspondent*. In it a man
> was assassinated by a pistol concealed in a camera. In my film a photographer said, "Just a
> moment," to a diplomat on the steps of a large building; then pointed his camera at him and
> shot him dead. It gave me a turn when, a year later, the same thing occurred in real life in
> Teheran.[26]

Haverstock chases the photographer, who periodically shoots at him. The
killer escapes in a waiting car, and Haverstock jumps into a second car to
continue his pursuit only to find himself in the presence of Mr. Herbert Folliott
(George Sanders) and Carol Fisher. They are led on a wild chase through the
streets of Amsterdam and out into the Dutch countryside, dotted with windmills.
Carol introduces Mr. Folliott, an English foreign correspondent, to Haverstock.

As they round a corner, they see an open area with three windmills. The car they have been chasing has disappeared. They pull up to one of the windmills and leave their car.

Haverstock notices a plane overhead and comments, "You don't suppose they could have got up that high, do you?"[27] A gust of wind blows his derby into a marshy area, and he goes to the edge of the pond to try to retrieve it. The loss of Haverstock's hat is a significant motif in the film; the windmill scene is its third occurrence. Upon his departure from the United States, two children had absconded with his hat, and after his conversation with Van Meer, Haverstock left his hat in the cab they had shared. The motif is a foreshadowing device to convey to the cinema audience the message that Haverstock will not keep things "under his hat"; he will uncover the truth and print it for the world to read.

Haverstock's attention is diverted to the windmill and its sails. He notices the sails are turning against the wind and rushes up to his two companions on the road to tell them what he has seen, and what we have seen through the use of the subjective shot. In the interim, however, the direction of the sails is reversed. He eventually persuades the others to go and get the police because he believes the killer is inside the windmill. They are reluctant but agree to his request. This leaves Haverstock free to investigate the windmill. He notices the sails are again reversed, and as a plane lands, he realizes that the movement of the sails is a signaling device.

He opens a large door in the windmill and finds the car the killer had used for his escape. Haverstock cautiously opens another door and enters the windmill. The hero and audience see a number of gears turning and two stairwells which lead to an upper room. Men speaking in German can be heard; they are located on the main level (ground floor) of the windmill. There is an open space through which Haverstock must pass if he is to go up the stairs, but this will expose him to Van Meer's murderer and the other Germans. Two men are seen approaching the windmill. To escape detection, Haverstock must somehow conceal himself. The situation forces him to pass through the open space, go up the stairs, and open and pass through a door. He is not discovered, but he is very startled when he finds Van Meer in the room.

HAVERSTOCK

Why, Mr. Van Meer! It can't be possible.

VAN MEER

(*Slightly slurred voice.*) I have just been given a drug.

HAVERSTOCK

I saw you shot just now outside the conference hall! I saw it!

VAN MEER

They gave it to me when they moved me from . . . How long has it been now?

HAVERSTOCK

The man I saw was a dead image!

VAN MEER

The man you saw shot wasn't me. He was a substitute.

HAVERSTOCK

But why? What?

VAN MEER

They want the world to think that I've been assassinated. Yes. You can see the fact that I am in their hands.

HAVERSTOCK

Who are they?

VAN MEER

I can't explain it. (*Strongly slurred voice.*) All that I can tell you is that they are going to take me away by plane.[28]

Van Meer starts to write a name, but it is not distinguishable since the drug has affected his motor activities. Men are heard coming up the stairs, and Haverstock hides himself behind some gears in the room.

Two Germans enter the room to check on Van Meer in his drugged condition. A suspenseful complication occurs at this moment as Haverstock's trenchcoat becomes caught in the moving gears of the windmill, threatening his life. Fortunately, he manages to remove his coat just in time to avoid harm and is then able to recover it undetected by the Germans. During this episode the Nazis look up twice. The first time they see a bird, and the second time they see light and empty space. The reporter has climbed out of a window and partially down the windmill. He then re-enters the windmill through another window. Simultaneously, the two Germans and Van Meer leave the upper room and start down the stairs. The previous dilemma is now reversed. The first time Haverstock was forced up the stairs; the second time he is forced down. He manages to pass undetected by the Germans on the first floor and escapes through the door which he had entered at the beginning of the sequence.

These three sequences are significant for their suspense, political propaganda, and historical accuracy. The first sequence, on the steps of the Peace Conference building, is the obligatory scene. It exposes both the hero and the audience to the ruthless political tactics being used in Europe. It is obligatory because it is the inciting incident that places the hero's life in jeopardy when he pursues the killer, and this jeopardy later heightens suspense in the windmill sequence. Haverstock's pursuit of the killer makes him worthy of the title "hero" because he makes the pursuit of truth and justice more important than his own life.

The rapid pace of the chase from the Peace Conference building to the windmills does not give the audience time to realize that an Englishman, Herbert Folliott, and an American, Huntley Haverstock, have been united in their pursuit of a political killer in Europe. This is political propaganda in that Hitchcock again subtly calls for unity between the United States and Britain to bring the Nazi criminal to justice, just as he called for political unity through the romantic relationship between Haverstock and Carol Fisher, whose presence in the car makes her a heroine for the same reasons that Haverstock is a hero. These three— Haverstock, Carol, and Folliott—work together to bring about justice in an international sense in much the same way the United States and England cooperated in bringing about the defeat of Nazi Germany.

The well-known and much-liked windmill sequence, at the dramatic level, allows the hero to arrive at the plot elements of recognition and reversal. Suspense arises from the possible discovery of the hero by the Germans and from our knowledge that at least one of the Nazis in the windmill would kill our adventurous, alter-ego friend, Huntley Haverstock. Political history is evident in the use of the windmill as a microcosm of the Nazi spy subterfuge perpetrated in Holland in the late 1930s.

When Haverstock discovers that the man killed on the steps of the Peace Conference building was not Van Meer, he recognizes the great difference between appearance and reality. This leads to the reversal, his commitment at the end of the windmill sequence to prove Van Meer was not killed and thus show to the world the reality of Nazi Germany's ruthless foreign policy:

HAVERSTOCK
I know I look a fool. But there is something fishy going on around here (Europe). There is a big story in this. I can smell it. I can feel it. I am going to get to the bottom of it if it is the last thing I do. Nothing is going to stop me, you understand? I am going to prove that it was not Van Meer who was assassinated, but his double.[29]

"Fishy" implies that a situation is questionable because it rests on a false foundation of deceit, like the character of Stephen Fisher. The above excerpt of dialogue using "fishy" and "smell" is a subliminal statement on Nazi ideological rottenness concealed in the character of Stephen Fisher.

There are three scenes of superb suspense in the windmill sequence. The first is when Haverstock is forced up the stairs by the Germans approaching the windmill from the outside while the other Nazi spies are on the main level. He manages to get up the stairs without being noticed. The second occurs in the upper room with Van Meer. Van Meer tries to write the name of a person, and the audience becomes agitated when the drug administered to him prevents his giving them greater knowledge. Also in the upper room, Haverstock's coat gets caught in the gears of the windmill. We fear for him because of the equally unfavorable alternatives of being crushed by the revolving gears or being discovered by the Nazis. When the two Germans look up to see what is happening in the gear area, the audience is dismayed in their certainty that Haverstock will be discovered. The last scene of suspense occurs when the Nazis carry out Van Meer and Haverstock is forced down the stairs and has to conceal himself from the Nazis already on the main floor. One Nazi on the main level is staring directly at the open area through which Haverstock must pass. The hero hesitates to avoid certain discovery, but the two descending Nazis are getting closer. He has no choice but to dash across the open space, which he does. He goes undiscovered because just as he moves across the space, the observant Nazi pulls a sweater over his head.

The suspense in this sequence is based on isolation and, according to Hitchcock, editing to "draw" the audience into the action by continually cutting from the hero to villains. This forces the audience to share the psychological trauma experienced by the hero. "The key figure in a suspense film is very often isolated and vulnerable. This person's dangerous solitude can be evoked quite strongly through the *mise en scene*, and the setting is a major factor, enclosing the potential victim in an atmosphere of latent menace."[30] As Hitchcock himself explains,

> The point is to draw the audience right inside the situation instead of leaving them to watch it from outside, from a distance. And you can do this only by breaking the action up into details and cutting from one to the other, so that each detail is forced in turn on the attention of the audience and reveals its psychological meaning. If you played the whole scene straight through, and simply made a photographic record of it with the camera always in one position, you would lose your power over the audience. They would watch the scene without becoming really involved in it, and you would have no means of concentrating their attention on those particular visual details which make them feel what the characters are feeling.[31]

The next sequence opens in Haverstock's Amsterdam hotel room. He is typing a letter to Mr. Powers. There is a knock at the door and Haverstock invites two men to enter. They inform the reporter that the Chief of Police wants to see him. He tries to call Carol on the phone, but there is no dial tone. He (and the audience through the courtesy of an insert shot) notices that the line on the phone has been cut. Haverstock excuses himself and goes into the bathroom to take a quick bath and shave. In the bathroom he kneels down, removes the key from the keyhole, and sees the two men handling guns. He turns on the water in the bath and exits the bathroom through the window. Cautiously, he makes his way across the top story ledge of the building, the Hotel Europe. His hand inadvertently strikes the letter "E" of "HOTEL," and there is a crashing and tinkling sound as the letters "EL" are extinguished. Now Hitchcock has transformed the neon sign to read "HOT EUROPE," indicative of the international subterranean espionage taking place in the film and, as we shall see, in Holland itself.

Haverstock leaves the hotel ledge by stepping through a window and unwittingly entering Carol Fisher's room. He is wearing his bathrobe and finds himself in the presence of a woman who is a friend of Stephen and Carol Fisher. Carol walks into the room to check on her friend, who had been looking for face powder. The presence of Haverstock, dressed as he is, in Carol Fisher's bedroom makes Carol appear promiscuous in the eyes of her woman friend—another case of appearance versus reality. The friend is embarrassed and demurely excuses herself, and rejoins the party outside leaving the hero and heroine in the bedroom. Carol becomes verbally hostile toward Haverstock because he has disgraced her before her friend. She repeatedly asks him to leave, not so much for her sake as for the sake of her father, who will be discredited if their apparent tryst is taken for reality.

HAVERSTOCK

I take it you don't believe I am in trouble?

CAROL

You'll be in plenty of trouble if you don't get out of here. Now for the last time, please go.

HAVERSTOCK

Okay. But I want you to know exactly what's going to happen when I do go. I'll go back to my room and get dressed and I'll try and shake those two fellows off, but I won't succeed. They'll stick to me like a couple of tattoo marks, until they get me. They'll stop at nothing. I seem to know too much, and they're right. I don't know the ins and outs of your crackpot peace movement, and I don't know what is wrong with Europe, but I do know a story when I see one; and I'll keep after it until either I get it or it gets me. Sorry you have those derogatory opinions of me, but I guess that can't be helped. Well, so long. It's been nice knowing you. (*A long pause.*) I said good bye. (*He starts to leave.*)

CAROL

(*In tears.*) Don't go.

HAVERSTOCK

Oh, I guess I could have handled those fellows all right with a little luck.[32]

The two of them team up to thwart the two Nazi agents' attempt to kill Haverstock. The hero uses Carol's phone to have his room inundated with hotel personnel. Then he sends the valet into his room to get his suit. Carol and Haverstock leave the hotel and book passage on a ship for England. On the journey across the channel, Haverstock proposes marriage to Carol and she accepts.

Foreign Correspondent is in harmony with Nazi Germany's actual influence in Holland in the late 1930s. Hitchcock and Walter Wanger, the producer, were very much aware of events in Europe. They wanted to make an internationally topical film because their political inclinations were interventionist, in opposition to the majority opinion of the citizens polled in the United States.

The book *National Socialism*, by Raymond E. Murphy et al., published in 1943, gives historical insight into the extent of Nazi organization in Holland.[33] Although a National Socialist party functioned in Holland, Dutch law did not allow German residents to organize themselves politically. According to Murphy's source material, the cover for the Nazi party was "an outwardly social and cultural body that went by the innocent name of *Reichsdentsche Gemeinschaft*, the German Citizens' Association."[34] The attaché of the German legation at The Hague, a Dr. Butting, was president of the association and, "as party leader for Holland he was in absolute fact the uncrowned king of every German national resident in that country."[35]

The German Citizens' Association, headed by Dr. Butting, was determined to undermine Dutch democracy. The Nazis used economic depression to manipulate the unemployed element of the society, sending the bright and radical out-of-work Dutch youth to Germany for jobs and social fellowship. Once in Germany, the young men were housed, fed, entertained, and given work. They received relatively good wages and special arrangements were made allowing them to send up to two-thirds of their income, in Dutch guilders, to their families. During their stay, generally not more than six months, the Dutch youth were exposed to Nazi propaganda via the "Strength Through Joy" movement. Up to 80,000 men went through this program.[36]

The Nazis had a significant spy network in Holland. Many of the Dutch workers who spent time in Germany in the "Strength Through Joy" program would join the Dutch National Socialist Party when they returned home. As members of this party or the German Citizens' Association, these men were used by Butting as intelligence sources to assist the professional spies of Admiral Wilhelm Canaris' bureau in providing the German High Command information vital to German military operations in Holland.[37]

In May of 1940, Germany invaded Holland and took control. *Foreign Correspondent* was a significant reflection of Nazi spy tactics in Holland; today the film serves as a valid historical document of free world entertainment with an anti-Nazi message in that it shows the German spy as a ruthless killer, kidnapper, and mind controller within Holland.

After the journey across the channel, several sequences are played in London. The first occurs in the home of Stephen Fisher and involves him, his daughter, Huntley Haverstock, and Mr. Kreuger. Haverstock and the audience recognize Kreuger as one of the Nazis from the windmill. When Kreuger excuses himself to wait in Fisher's study, Haverstock tells Fisher and his daughter that he saw Kreuger in the windmill. Fisher appears skeptical and is called away by Kreuger. The following scene is played between Kreuger and Fisher.

FISHER
I don't want to seem inhospitable, Mr. Kreuger, but I must ask you to leave my house. I'm sure Mr. Haverstock is going to suggest that I turn you over to the police.

KREUGER
Mr. Haverstock seems to be something of a trouble maker.

FISHER

I thought you said he had been taken care of by our agents in Amsterdam?

KREUGER

I thought so, too. I don't understand. Perhaps Miss Fisher being with him may have caused complications. It would have been ideal if she had been in our confidence.

FISHER

Please leave my daughter out of this.

KREUGER

Someone has to take care of the sordid details.

FISHER

This is too close to home. In fact it is my home. I can't do away with a guest in my own house.

KREUGER

I have an idea. You remember Rolley?

FISHER

Rolley? Oh yes! The fellow who used to run your father's stables in Moscow. I think he was present when a mutual friend of ours accidentally fell off a high bridge at Bellow.

KREUGER

He's retired now. He's living here in a flat in London. If Mr. Haverstock could be induced to hire him as a private detective . . . You should warn him [not] to go about London with the knowledge that he has.

FISHER

Yes, I see.

KREUGER

I shall look Mr. Rolley up at once and give him his instructions.[38]

Through this obligatory scene, the audience is in a superior position because it learns that Fisher is a Nazi and is the master antagonist who intends to have Haverstock murdered. Fisher returns to Carol and Haverstock and persuades Haverstock not to print the Van Meer story. Then he tries to convince him to hire a bodyguard:

FISHER

I don't like you dashing about without some kind of protection.

HAVERSTOCK

Oh, forget it.

FISHER

If what you say is true, you'll need protection.

HAVERSTOCK

Listen, Mr. Fisher. I've covered beer mob killings and race riots since I was a cop without even carrying a rabbit's foot.

FISHER

These people are criminals—more dangerous than your rumrunners and housebreakers. They're fanatics. They combine a mad love of country with an equally mad indifference to life; their own as well as others'. They're cunning and unscrupulous, and . . . inspired. *("Inspired" is whispered in a mesmerized state.)* I wouldn't be able to talk with Mr. Powers again if you didn't live long enough to turn in the best story of the year.

HAVERSTOCK

I'll be a fine correspondent hiding in an attic somewhere.

FISHER

I'm not suggesting you hide anywhere. Just get somebody to watch out for you.

HAVERSTOCK

A nurse, huh. Johnny Jones goes to Europe and hires a nurse. That's going to look great on the expense account.

FISHER

I know a very efficient private detective agency where we can get just the man.

HAVERSTOCK

Okay. Whatever you say.

FISHER

I can arrange it all for you. And if it will make you feel any better, I won't mention it to anybody.

HAVERSTOCK

Listen, if anybody finds out I hired a bodyguard, I'll shoot myself.[39]

This dialogue and the events that preceded it reveal the difference between Nazi ideology and British and American democracy. The character of the American, Huntley Haverstock, is naive to the fanatical and insidious tactics of the Nazis revealed in the character of Fisher. Hitchcock creates an adventurous journey where Haverstock and the free-world audience experience the deception and danger of Nazi foreign policy. Both Haverstock and the audience must come to terms not only with Nazi ideology but, more important, with their own democratic values as embodied in the Declaration of Independence.

In a propaganda film, the protagonist and antagonist are more than characters of a plot; they symbolize conflicting ideologies. Stephen Fisher, the antagonist in *Foreign Correspondent*, has fallen prey to the Nazi totalitarian state of mind, as did the English writer Houston Stuart Chamberlain, who in the late 1800s left England to become a citizen of Germany and married a German woman. He states in one of his books that "It is because of the lack of a true religion that our whole Teutonic culture is sick unto death, and this will mean its ruin if timely help does not come."[40] Years later, when Chamberlain met Hitler, he felt that Hitler would satisfy Germany's need for a leader who could give her a "true religion." Hitler would create an Aryan race and a political religion. This is the essence of the Nazi ideology present in the character of Stephen Fisher.

Huntley Haverstock, the protagonist, represents democratic ideology and is not aware of the difference between appearance and reality in the character of Stephen Fisher. Haverstock's lack of political perception almost leads to his demise as he is caught in the middle of political revolution against royal despotism. He has been and will be confronted with the need for self-preservation. A direct attack on Haverstock is a direct attack on American democracy because the individual is of paramount importance in American society. Edward G. McGrath, a political scientist, exposes the essence of what becomes Haverstock's political position, and what became the United States foreign policy: "American democracy allows anyone to state his case. But it does not allow him to conspire to teach or advocate the overthrow of the system by force or violence. American democracy does not recognize an obligation to serve its own destruction."[41]

In the next suspenseful sequence of *Foreign Correspondent*, Haverstock sees beyond the peace organization front to the reality of Fisher, the Nazi, and in this clarity of perception Haverstock ceases to serve his own destruction.

At the beginning of the sequence, Mr. Rolley arrives at Fisher's home and waits outside for Fisher and Haverstock. He holds up his hands and looks at them, foreshadowing how he intends to kill the American hero. The suspense arises from the audience's knowledge that Rolley intends to kill Haverstock and their hope that Haverstock discerns this before Rolley's mission is successful. This places the audience in a superior position and compounds suspense, while also giving the unexpected complication and dreadful alternative.

Fisher and Haverstock greet Rolley on the sidewalk. Haverstock is reluctant to accept Rolley as a bodyguard because of his small stature. However, Fisher leaves them and returns to his home. Haverstock and Rolley then walk down the sidewalk together in pleasant conversation. As they start to cross the street, Rolley sees a truck approaching. Here Hitchcock shows Rolley rushing forward with upraised arms and hands. Both we, the audience, and Haverstock are being pushed in front of the oncoming truck.

HAVERSTOCK
Did you see that? Someone deliberately pushed me.

ROLLEY
Why that was me, sir. If I had pulled you back you would have been caught. It was push or nothing.

HAVERSTOCK
Well, that's smart work, Mr. Rolley. Thank you very much.

ROLLEY
Oh, after all, that's what I'm here for, eh.[42]

Rolley and Haverstock take a cab. By pretending that someone is following them, Rolley persuades Haverstock to leave the cab and take sanctuary in a church which has a large adjoining tower. The assassin convinces Haverstock to take the elevator to the observation deck of the tower to avoid the men who are supposedly following them.

The two men's solitude at the top of the tower is broken by a small group of school boys who crowd around an open viewing area. Rolley holds up one boy to give him a better view and the youngster inadvertently loses his hat. The boys take the elevator down after a young couple get out, but the girl has vertigo, and they take the stairs down. Now the two men are alone again. The suspense states of phobia—vertigo—and isolation are present. Rolley directs Haverstock's attention to an area of distant landscape and then rushes toward him to push him from the tower.

These two characters spend slightly less than four minutes at the top of the tower. The two interruptions—boys and the couple—have extended and heightened the suspense. As Rolley rushes toward Haverstock, a woman screams, and we see a second shot of a woman screaming among a group of people on the ground. Then religious choir music corresponds with a shot of two nuns crossing themselves. Like the Albert Hall sequence in *The Man Who Knew Too Much* and the Hannay-Jordan sequence in *The Thirty-nine Steps*, Hitchcock does not reveal the fate of the hero until the subsequent scene. This is a deliberate extension of suspense.

The next scene opens with conversation between Stebbins and Haverstock.

HAVERSTOCK

I heard the lift coming up and I turned. I saw that look in his eye as he came toward me. In that split second the whole thing flashed through my mind. All I could think of was Fisher. Fisher planned this. And I guess I just stepped aside and over he went.[43]

Folliott enters the room and informs Haverstock he has been aware of Fisher's treason for a year. He also tells him that Van Meer has memorized an unwritten part of a peace treaty and that his Nazi abductors are going to torture him until he gives it to them. This scene becomes obligatory when Folliott asks Haverstock to abduct his fiancée, Carol Fisher. Folliott will then go to Fisher and suggest a trade of Van Meer for Carol Fisher. Haverstock is reluctant to comply. Carol enters the room and suggests that Haverstock leave London. She calls home and leaves word for her father that she is going to her Aunt Martha's in a town south of London. They leave, and the audience is prepared for Folliott to play a suspense scene with Fisher.

Folliott does confront Fisher, in his own home, with the news that Carol has been kidnapped. Fisher calls Martha and finds out that Carol has not been there recently. Folliott tells him that he wants to know what he has done with Van Meer. He explains that Fisher will only see his daughter if the whereabouts of Van Meer are made known. Fisher picks up a pencil and paper and writes a note. As he finishes, Carol walks into the room. Folliott takes the note out of Fisher's hand and excuses himself. The camera follows Folliott through the house and out into the street, where he and the audience finally read the note: "Sorry, but I heard my daughter's car coming."[44]

Carol explains to her father that a disaffection has occurred between herself and Haverstock. She has misconstrued his intentions as immoral because he ordered two adjacent rooms with an adjoining door at the hotel where they intended to stay before traveling on to her aunt's home. Fisher informs his daughter that they will be leaving London the next day on a plane for Washington, D.C. She agrees to go, and her father leaves the house. He takes a taxi to the building where Van Meer is being held hostage.

The estrangement between Haverstock and Carol symbolizes that which occurred between the United States and Britain following World War I, and which resulted in the legislation of the Neutrality Acts. In the 1920s and early 1930s, many people were saying that the United States had entered the war for profit, not to "make the world safe for democracy."

> In 1934 a great many books and articles were written describing the intrigues and profits of munitions-manufacturers. In the spring of that year the Senate set up a committee with Gerald Nye as its chairman to investigate the activities of the American munitions industry. The committee showed that excessive profits had been made during the first World war by bankers and armament-makers. The investigation revealed the profits that had been gained by J. P. Morgan and Company as agents for Allied purchases in the United States and showed that American industry was prosperous largely because of orders from the Allies. It also demonstrated that an Allied defeat would have struck a severe blow to American prosperity. The question then arose as to whether the country had gone into the war as a free agent to save democracy or whether it had been shoved into the war by selfish international bankers and munitions-makers.[45]

Following the indicting publicity and the Nye committee's investigation, Congress moved toward neutrality legislation to prevent America's involvement in another world war, enacting four Neutrality Acts from 1935–1939.

On September 3, 1939, a state of war existed between the Allied powers and Germany, touched off by Germany's invasion of Poland. Less than three weeks later, Roosevelt called a special session of Congress to seek the power to assist the Allies, by sending them arms and ammunition, through a repeal of the Neutrality Act of 1937. The Congress concurred with his wishes.[46]

From 1939 to the attack on Pearl Harbor, two groups polarized the American political scene: isolationists and interventionists. The isolationists organized the America First Committee, and the interventionists organized the Committee to Defend America by Aiding the Allies (CDA). Each group comprised members of both political parties. Bill White, Chairman of the CDA, was a staunch member of the Republican Party who threw full support behind Roosevelt's interventionist foreign policy. The following synopsis reviews these two groups' respective objectives:

> In President Roosevelt's open stand for all-out aid for the Allies short of war, and in his unpublicized belief that war itself would be a lesser evil than an Axis victory, he had important segments of public opinion both with him and against him. The isolationist sentiment that had promoted the neutrality laws was still strong. It opposed aid to the Allies as a step toward war, and it felt that America's sharing in "Europe's wars" was the greatest of evils. It was organized most effectively in the America First Committee, with General Robert E. Wood of Chicago as president and Colonel Charles A. Lindbergh as leading orator. It received the support of, among other journals, the *Chicago Tribune* and the Hearst newspapers. The America First Committee was "going strong" up to the afternoon of the Pearl Harbor attack.
>
> On the other side, the most important organized vehicle for the expression of public opinion was the Committee to Defend America by Aiding the Allies, headed for some time by the well-known Kansas editor, William Allen White, and often referred to as the White Committee. Organized in the spring of 1940, it stood for all material aid to the Allies short of war; part of its membership favored outright participation in the war. Some persons sharing this latter view, from both within and without the White Committee, formed the Fight for Freedom Committee in April 1941. They held that, in asking others to do all the fighting, America was playing an ignoble role, and urged that America take its place as a fullscale belligerent in the "fight for freedom."[47]

Strong debate about the reversal of the original Neutrality Act was the political atmosphere in the United States when *Foreign Correspondent* was released. This propaganda-entertainment film was part of the new vanguard of politically-oriented films exposing the Nazi menace while calling for military alertness through rearmament. Hollywood's motto had been for many years, "If you want to send a message, send a telegram." At first, Will Hays, President of the Motion Picture Producers and Distributors of America, supported pure entertainment and opposed propaganda in film. Placing side by side the statements he made in 1938 and 1939 shows the significant shift of the motion picture industry toward treatment of political issues in film.

> [March 28, 1938] The industry has resisted and must continue to resist the lure of propaganda in that sinister sense persistently urged upon it by extremist groups. The function of the entertainment screen is to entertain by whatever wholesome theme or treatment writers, artists, and dramatists can create. There is no other criterion.
>
> Entertainment is the commodity for which the public pays at the box-office. Propaganda disguised as entertainment would be neither honest salesmanship nor honest showmanship. The movie theatre can afford the soft impeachment that most pictures reflect no higher purpose than to entertain, with escapist entertainment if you please. If entertainment and recreation are what 85,000,000 people weekly seek in American motion picture theatres, and they do, so much the better for the screen and the universal public which it serves.
>
> [March 29, 1939] Today competent critics, in and out of the industry, are able to point to a succession of pictures which dramatized present-day social conditions, which exposed slum areas in many of our great cities, which placed in true perspective the problems of medicine and medical care, which dealt with issues of war and peace, which treated of crime and crime-

breeding, which showed human beings struggling for individuality against the forces of an increasingly complex civilization, which discussed the values of our present-day democracy and emphasized the traditions that have made this nation great, which exposed racketeering, which treated of the problems of adolescence and which dealt with themes notable for their educational value.[48]

This is a complete about-face on the part of the film industry. But more important, it reflects what the movie patrons were willing to buy and what their international political interests were at this time. It reflects "the movement of the American mind."[49]

Hitchcock was very much concerned that the American mind move toward an awareness of the growing tyranny in Europe. In the next sequence of *Foreign Correspondent*, he shows his high regard for the indomitable character of the little people of the free world.

Folliott takes a cab and follows Fisher to the Nazi hideout where Van Meer is being held captive. Folliott has left word for Haverstock to come to the Tottenham Court Road restaurant, where Van Meer is being tortured. As Fisher talks with Van Meer to try to get him to reveal the secret clause of the treaty, Folliott is brought into the room at gunpoint. One of the spies in the downstairs restaurant captured him. Folliott sits down, and Fisher continues with his interrogation of Van Meer. Fisher tries to get Van Meer to divulge the secret clause on the basis of their friendship, but Folliott speaks out against this ruse:

FOLLIOTT
He's not your friend, Mr. Van Meer. Don't tell him.

VAN MEER
What's that? Someone just said you're not my friend. Why didn't you bring the police? Why aren't you taking me away from here? Help me, Fisher. Help me. There's no help. No help for the whole, cruel, suffering world. You lied to me, Fisher. You have cried peace and there is no peace, only war and death. You're a liar, Fisher, a truly true liar. You can do what you want with me—that's not important. But you'll never conquer them, Fisher—little people everywhere who have been taught to be brave. Lie to them, hurt them, whip them, force them into war. When the beasts like you will devour each other, then the world will belong to the little people.[50]

There is a direct parallel between Fisher and Hitler. Fisher's mind has been consumed by the Nazi ideology advanced in the speeches and writings of Hitler. Van Meer's words "You have cried peace and there is no peace, only war and death" are true of Hitler. The German Four Year Plan of 1936 and a speech Hitler gave in 1939 revealed his ultimate objective of aggression and war.

As the "final solution" of the German struggle for existence [the Four Year Plan] named the "expansion of living space, that is, of the raw material and food basis of our people," demanded that war be prepared in peacetime, and closed with the words: "I hereby set the following task: I. The German army must be ready for action in four years; II. The German economy must be ready for war in four years."[51]

Hitler's speech of August 22, 1939, revealed his true character. Gone was the pretense of his earlier peace speeches; in its place was his pronouncement that

> We must close and harden our hearts. He who has pondered on the order of this world realizes that its meaning lies in the warlike survival of the fittest. But the German people are among the fittest people on earth. Providence has made us the leaders of this people, thus it is our task to provide the German people, crowded together with a hundred and forty inhabitants to the square kilometer, with necessary living space. In carrying out this task, the greatest severity can be the greatest kindness.

Nolte comments that

> This could have been written word for word in *Mein Kampf*. And it only confirmed what was in fact obvious to all: it removed the accidental nature from the incipient war and stamped it with the mark of timely decision. Not long afterward he made the connection clear when he said, looking back: "Basically I did not set up the Wehrmacht [army] in order not to strike. The decision to strike was always in me."[52]

A line indicates that what is true of Fisher is true of Hitler. "You're a liar, Fisher, a truly true liar." England, Germany, and most of the free world had failed to grasp the undercurrent of Nazi totalitarianism and its compulsion to world conquest. But through the character of Fisher and his torture of Van Meer, we grasp the true nature of Nazi Germany's ideology.

Van Meer is tortured off camera, and he divulges the secret section of the peace treaty. Meanwhile, Haverstock sees a fight through the window of a room above the restaurant. Folliott jumps out of the second story window and his fall is broken by a cloth store-window awning. He asks Haverstock to follow him.

The relationship between Folliott and Haverstock parallels that between England and the United States. Britain wanted the United States to join her in stopping the international tyranny of Nazi Germany. The Marquess of Lothian, a British aristocrat who addressed the American Farm Bureau at Baltimore on December 11, 1940, stressed Britain's role as a democracy and called for the support of the United States in opposing Nazi German tactics:

> You have already declared your interest in the survival of Britain. It is for you to decide whether it is to your interest to give us whatever assistance may be necessary in order to make certain that Britain shall not fall.[53]

> The plain truth is that peace and order always depend not upon disarming the police but upon there being an overwhelming power behind just law. The only place where that power can be found behind the laws of a liberal and democratic world is in the United States and in Great Britain supported by the Dominions and in some other free nations. The only nucleus round which a stable and peaceful and democratic world can be built after this war is if the United States and Great Britain possess between them more airplanes and ships of war and the key positions of world power . . . than any possible totalitarian rival.[54]

Folliott, Haverstock, and a cadre of men run up to the room where Van Meer is being held captive. They rescue him, but Fisher escapes and there is insufficient evidence to arrest him. Van Meer cannot speak because he is in a coma. Folliott and Haverstock decide to book a flight on the plane Fisher and Carol are taking to Washington, D.C. On the trans-Atlantic flight, Haverstock approaches Carol and attempts a reconciliation. However, a Nazi ship fires on the plane which crashes into the ocean. Stephen Fisher leaves the wing of the plane, upon which the survivors are clinging, to preserve their lives by preventing the wing from sinking. Folliott and Haverstock dive into the sea and try to save his life, but they are unsuccessful. The survivors are picked up by an American ship returning to England. Haverstock and Carol are reconciled, and Haverstock manages to send his story to the *New York Globe*. I quote the short final sequence in full.

RADIO ANNOUNCER

This is London. We have as a guest one of the soldiers of the press. One of the little army of historians who are writing history from beside the cannon's mouth. Foreign correspondent of the *New York Globe*, Huntley Haverstock.

HAVERSTOCK

Hello America. I've been watching a part of the world being blown to pieces. A part of the world as nice as Vermont, Ohio, Virginia, California and Illinois lies ripped up bleeding like a steer in a slaughterhouse. And I've seen things that make the history of the savages read like Pollyanna legend.

RADIO ANNOUNCER

We're going to have to postpone the broadcast. (*At this point sirens begin to wail and lights flash as bombs begin to burst outside the studio.*)

HAVERSTOCK

Don't postpone nothing; let's go on as long as we can.

RADIO ANNOUNCER

(*To Carol*) Ma'am, we've got a shelter downstairs.

HAVERSTOCK

How about it, Carol?

CAROL

They're listening in America, Johnny.

HAVERSTOCK

Okay. We'll tell them. I can't read the rest of this speech I have because the lights have gone out. So I'll just have to talk off the cuff. All that noise you hear isn't static, it's death coming to London. Yes, they're coming here now. You can hear the bombs falling on the streets and homes. Don't tune me out—hang on—this is a big story—and you're part of it. It's too late now to do anything except stand in the dark and let them come as if the lights are all out everywhere except in America. (*The music "America" begins to play softly in the background and through the end credits.*) Keep those lights burning, cover them with steel, build them in with guns, build a canopy of battleships and bombing planes around them and, hello America, hang onto your lights. They're the only lights in the world.[55]

The final sequence of *Foreign Correspondent* is a bold balance of patriotic music and propagandistic dialogue. The film was released by United Artists in New York City on August 28, 1940.[56] Ten days later, on September 7, 1940, the Germans began their massive air offensive against London.[57] *Foreign Correspondent* had predicted the London blitz.

Criticism of *Foreign Correspondent*

Hitchcock's *Foreign Correspondent* was virtually a call to arms by an Englishman who was anxiously concerned about the freedom of his own country and the world. Not only did its release coincide with the London blitz and the fall of Western Europe, it was a deliberate attempt by Hitchcock and the script writers to "shake the United States into awareness of what must threaten her if she turned her back on Europe."[58] Hitchcock knew exactly what he wanted in *Foreign Correspondent* right down to the cuts and sound effects—everything was preconceived.[59] Philip Dynia says that the "political message at the end is spoken directly" to the movie-going public. Hitchcock "set out to give American public opinion a nudge in favor of active intervention in the war against Hitler's Germany."[60]

Reviewers are quick to praise *Foreign Correspondent*. *Time* magazine claimed *Foreign Correspondent* to be "one of the year's finest pictures," noting that Hitchcock's camera was the best reporter—being in the right place at the right time as when a diplomat is shot and when a man is about to fall from a tower, the camera watches a hat take the plunge first. More than anything the camera has "the supreme gift of not telling everything."[61] *The New York Herald Tribune* declared it "a stunning melodrama" in which "no punches have been pulled in describing the Gestapo or the fifth columnists, while the ending of the film is as challenging a call to arms as the screen has issued to democracy."[62] Reich propaganda minister Joseph Goebbels, arch enemy of democracy, liked the film for its outstanding propaganda technique. He considered it "a first class production, a criminological bang-up hit, which no doubt will make a certain impression upon the broad masses of the people in enemy countries."[63]

Leo Rosten, film critic and researcher, distinguishes propaganda films from educational or merely patriotic films:

> A movie on physiology or golf or arithmetic is an educational film. A movie which dramatizes the prevailing civic emotions about our country, its institutions or national heroes, is a patriotic film. But a movie made for the *purpose* of changing attitudes about, say, American foreign policy or socialized medicine or monogamy would be a propaganda film.[64]

His definition of the propaganda film fits *Foreign Correspondent* in that the majority of Americans were against the United States entering World War II in 1940. But the film was not propaganda only. The strong, independent character of Johnny Jones and his struggle to uncover and print the truth (freedom of the press) suggest that *Foreign Correspondent* represents a new patriotism. It is educational insofar as it foreshadows the night air raids as part of the blitz over London. Beyond this, the film is entertaining because the audience derives pleasure from the suspense sequences, the comedy of Stebbins, and the romance between Haverstock and Carol.

The isolationists viewed *Foreign Correspondent* as propaganda because it attacked non-involvement; the interventionists viewed it as patriotic because it called for support of Britain in her fight for freedom against Nazi Germany. In the 1940s, the public expected the mass media to follow certain unwritten guidelines about information flow. Newspapers and radio were to give news; feature films were to give programming and entertainment. A film that mixed entertainment and a political position, as *Foreign Correspondent* did when it called for intervention in World War II, was considered propaganda.

From 1939–1941, Hollywood produced approximately fifty films that were anti-Nazi in theme and content.[65] Isolationists, especially politicians, were appalled at the possibility that five or six movie company presidents could be influencing foreign policy through propaganda films seen by a movie-going public of eighty million people a week. Joseph P. Kennedy, United States ambassador to Great Britain, was against the anti-Nazi films: In November 1940, Kennedy visited Hollywood and at a private dinner attended by motion picture industry leaders insisted that the production of anti-Nazi films must stop because we would have to make peace with Hitler since the fall of England was inevitable. Kennedy noted that many industry leaders were Jewish and allegedly suggested that their fate might eventually be as tragic as that of European Jews if they were not more careful in their pro-Allied film treatments.[66]

But Hollywood's interventionist position continued, to the annoyance of a growing number of United States senators in the isolationist camp. Chief among them was Burton K. Wheeler, Chairman of the Committee on Interstate Commerce. In September 1941 he instigated Resolution 152 to facilitate a subcommittee investigation of propaganda in films.

The Senate subcommittee's hearings began on September 9 and continued through September 26, 1941. Senator Gerald P. Nye, isolationist and main formulator of the First neutrality Act in 1935, was the first person to give testimony before the subcommittee. He used the word "propaganda" freely, and he echoed the common fear that so few men as filmmakers could exert such great influence over the public's opinion on foreign policy.[67] Senator Clark, a Republican from Idaho, gave the subcommittee two common usages of the term "propaganda picture": "a war propaganda film has been characterized as a means to incite hate for the people of another nation,'' adding that propaganda pictures could also ''incite the desire of those who saw it, or some of those who saw it, to go to war.''[68]

Wendell L. Wilkie, a lawyer and Republican who lost the presidential election to Franklin D. Roosevelt in 1940, served as legal counsel for the four Hollywood executives who testified before the subcommittee: Barney Balaban, President of Paramount Pictures; Nicholas Schenck, President of Loew's; Harry M. Warner, President of Warner Brothers Pictures; and Darryl F. Zanuck, Vice-President of Twentieth Century-Fox. The most direct and unabashed testimony concerning the ''propaganda film'' and the European war situation was given by Wilkie, Warner, and Zanuck. Wilkie acknowledged the motion picture industry's awareness of the worthlessness of Nazi pledges and promises, citing the fate of half of Europe as support. He considered the freedom of the industry, as well as the country, to be in jeopardy should Nazism triumph and brushed aside the thesis that ''America's trade hopes lie in a world where Nazism survives.''[69] In his closing comments, Wilkie summed up the industry's philosophy:

> The impression has now arisen, and very naturally, that one of the hoped for results of the pressure of your investigation will be to influence the industry to alter its policies, so that they may accord more directly with the views of such of its critics as Senator Nye. The industry is prepared to resist such pressures with all of the strength at its command.[70]

Warner, on a more personal level, reiterated Wilkie's stand:

> I believe nazi-ism is a world revolution whose ultimate objective is to destroy our democracy, wipe out all religion, and enslave our people—just as Germany has destroyed and enslaved Poland, Belgium, Holland, France, and all the other countries. I am ready to give myself and all my personal resources to aid in the defeat of the Nazi menace to the American people.[71]

He went on to express his support of President Roosevelt's foreign policy believing the world struggle for freedom to be ''in its final stage.''[72] His final comment which he first made in September 1939, predicted the end of isolationism: ''I said publicly then, and I say today, that the freedom which this country fought England to obtain, we may have to fight with England to retain.''[73]

And Zanuck defended Hollywood's right to choose its subject matter in the making of films:

> To condemn the motion-picture industry for dealing with subjects as timely, as vital, and as important as the current upheaval in the world is to subject the industry to an impossible censorship. It would deny us access to the same vital developments which today fill our newspapers, magazines, books, the radio, and the stage. It would leave the American motion picture as worthless and sterile as those made in Germany and Italy.
>
> The daily newspaper has always furnished me and my associates ideas for motion pictures. I made the first gangster pictures which helped uncover the rottenness of the underworld in our various cities. Perhaps some of you saw *Public Enemy No. 1*, which was the first exposé on the

screen of the underworld. We received many protests against that film. I suppose the underworld thought this was unfair propaganda against the gangster, just so some now feel our war pictures are unfair propaganda against Hitler.

Hollywood didn't create the underworld, nor did it create Hitler and the Nazis. We have portrayed them no differently than they are pictured daily in newspapers, magazines, books, and all other mediums of expression. In fact, we have merely portrayed them as they are.[74]

Hitchcock's *Foreign Correspondent* was mentioned twice in the subcommittee's hearings. It was a small but significant part of the national debate over foreign policy. The subcommittee provided a government-authorized forum where isolationists and interventionists were able to voice their views. This special group of senators adjourned on September 26, 1941, never to reconvene in this capacity. The Senate became engaged in more pressing duties and pushed aside the hearings of this subcommittee. Ten weeks later, the Japanese attacked Pearl Harbor.

It is interesting to note Hitchcock's unflappable reaction to the Pearl Harbor attack:

During the shooting of *Saboteur* there was one small, slightly untoward incident. One Sunday in December, when the rest of the studio was deserted, Hitch was working with his art director, Robert Boyle, on story-boarding some sequences for the following week. Suddenly in burst one of the studio guards, clearly surprised to find anyone on the lot. He was wearing the air-raid warden's outfit that had already, just to be on the safe side, been widely issued. "Haven't you heard, the Japs just bombed Pearl Harbor!" he blurted out, and vanished as quickly as he had come. There was a short silence. "Hm," said Hitch; "curious hat the fellow was wearing . . . " and went right on with what he was doing.[75]

On December 8, 1941, the United States Congress, at the request of President Roosevelt, declared war on Japan. On December 11, 1941, Germany declared war on the United States in support of her Axis ally, Japan. The plea of Alfred Hitchcock and Walter Wanger, through Johnny Jones in the last sequence of *Foreign Correspondent*, for the United States to come to the aid of the Allied Powers had finally received an affirmative response.

Conclusion

In *Foreign Correspondent*, Hitchcock took his audience to Europe through the news-gathering odyssey of his hero, Johnny Jones. The odyssey could have ended where it began, in New York City, but its termination point was London. Hitchcock's position was that England was the mother of the United States and of her democratic form of government. The United States' rightful responsibility in world politics was to help her mother country, whose present democratic existence was in jeopardy under the air raid onslaught of Nazi Germany. Hitchcock's political intent in *Foreign Correspondent* was to manifest the mutual democratic values of the English and the Americans. He suggested that political and military alliance of the two countries could defeat the German menace, just as the unification of the film's protagonists had outsmarted and partially disrupted the Nazi spying efforts in Holland.

Hitchcock adroitly applied the ten elements of suspense in *Foreign Correspondent*. The Nazis and those who succumbed to their ideology were always the antagonists. In the final sequence, the hero and heroine risked their lives to broadcast the truth of the European war situation to the United States, and to request her assistance. There was no final resolution of suspense because that resolution would come in the real world through the United States' declaration of war and her military intervention on behalf of global peace.

3

Saboteur

Production: Universal, 1942. *Producers:* Frank Lloyd and Jack H. Skirball. *Director:* Alfred Hitchcock. *Scenario:* Peter Viertel, Joan Harrison and Dorothy Parker, from an original subject by A. Hitchcock. *Director of Photography:* Joseph Valentine, A.S.C. *Sets:* Jack Otterson. *Music:* Charles Previn and Frank Skinner. *Editing:* Otto Ludwig. *Studio:* Universal. *Distributor:* Universal, 1942, 108 minutes. *Principal Actors:* Robert Cummings (Barry Kane), Priscilla Lane (Patricia Martin: "Pat"), Otto Kruger (Charles Tobin), Alan Baxter (Mr. Freeman), Alma Kruger (Mrs. Van Sutton), and Vaughan Glazer, Dorothy Peterson, Ian Wolfe, Anita Bolster, Jeanne and Lynn Roher, Norman Lloyd, Oliver Blake, Anita Le Deaux, Pedro de Cordoba, Kathryn Adams, Murray Alper, Frances Carson, Billy Curtis.[1]

In *Foreign Correspondent*, Alfred Hitchcock stated in suspenseful cinematic terms that the major external threat to the democratic free-world ethic was Nazi Germany. His next political film, *Saboteur*, focused on sabotage in the U.S. as German intelligence sought to weaken America's internal security.

Saboteur is an adventure film that also contains the classical cinematic suspense elements. The lead character, Barry Kane, is accused of sabotaging the airplane factory where he works in California, but the real culprit is Frank Fry, a sabotage agent. Kane takes a perilous journey across the United States in pursuit of Fry. Along the way he meets people who either help or oppose him in his main objective of capturing Fry and clearing his own name.

Numerous incidents of suspense hold the audience's attention, especially the final sequence on the Statue of Liberty. Hitchcock manages to thrill his audience and at the same time create a strong patriotic message, admonishing Americans to support United States democracy and freedom by detecting and destroying any Axis factions within their country.

Saboteur's release in 1942 by Universal Studios was timely. Although Hitchcock had gone into production on this film before the United States entered World War II, releasing it after the war began silenced further attacks by isolationists, who accused Hitchcock of using his films as propaganda for interventionism and thereby trying to change foreign policy. *Saboteur*, which would have been considered blatant propaganda a year earlier, was received as a positive entertainment vehicle and a supportive patriotic document while being lauded as "a strongly anti-Nazi film."[2]

Saboteur and the Threat and Reality of Nazi Sabotage in the United States

The exposition sequence of Saboteur opens in a Glendale, California airplane factory. A whistle blows and two large doors slide apart. Three characters appear: Barry Kane (Robert Cummings), Ken Mason (Virgil Summers) and Frank Fry (Norman Lloyd). A cafeteria worker has the opening line—"Here come the wolves."[3] The idea of wolves has three levels of meaning: the men are hungry; Ken Mason is attracted to a pretty blonde who smiles at him; and Frank Fry, the antagonist, is a saboteur with the instincts of a wolf. Mason, watching the young girl, bumps into Fry, and they both fall to the ground. This fall foreshadows the fate both men will suffer before the end of the film—death. Mason quickly gets up and he and Kane help Fry to his feet. Kane then picks up some of Fry's possessions scattered in the collision—a wallet, several hundred-dollar bills, and an envelope addressed to Fry at Deep Springs Ranch, Springville, California.[4] He returns these items to Fry, who walks away. Mason picks up yet another hundred-dollar bill belonging to Fry and returns it. This gesture establishes the integrity of Kane and Mason.

The action continues as a fire breaks out in the factory and the three men run to put it out. Fry lifts an extinguisher from the holding bracket and hands it to Kane. Mason grabs it from Kane, rushes into the paint shop, and starts to put out the fire. A subjective shot from the point of view of Kane shows Mason consumed by flames. Shortly thereafter, Kane is interrogated by detectives. He leaves the factory to visit and console Mason's mother, and after speaking with her for a few minutes, he goes next door to borrow some brandy for her. During his absence, two detectives come to arrest Kane for Mason's murder—gasoline was found in the fire extinguisher Kane gave to Mason. The detectives leave, Kane returns, and Mrs. Mason tells him what has happened and explains that the police are unaware of his visit. Kane wants to know why they didn't talk with Fry; he learns from Mrs. Mason that according to the detectives, no man named Fry was employed at the defense plant. Kane leaves the home of his murdered friend's mother, deciding to seek out Fry in order to clear his own name. This action sets up the double chase that is so prevalent in Alfred Hitchcock's films:[5] Kane chases Fry and the police chase Kane. Remembering that Fry's address is Springville, California, Kane begins his search there.

The exposition sequences of Saboteur closely parallel actual events reported to the American public by the press. The historian Hans L. Trefousse reviewed what U.S. citizens were reading about espionage and sabotage in their country and identified five goals German intelligence was seeking to accomplish, namely, evaluate political trends in the U.S. relating to foreign policy; track scientific and technological developments, particularly regarding airplane production; assess the strength of America's war potential; monitor maritime activities; and create economic insecurity through sabotage.[6] Prior to the outbreak of war, most Americans were naive concerning the breadth and depth of Nazi sabotage. It was only when they learned through the media that sabotage involved direct attacks against key targets, passive action aimed at their morale or material resources, and psychological manipulation of themselves to "cause strikes, panic, or riots,"[7] that they experienced fear of the Nazi menace. Hitler had already fabricated an act of sabotage at the Polish German border to make Poland appear to be the aggressor at the beginning of the war in 1939.[8]

Moreover, evidence pointed toward serious acts of espionage, or indirect action sabotage, being committed by Abwehr, the German Secret Service, against the U.S. In the 1930s America was flooded with Nazi German spies seeking technological secrets. They were especially keen to gather industrial knowledge and blueprints of innovations in aviation. In fact, the German Air Force was made combat-ready much earlier than many had expected because they stole aviation secrets from the United States. This was the backbone of the blitzkrieg war tactics that were so successful in Europe in 1939 and 1940.[9]

One of the new devices developed by the United States aviation industry in the 1930s was the Norden bombsight. The German Air Force needed this innovation if they were to launch successful air attacks in the near future. The Abwehr, headed by Admiral Canaris, was commissioned to procure the blueprints of this top-secret bombsight. An agent of the Abwehr named Ranken was successful in the espionage venture early in 1938, and Canaris was presented with the Norden bombsight blueprints.

> The Admiral was agog. At once he summoned his chief technical advisor who promised to report in twenty-four hours. The following afternoon Ranken was summoned to Canaris' office where he found the admiral pacing the room with his technical chief.
>
> "My God, man, do you know what you've got?" demanded Canaris as soon as Ranken appeared. Before the admiral could continue, the technical expert intervened:
>
> "This is what we have been looking for, for months. We had heard whispers about a new American bombsight which was claimed to be the last word. But no one could find out anything. And between ourselves I'll tell you something more. The present high-level bombsight of the *Luftwaffe* is useless—that is why we are building so many dive bombers like the JU 87, because they are the only planes with which we have been able to be certain we could hit a target. This will revolutionize our whole bombing strategy."[10]

A second example of espionage tactics is the Abwehr communication network itself. In 1934, Rudolph Hess, right hand man to Hitler, came up with a three-part slogan that became the official dictum of the Abwehr: "Everyone can spy. Everyone must spy. Everything can be found out."[11] At that time there were approximately "fifty thousand individuals" in the United States involved in espionage for Nazi Germany.[12] Espionage of this magnitude required an excellent communication network. The Abwehr was to devise a unique method for important espionage communication among its agents, the microdot. J. Edgar Hoover called the microdot "the enemy's masterpiece of espionage." Fortunately for us, in early 1940 a double agent alerted the FBI that the Germans had invented a new "gimmick" that would enable them to "communicate back and forth throughout the world with impunity." Eighteen months later a "suspicious letter" came into the hands of the FBI labs in Washington. The laboratory agent examining it "suddenly noticed a tiny gleam—a dot reflecting the light." Closer examination "under a powerful microscope revealed that it was the infinitesimally reduced image of a full-sized typewritten letter" to be delivered to a German agent in New York.[13]

Another incident occurred in early 1940 when two Nazi saboteurs made their way, almost simultaneously, to the German Embassy in Washington. On May 20, an Abwehr saboteur, Walter Von Hausberger, walked into Dr. Hans Thomsen's office to seek financial aid. Thomsen was the chargé d'affaires officer at the embassy. Hausberger had repeatedly requested funds from the Abwehr, but they failed to respond to his pleas. A few days later, Thomsen was confronted by still another Abwehr agent, Julius Bergman, who had also become financially destitute.[14] Thomsen sent a cable to the Foreign Ministry in Germany to verify the story of the two men. The Foreign Ministry sent Thomsen a cable that the two men in question were not sabotage agents of the Abwehr. Thomsen knew full well that Von Hausberger and Bergman were Abwehr agents and cabled again for further clarification. A member of the German Foreign Ministry suddenly remembered that the men mentioned by Thomsen had been sent to America by his department, but merely as "observers." They had strict orders to refrain from doing anything that even remotely resembled sabotage.[15]

The Norden bombsight theft, microdot communication, and potential saboteurs were a direct result of Nazi Germany's Abwehr operations. Hitchcock's film, *Saboteur*, is a clear representation of the sabotage realities perpetrated by Nazi Germany against the United States. The opening sequence of *Saboteur* illustrates America's growing awareness that Nazi Germany was not above using sabotage to achieve international objectives. Hitchcock intentionally implemented direct action sabotage in *Saboteur* because of its ability to produce dramatic action and strong suspense. He also applied many of the elements of suspense in the expositional foundation: conflict between Kane and Fry; Fry as master antagonist; the unexpected complication of gasoline in the fire extinguisher; fire representative of fear; the mind of the murderer revealed through Mason's death; the dreadful alternative being Kane's freedom and life dependent upon Fry's confession; and isolation mirrored in Kane's lonely battle against the police and Fry to heighten Hitchcock's message.

The next sequence of *Saboteur* opens with Kane riding in the cab of a truck. He is hitchhiking to Springville, California, hoping to find Fry. The driver

(Murray Alpen) is a loquacious, cheerful, inquisitive person. The dialogue accentuates the possibility of sabotage in U.S. defense plants:

DRIVER

Where you from, Bud?

KANE

Los Angeles.

DRIVER

You work down there?

KANE

Yes. Well—I did.

DRIVER

What doin'?

KANE

I was working in an airplane factory.

DRIVER

They say that's pretty good. I was wondering why you weren't in the army.

KANE

Yeah?

DRIVER

I understand they're doggone particular about the fellows they hire in those big defense plants. Well, that's no more than right. They got to be careful they don't get blown up.[16]

During this conversation a motorcycle siren is brought up on the soundtrack. The truck driver pulls over and stops his truck.

OFFICER

I'd like to have a little talk with you. Out here.

DRIVER

Yes sure. Sure, officer. Stay here a minute, will you. I'll be right back.[17]

Kane, in fear of capture, leaves the cab on the passenger side. He is cautiously walking away when the driver calls to him: "Hey bud! Come on in. Everything's fixed. Good-night, officer."[18] They climb back into the truck and continue their journey. According to the truck driver, the police officer pulled them over because the truck was missing a tail light.

This is a short sequence of suspense. The motorcycle siren is the "inciting sound" of suspense. The police officer's request for the truck driver to leave the cab and his compliance isolates the hero, Kane. The police officer is the catalyst character who causes the suspense elements of conflict, unexpected complication, fear, and the dreadful alternative. The suspense element of the dreadful alternative is created through the possibility of arrest and a death penalty

conviction of Kane, and vicariously, the audience. The words—''Hey Bud!''—
spoken by the truck driver after he has finished talking with the police officer
explodes a collective psychological bomb within the audience, whose immediate
thought is, ''I'm captured.'' The elements of suspense are placed in a temporary
state of resolution when the two men leave the police officer to continue on their
journey. The policeman's radio is heard at the end of the sequence to establish
Kane's close call with the law:

RADIO

Calling all Highway Patrolmen—calling all highway patrolmen. Be on lookout for a man named
Barry Kane. Last seen on Highway 99—He has dark brown hair, blue eyes, height about six feet
two—no hat—about twenty-five years old. Calling all highway patrolmen—calling all highway
patrolmen.[19]

The police officer did not see Kane well enough to match the radio
description with him, so the police officer drives away in the opposite direction.
The audience receives a temporary reprieve but the capture of Kane seems
imminent.

Kane waves goodbye to the truck driver and enters the gateway of Deep
Springs Ranch. He knocks at the door of the main house of this spacious ranch
and, when the maid answers, asks to see Mr. Frank Fry. Kane is eventually led
to the backyard where he meets Mr. Tobin, owner of the ranch, who is playing
catch with his granddaughter beside a swimming pool. Tobin denies knowing
Frank Fry, but mentions that his next-door neighbor who lives twenty miles away
may know Fry. Tobin leaves Kane to watch the little girl on the pretense of
phoning his neighbor. Actually he calls the police. During Tobin's absence, his
granddaughter, Susie, takes some envelopes from Tobin's coat on the back of a
chair. Kane takes the letters from Susie and unintentionally glances at the
following telegram message: ''All finished here. Joining Neilson in Soda City.
Frank.''[20] Tobin is a liar. He returns from phoning in time to see Kane replacing
the letters in his coat. The major suspense of this sequence is whether or not
Tobin will catch Kane with the letters—and he does.

KANE

Where's Frank Fry?

TOBIN

Well, really you must do something about that memory of yours. You know it wasn't a minute
ago that you read a telegram that Fry sent me and it said he was on his way to Soda City.[21]

The sequence ends when Kane is arrested, handcuffed, and taken into custody by
the local police.

Hitchcock has taken substantial time in the Deep Springs Ranch sequence to
make a strong connection between Fry, a Nazi saboteur, and Tobin, an affluent

rancher in rural America. Although never specifically stated in the film, Tobin was a representation of a member of the America First Committee (AFC). This is verified in an interview with Hitchcock conducted by the film critic and director, François Truffaut, when Hitchcock confirms:

> We were in 1941 and there were pro-German elements who called themselves America Firsters and who were, in fact, American Fascists. This was the group I had in mind while writing the [*Saboteur*] scenario.[22]

Kane is then taken to the county jail. He complains that he cannot be held without a warrant. Moreover, he argues that time is running out allowing the real saboteur to escape. He is interrupted by an ironic comment made by one of the detectives: "Time's the one thing you don't need to worry about. You'll have it to burn. You'll have twenty years, nice and quiet—if you get the right lawyer. And if you don't you'll have all the time there is."[23] The police car pulls to a stop—a parked truck and car block the flow of traffic. The owner of the car helps the truck driver change a flat tire. Kane uses this distracting situation to escape. He jumps out of the car and runs past the truck driver, the same one with whom he rode to Deep Springs Ranch. Kane leaps from the bridge and lands in the water. He hides himself behind some rocks situated near the shore of the fast-flowing river. One of the detectives happens to stand on a rock right above Kane, who pushes the detective into the water and the other detectives mistake their comrade for Kane and pursue him. The temporary decoy gives Kane ample time to escape. The truck driver and Kane wave to each other as Kane, the supposed saboteur, disappears into a forest.

This sequence has many suspense elements as internal structure. There is conflict in the relationship between Kane and the police. The master antagonist is the police in this sequence. The dreadful alternative is emotionally present here because Kane faces a long prison sentence or execution if he fails to escape. Paradoxically, the mind of the murderer is the progressive process of police and legal system action. Circumstantial evidence and negative community emotions, motivated by a sensational press, may be combined forces necessary to convict this innocent man. A subjective shot is used when Kane is completely submerged in the stream and looking at the detective on the rock above him; the technique forces the audience to submerge in the water with the hero. Isolation occurs on three levels: social isolation when Kane is taken into police custody, social isolation linked with mental isolation when the police fail to listen to him, and social and mental isolation compounded with physical isolation when he escapes and the sequence ends. Not only does Hitchcock use the elements of suspense, but he is masterful in his ability to originate levels to which these dramatic techniques are used, as he has done with isolation.

The theme of appearance versus reality is also present in this escape sequence. Kane, a fugitive from justice, appears to be guilty of both sabotage and murder in the eyes of fellow workers, Mason's mother, the police, and the general public because of his flight, whereas in reality he is seeking to clear his own name by finding Fry, the real murderer. Tobin appears to be a respectable citizen, but is in reality a traitor to United States autonomy. The appearance versus reality theme is politically timely. *Saboteur* warns "Americans . . . that fifth columnists [those who support an enemy that engages in sabotage and espionage] can be outwardly clean and patriotic citizens."[24]

After Kane escapes, he finds a cabin in the woods. It is raining and a barking dog within the cabin brings the occupant to his door. Philip Martin (Oliver Blake) calls out, and when Kane answers, invites him in. Kane introduces himself as Mason—the name of his dead friend. Martin is both benevolent and blind; he cannot see Kane's handcuffs. Eventually, Patricia Martin (Priscilla Lane), the blind man's attractive niece, returns to the cabin. She is a model who is currently working in billboard advertising. Pat relates that she was just informed by some detectives on the road that a dangerous criminal had escaped. At this point she notices Kane's handcuffs and is startled.

MARTIN

What's the matter, Pat? Have you just seen his—handcuffs? I heard them as soon as he came in.

PAT

Uncle Philip—he must be the man they're looking for!

MARTIN

Yes. Very probably.

PAT

But you should have given him to the police!

MARTIN

Are you frightened, Pat? Is that what makes you so cruel?

PAT

But you've got to! He's a dangerous man!

MARTIN

Oh, Pat, come on! Mr. Mason may be many things, but he's certainly not dangerous. In fact, I'm not at all convinced that he's guilty.

PAT

Uncle philip, it's your duty as an American citizen—

MARTIN

It is my duty as an American citizen to believe a man innocent until he's been proved—guilty. Pat, don't tell me about my duty—it makes you sound so stuffy. Besides, I have my own ideas about my duties as a citizen. They sometimes involve disregarding the law.[25]

Martin tells his niece that he is capable of seeing intangible things such as innocence. Much like Sophocles' Teiresias, who can see into the heart, Hitchcock has created a blind, kindly person who has weighed Kane's character in his

(Martin's) scales of justice and found him innocent. Martin tells Pat to take Kane to the local blacksmith and have him remove the handcuffs. Kane thanks Martin and leaves with his reluctant niece.

As Kane and Pat are traveling to the blacksmith's shop, Pat uses subterfuge to get a closer look at Kane's handcuffs and manages to pull his arms over the steering wheel to prevent him from escaping. She tells him that she is taking him to a police station. To thwart her intention, Kane steps on the accelerator, grabs the steering wheel, and steers the car from the main road down a side road. The car comes to a stop in the next shot. Pat jumps out of the car and tells Kane that she will stop the first car she sees. Her statement and concurrent action maintain the suspense. Kane rubs the handcuff chain against the steering wheel and gets an idea. He turns on and accelerates the engine, sets the brake, and gets out of the car. He comes around to the front of the car and lifts the hood. He then slowly places the handcuff chains against the whirling radiator fan. The first grinding sensation causes him to draw back. He sets his jaw with determination and places the chain against the whirling blades as sparks fly. The next shot is of Pat waving her arms at an approaching car. Kane becomes anxious and presses harder against the fan. The shot structure is triangular: Kane looks at Pat, Pat waves at approaching car, and handcuff chain and sparks fly from whirling blades of the radiator fan. This triangular shot structure is repeated four times, but the shot duration is shortened each successive time to heighten the suspense for the audience by creating the idea that time is indeed running out for the hero, themselves, and their country. Temporary release from suspense occurs when the car passes by. Kane is relieved, smiles and continues to work. In the next shot, Kane looks up and is alarmed because another car is approaching. Pat is standing in the middle of the highway frantically waving her arms. Kane looks down as the chain is cut in two. His hands are physically free. He lowers the hood, jumps in the car, and drives up to Pat, who is forced to the right side of the road as the cars stop adjacent to each other. Kane jumps out of the car, grabs Pat, opens the passenger door, gets in, and pulls Pat in beside him. The scene ends as the stupified elderly couple in the other car listen to what they believe is a lover's spat!

PAT

Help!

KANE

Sorry, honey, I can't get along without you.

PAT

Let me go! Help! Help! Get the police! Help!

The elderly woman stares at the hero and heroine's car traveling down the road and says to her companion, "My, they must be terribly in love."[26]

There are eight suspense elements in this sequence. The basic conflict is between Kane and Pat. She intends to leave him, contact the police, and make his present location known to them. Compounding suspense and the unexpected complication happen twice when the two cars successively threaten Kane's future freedom. The master antagonist is a combination of time and space. Kane struggles to break his fetters in time to cover the distance between himself and Pat to prevent her from revealing his identity and notifying the police. The audience is in the superior position because, unlike Pat, they know Kane is innocent. Subjective shots are used to show Kane looking at Pat on the road and then looking at his handcuff chain against the radiator fan blades. The audience is forced into Kane's mind to share his dilemma. He fears injury to his arms and hands and subsequent capture if Pat is picked up by a passing car. Again, Hitchcock uses the suspense elements to entertain his audience.

Having left the overheated car, Kane and Pat begin to walk toward Soda City. A convoy of circus trucks slowly moves past them as it climbs up a steep grade of road. Kane jumps onto the back of the last truck. Pat, not wanting to be left in the desert at night, follows him. Their commotion causes the occupants of the truck to wake up—they are circus side-show people. A midget called Major steps from the truck onto the platform on which the couple are standing and commands them to get off. Bones, the human skeleton and leader of the group, is in favor of the couple remaining on the truck. The essential conflict of the sequence is set. Soon the police stop the convoy and begin searching it from the front. This action gives the circus side-show people time to decide what to do with the two stowaways; Kane in particular, since he has admitted to them that he is wanted by the police for something somebody else did. The side-show people are a microcosm of the world situation:

MIDGET

Well, what are you waiting for? Hand him over to the police.

MARIGOLD

He's perfectly right.

MIGNONETTE

He's a little stinker.

TITANIA

Seems like a terrible thing to do but it would be terrible, too, if we got into trouble.

MIDGET

All right, Bones—call the cops!

BONES

Just a minute, Major—In this situation I find a parallel in the present world predicament—we stand defeated at the outset. You, Esmeralda, have sympathy and yet you are willing to remain passive and let the inevitable happen. I have a belief and yet I am tempted to let myself be overridden by force. The rest of you, with the exception of this (*looks at the Midget*) malignant jerk—are ignorant of the facts and therefore confused. Thank heavens we're still members of a democracy. We'll put the matter to—a vote.

MIDGET

No vote— I'm against voting.

BONES

Fascist. You know how the matter stands so far. The twins, as usual—are on opposite sides—and so their votes pair Titania's, on both sides—so therefore, neutral. The Major—is for delivering these young people to the police— and I, frankly, am against it. Esmeralda, the decision is up to you.

ESMERALDA

Well, I don't want any trouble, any more than anybody else. But while you've been talking, I've been looking at something—something pretty fine, too. I've been looking at that little girl— standin' right beside that poor young man—Never a word—never a question—Taking everything he's had to take— stringing along with him, no matter whatever happens—and I've been thinking it's the good people that stick when anybody's in trouble and there aren't many good people in the world. I guess we—all of us—know that better than most—it isn't something you see every day of the week—so I vote—

BONES

We don't give them up! Good girl, Esmeralda!

MIDGET

This is subversive—I won't stand for it—I'll—

BONES

Oh no, you don't, cuddles. You'll abide by the will of the majority.[27]

The dialogue renders a facsimile of the World War II situation. Major, the midget with the moustache and military nickname, is a caricature of Hitler who as soon as he became Chancellor and Head of State abolished competing parties.[28] The midget is against voting and is labeled a fascist by Bones, who is in favor of settling the matter through a democratic vote. There is a leadership parallel between Bones and Roosevelt, who used the democratic system to get elected four times to serve as President of the United States. Moreover, both political men are perceptive and forthright when dealing with the Nazi menace. Marigold and Mignonette, the two Siamese twins who are physically united but ideologically separated, seem to be Hitchcock's fictional counterparts to the U.S. America First Committee (Isolationists) and the Committee to Defend America (Interventionists). Esmeralda's decision to help Kane is an affirmation of United States democracy to thwart Hitler and his police world. The police come, but leave when they are satisfied that Kane is not in the truck.

The next sequence reveals Pat to be no longer a static character; through recognition and reversal, she becomes a dynamic heroine.

PAT

I'm sorry.

KANE

What for?

PAT

For being such a dope.

KANE

You'd have been a dope if you hadn't been scared. You're tired and that's all that's the matter with you. Get some sleep—you'll be fine.

PAT

I can go to sleep all right. I'm so tired. I want to tell you something. I believe you.

KANE

Do you, Pat? You didn't, you know.

PAT

It's a free country. A girl can change her mind, can't she?

KANE

Sure she can. Thank you Pat.

PAT

They made me so ashamed. They were so nice and trusting. They're wonderful people—all except that nasty little Major and that mean twin.[29]

Pat comes to perceive Kane as a wholesome person for three reasons: Pat is treated by the Major the way she has treated Kane; she sees a reflection of her own character in the Major and Marigold; and Esmeralda's spoken perception of an honorable character in Pat gives her a new identity which she readily adopts. She recognizes that her behavior is wrong and that she must reverse it and help rectify a society that hunts an innocent man and lets saboteurs and traitors continue their destructive work. Although she has no real proof of Kane's innocence, she accepts the "innocent until proven guilty" ethic, which is characteristic of republican democracy. As friends, Pat and Kane take their journey to Soda City in search of Fry, the saboteur.

To get a closer look at Nazi German sabotage in the U.S. and through it this film's theme, let's review the most famous Nazi German sabotage in the United States, "Operation Pastorious." Operation Pastorious was allegedly the brainchild of Adolf Hitler himself. The name of the operation was taken from Daniel Pastorious, "a decent teutonic pioneer who was among the first German immigrants to try his luck in this country."[30] Admiral Wilhelm Canaris and Colonel Erwin von Lahousen were summoned to Hitler's headquarters and given direct orders to land saboteurs in the United States. Both Abwehr leaders left Hitler's headquarters in a dejected state of mind. They felt that ineffectual members of the Nazi Party had concocted a suicide scheme and influenced Hitler to accept it. Canaris spoke the following words to Lahousen: "You know that I always say that any undertaking with more than three or four men is doomed. Someone always talks. This can lead only to a catastrophe, but what can we do about it?

The Party amateurs have taken over.''[31] Eight men were eventually chosen to take part in Operation Pastorious. They were men who met four essential prerequisites: they had lived in the United States, they spoke American English, all had a high aptitude for sabotage, and all were willing to go on this dangerous mission. Moreover, all these men had been excellent students at a Berlin special school for saboteurs.[32] The final part of their training was to practice mock infiltration and sabotage of installations in Germany that were similar to the type they would encounter in the United States. They were also schooled not to visit family, friends, or Nazi elements in the United States.

On May 26, 1942, four saboteurs (Dasch, Burger, Heink and Querin) boarded U-202. Two days later Captain Wagner received the other four saboteurs (Kerling, Haupt, Theil, and Neubauer) aboard U-170 and headed for the coast of Florida. The cruise was pleasant and the saboteurs were put ashore near Jacksonville.[33] The men aboard U-202 were not as fortunate. Two destroyers searched out and attacked U-202 and withdrew after supposedly making a direct hit. The submarine had merely lost oil and the remainder of the sea voyage to Long Island was uneventful.[34] Saboteurs aboard U-202 were anxious to end their secretive cruise and begin the destructive work they had been trained to accomplish.

Hitchcock's saboteurs were also anxious to bring their goals of internal destruction to fruition. At this point in the film, Kane and Pat leave the circus convoy and enter Soda City, their next lead to Fry. Once there they hear a phone ringing and enter a decrepit shack. Kane goes inside, picks up a field phone only to hear the line go dead. Pat joins Kane, and they find a tripod and telescope. After they place the telescope on the tripod, they notice that they have an excellent view of a dam a few miles away. Suspense builds as they hear the engine of an approaching car. Kane hides Pat in an adjacent room while Freeman (Alan Baxter) and Neilson (Clem Bevans) enter the shack and interrogate Kane. He convinces them that he is an associate of Fry and Freeman decides he will take Kane to the East coast with him. Freeman is pressured into this decision by Kane, who hopes to locate Fry. Pat, meanwhile, has left the shack and sought out the local police, telling them that Kane and Freeman are going to New York City. Pat believes the police will lead her to Kane and she will be able to assist him in clearing his name.

Kane is first taken to the dam because Freeman wishes to take one last look at it. During the conversation, Freeman begins to reflect on the behavior of his two sons.

FREEMAN

I have two boys. Nice little fellows—aged two and four. The four-year-old is naughty at times—he's quite a problem. We get him a new toy and within half an hour it's smashed to bits. And then, sometimes after it's all over he seems almost sorry. Sometimes I wish my younger child had been a girl. In fact my wife and I argue over a little idiosyncrasy I have—I don't want his hair cut short until he's much older. Do you think that will be bad for him?

KANE

I don't know—it might be.

FREEMAN

When I was a child, I had long golden curls. People used to stop me on the street to admire me.

KANE

Things are different nowadays. If you gave the kid a haircut, it might save him a lot of grief.[35]

These "nice little fellows" are not what they seem. The older child is remorselessly destructive while the younger child's masculinity is questionable. A major implication in this dialogue is that an adult, indoctrinated with Nazi ideology, becomes destructive (a saboteur) without any remorse for the loss of property and life. This destructive capacity is then passed on to the next generation as with Freeman's four-year-old. Freeman's two-year-old represents the trauma caused by sexual confusion through parent identification. There is a "like father, like son" perspective advocated by Hitchcock. The Master of Suspense has created Freeman and his immediate posterity as casualties of Nazi Germany's ideological war.

Adolph Hitler, primary author of Nazi ideology, was not what he seemed. His icy demeanor belied the strong mother-son relationship that caused him to bargain with death as his mother lay dying of cancer.[36] Had Hitler's mother lived, the arch destroyer may never have emerged. Hitler's friend and biographer, August Kubicek, considers how fantasy became the unconscious motivation of Hitler's political ideology in the 1920s:

At this point Hitler commits himself to his life-work: to "save" Germany from death. Where his mother died, Germany shall live. Where the forces of destruction attacking his mother's body could not be mastered, Hitler shall master the forces of destruction attacking Germany; where doctors were unable to cure the disease from which his mother suffered, he shall cure the disease from which Germany is suffering, and, finally, where Hitler was helpless in the face of his mother's plight, now, in the case of Germany, he shall *act*, and act decisively.[37]

Kubicek goes on to point out that in time Germany became Hitler's symbolic mother and the Jew her cancer.[38]

The sexual confusion and destructive tendencies created by Hitchcock within the psyche of the Nazi saboteur, Freeman, and his children is a surprising reflection of Hitler's psychological character. Hitchcock has placed Kane in a foreboding situation because of physical danger emanating from Nazi ideology.

Freeman and Kane next arrive in New York City. Freeman learns that his phone has been disconnected, a sign that the police are watching his office. Kane learns that an act of sabotage is planned for the Brooklyn Navy Yard the next day. Still believing Kane to be on his side, Freeman decides to take him to a mansion owned by a Mrs. Sutton. In the New York City mansion sequence, Hitchcock creates another union between the America Firsters and the Nazis. This is the longest unit of the film, and may be divided into four sequences: the meeting of Mrs. Sutton and the unexpected presence of Pat, plus the arrival of Tobin; the ironic ballroom sequence involving Pat and Kane; the disappearance of Pat and the confrontation between Kane and Tobin; and the escape of Kane and Pat from the Sutton mansion. The two most relevant are the ballroom scene, which illustrates the appearance-versus-reality theme and the attitude of the America First Committee of New York City, and the confrontation between Tobin and Kane, which highlights the differences between Nazi and democratic ideologies.

The obligatory sequence preceding the ballroom action is played in one of the upper rooms of the mansion. Pat is there because, unbeknown to her, the detective she went to see when she fled from Soda City was in fact in league with the saboteurs and wants to prevent her from harming their cause. Tobin arrives to affirm the innocence of Freeman's companion, thus placing the lives of the hero and heroine in jeopardy. An unexpected visit by one of the guests from the ballroom party on the main floor allows Kane and Pat to flee the room and seek the safety of the ballroom floor, occupied mostly by guests unconnected with the sabotage conspiracy.

Kane and Pat decide to talk with the guests and persuade them that Mrs. Sutton is involved with the conspirators.

KANE

Excuse me. This may sound sort of crazy to you—in fact, I don't even know how to start—but this whole house is a hotbed of spies and—saboteurs. I'm not being silly, I assure you. Even our hostess, Mrs. Sutton—

ELDERLY MAN

What's the matter with you, sir? You're drunk! You're not even dressed.

PAT

What did he say?

KANE

Oh, he thinks I'm drunk.

MAN

When I read in the papers what those Japs are doing, I feel like going right down to Washington and getting a job.

BOY

Beat it out—yea, man! Give me that jive—

KANE

Pardon me. Did you pay twenty-five dollars to get in here tonight?

BOY

Not exactly. My boss gave me a ticket. Why?

KANE

I need your help very badly. You're right in the middle of the biggest bunch of Fifth Columnists in this country.

BOY

Are you kidding? What's the gag?

KANE

No. I'm on the level. This is it.

BOY

Aw, you're kidding! Forget it. You've got a wag in the joint. (*To his girl*)—the guy's trying to rib me.

GIRL

Ah, he's slinging you a curve.

BOY

Beat it out, son, beat it out.

KANE

Excuse me, sir. I'd like to talk to you about something very important.

MAN

What is it, Mr. Kane?—You know it's hopeless. Why don't you join Mr. Tobin upstairs in a little supper?[39]

The appearance-versus-reality theme is overt in this sequence. The elderly gentleman Kane first speaks to thinks that he is drunk. He then comments on the fact that Kane is not dressed for the occasion. Obviously, the appearance of a man is more important than the reality of his allegiance. Jazz is the main concern of the young couple Kane tries to speak to in a second attempt to communicate the reality of the situation. The couple treat Kane's communication as a ruse and resubmerge into the music. Hitchcock is making the statement that people are locked into their classes and personal interests and fail to perceive and fight the threat of sabotage in their environment. The third person with whom Kane tried to communicate was, of course, part of that very threat.

Unable to convince anyone of their problem, the hero and heroine begin dancing and end up expressing their mutual love for each other. A stranger comes up to Pat and asks her to dance. She does so and Kane loses sight of them. He then realizes that Pat has been abducted by one of Tobin's men. Kane decides to make a public announcement to expose the conspiracy but is interrupted by a butler who warns Kane that a gun is being pointed at him by a person on the balcony. An auction is to be part of the evening's festivities. Kane turns auctioneer before handing the task over to a United States admiral, and going upstairs to meet with Tobin, who is preparing to take a trip to the Caribbean and Central America to evade the FBI. Pat's uncle had reported Tobin's activities to the police, but Tobin had so far managed to avoid arrest.

Tobin represents the ideology and intellect of the Nazi organization, whereas Fry is the agent of sabotage action. Kane, a representative of democratic ideology and action, is ready to counteract Tobin ideologically and Fry physically. Kane enters the room and demands to know Pat's whereabouts. Tobin calmly responds.

TOBIN

You seem to have a soft spot for that young lady. You can't afford to make yourself that vulnerable, not when you are out trying to save your country.

KANE

Why is it that you sneer every time you refer to this country? You've done pretty well here. I don't get it.

TOBIN

No, you wouldn't. You're one of the ardent believers—a good American. Oh, there are millions like you—people who plod along without asking questions. I hate to use the word stupid, but it seems to be the only one that applies. The great masses—the moron millions. Well, there are a few of us who are unwilling to just troop along—a few of us that are clever enough to see that there is much more to be done than live small complacent lives. A few of us in America who desire a more profitable type of government. When you think about it, Mr. Kane, the competence of the totalitarian nations is much higher than ours. They get things done.

KANE

Yes—they get things done. They bomb cities, sink ships, torture and murder—so you and your friends can eat off of gold plates. It's a great philosophy.

TOBIN

I neither intend to be bombed nor sunk, Mr. Kane. That's why I'm leaving now. And if things don't go right for you—if we should win—then I'll be back. Perhaps I can get what I want then—power. Yes, I want that just as much as you want your comfort or your job—or that girl. We all have different tastes as you can see, only I'm willing to back my tastes with the necessary force.

KANE

You certainly make it sound smooth and easy. Well, that's a trick. I know the results of that power you believe in. It killed my friend and it's killed thousands like him. That's what you're aiming at, but it doesn't bother you. I can see that. Because you really hate all people. Let me tell you something. The last four or five days I've learned a lot. I've met guys like you and I've met others—people who are helpful and eager to do the right thing. People that get a kick out of helping each other fight the bad guys. Love and hate. The world is choosing up sides. I know who I'm with and there are a lot of people on my side—millions of us in every country. We're not soft. We're plenty strong. And we'll fight standing up on our own two feet and we'll win. Remember that, Mr. Tobin—we'll win no matter what you guys do. We'll win if it takes from now until the cows come home![40]

The dialogue between Tobin and Kane illustrates both Nazi and democratic ideology. A polarization of what Tobin and Kane represent had already taken place in the world when *Saboteur* was released on May 7, 1942.[41] Tobin considers millions of Americans to be stupid because they are satisfied with their lives. These citizens are viewed as the "moron millions." Hitler had similar views of the Americans. Shortly after he became Chancellor of Germany, he scoffed at the suggestion that it would be advantageous for him to visit the United States: "What is America but millionaires, beauty queens, stupid records and Hollywood. . . ."[42] Tobin is taken by Hitler's "clever" mind; there are a few who seek a more "profitable type of government." He adds that totalitarian nations are more competent than the United States. The idea of Aryan supremacy is the foundation of Tobin's words; so-called Aryan supremacy led to a supposed military supremacy that Hitler tried to prove through world conquest.[43]

Tobin's main goal is attainment of power and, like Hitler, he will use force to obtain this end. He also intends to obtain power through the elite class, or clever group, the America First Committee.

Unlike Tobin, Kane is a hero of the democratic way of life. The democratic way of life preceded the democratic way of government, this way of shared life and mind being a product of the American frontier. Kane and Pat have traveled across the United States meeting the posterity of the American frontiersmen. Some are corrupt and others are helpful and eager to do the right thing. The exodus has forced them to rediscover and fight for their individual liberty and freedom on a national scale. The frontier values of self-reliance, independence, and interdependence are awakened in them, being necessary for personal, national, and international survival.

Hitchcock's intention was to awaken these same values in his audience. Moreover, he revealed his political perception of the real internal enemies of democratic life values and republican government to his film clientele. Since the original idea for this film was Hitchcock's,[44] the positive values and democratic ideology of the hero is an expression of Hitchcock's democratic value system. In short, the hero is Hitchcock.

Kane, the fictional embodiment of Hitchcock's ideology, is struck on the head by Tobin's butler and rendered unconscious. He is then locked in a storage room. The following morning Kane sets off a fire alarm and manages to escape during the resulting general confusion. He is now free to go to the Brooklyn Navy Yard to try to stop the planned sabotage.

Kane's quest to thwart a major act of sabotage in the Brooklyn Navy Yard ties in closely with events surrounding the final stages of Operation Pastorious. The executors of the real, historical sabotage, George Dasch and his three comrades, landed on a fog-shrouded shore near Amagansett, Long Island. Dasch moved away from the other three men to make sure the coast was clear. Suddenly, a flashlight beam appeared in the fog moving right toward him. He did not have time to conceal himself or warn the others. Dasch said good morning to a young Coast Guardsman (Culley). The young fellow was startled because he had never met anyone while on patrol. Dasch spoke to him in English; however Burger approached and addressed Dasch in German. The German leader actually had the audacity to offer the young Coast Guardsman money to remain silent about their presence. They spoke a few more minutes and Culley left to return to his station. Culley notified his superiors and a few hours later the FBI in Washington was aware of strange men on the coast of Long Island.[45]

On Sunday, June 14, 1942, a nationwide alarm was sounded by the FBI. George Dasch and Peter Burger were visiting American Nazis in New York City. They had absolutely no fear they would be discovered. The other two men of their party had proceeded to their preassigned destination. Hundreds of miles south of them near Jacksonville, Florida, the Edward Kerlin group had landed without incident. Now there were eight saboteurs ready to wreak havoc against the military industrial complex of the United States. Hitler had achieved the first part of his objective.

Dasch and Burger checked into the Governor Clinton Hotel in New York City. Dasch had a "key" to the location of the other six men who had divided up into groups of two. Most historians view Dasch as an ambitious, vain, and greedy man. He had been given $160,000 by Colonel Lahousen. The money became a great temptation for him. Dasch began to think that if he turned himself over to the FBI and informed on his comrades he would be treated as a hero and be allowed to keep the sabotage money. The following day Dasch called the nearest FBI agency, identifying himself as Franz Daniel Pastorious. He asked that Washington be notified that he had a vital message to relay to Director J. Edgar Hoover in person within a few days.[46] Dasch and Burger took their journey to Washington, D.C. They met with J. Edgar Hoover. Dasch walked up to Hoover, took a handkerchief out of his pocket, and handed it to the chief of the FBI. This was the key to the location of the other six saboteurs.

> "I was given the handkerchief just before I left Berlin. Kerlin has an identical one. If you damp it in iodine vapor you will find written in invisible ink the names and telephone numbers of Abwehr contacts. We were told to use these links to communicate with the Abwehr headquarters in Lisbon until radio operators could be sent later."[47]

Hoover kept President Roosevelt abreast of all new developments of this case. Roosevelt earnestly desired the arrest, trial, and conviction of these saboteurs. Dasch's handkerchief was a monumental break in this case. Hoover's best agents were sent into the field to locate and arrest the men involved. They were successful.

The Brooklyn Navy Yard sequence in *Saboteur* embodies as much suspense as did FBI intervention in Operation Pastorious. As Kane takes a cab to the yard, he listens to a commentator on the radio giving an account of the preliminary events of a ship launching. Previous scenes have given the obligatory information that the saboteurs plan to dynamite and sink the U.S. Alaska at 10:00 A.M. as it slides down the launch rails into the sea. Radio speakers in the yard enable Kane and the yard workers to hear the broadcast of the launching. Kane frantically searches for the saboteurs before time runs out. He approaches what looks like a legitimate radio truck and sees Fry sitting at a control board. Fry has a radio in the truck so he can listen to the broadcast. He will detonate dynamite placed beneath the launching rails when the ship starts down the rails and thereby cause it to sink. Kane bounds into the truck and fights with Fry. Fry whispers to the truck driver to lock the back doors quickly and to pull out as soon as the ship goes. Kane and Fry continue to struggle inside the truck and Fry keeps reaching to press a button to detonate the explosives while Kane keeps pulling Fry's hand away from it. Meanwhile, the ship is christened and slips slowly down the rails toward the sea. Finally, Fry reaches and presses the button. A huge explosion conceals the ship in a curtain of smoke and debris. There is a montage of six reaction shots of spectators, followed by a shot of the ship floating safely offshore. Fry draws a gun, Kane ceases to fight, and the truck exits through the front gate of the yard to end the sequence.

All ten elements of suspense are present in the Brooklyn Navy Yard sequence. Conflict on three levels is the essence of the relationship between Kane and Fry: first there is the conflict of justice because Kane seeks Fry for the murder of Mason; second, Fry's Nazism versus Kane's democratic inclination is an ideological conflict; and third, the justice and ideological conflicts lead to physical conflict. The Master Antagonist is Fry, who has managed to elude Kane and make it appear that he, Kane, is a murderer. Elements of suspense— unexpected complication, compounding suspense, the dreadful alternative, claustrophobia, and mind of the murderer—occur when Kane sees Fry in the truck. The audience is in the superior position because they know that if Fry presses the button an explosion will destroy the ship and possibly the lives of all men who are aboard. The subjective camera is used when Kane sees Fry in the truck and again repeatedly when Fry reaches for the button to detonate the bomb. Herbert Lightman states how the subjective camera is used: "The *subjective* approach, when well executed, tends to bring the audience *into* the picture. The audience is allowed to see part of the action as it appears to one of the characters, and it will subconsciously experience the same reaction he does."[48] Social isolation begins when Kane is locked in the truck with Fry. Hitchcock has managed to employ all ten elements of suspense, with an extra bonus for his audience: the use of the radio. It is used in the cab, shipyard, and in the truck with Kane and Fry. The audience and Kane realize that if he does not succeed, death, the dreadful alternative, may also include the men in the ship and possibly others nearby. The radio forces the audience to constant and personal cognizance that time is running out. The radio is a documentary device that adds a strong level of apparent reality to an entertainment film. Hitchcock uses the reality of the radio to intensify suspense and lend credence to his political perception that sabotage is a real threat to the United States' objectives of maintaining democratic autonomy and aiding the Allied effort in winning World War II. Achieving the objective of communicating his political awareness and ideology through the use of the radio in this sequence is another artistic stroke of the master filmmaker.

Kane is taken through the truck entrance of Rockefeller Center Newsreel. Fry and his two men lead Kane down a corridor to the newsreel office. Confronted by several police officers when they open the door, they all run back down the corridor. They separate when one of Fry's men advises Fry to enter the Music Hall where a film is being shown. Fry complies, hoping to avoid arrest. Fry is forced across the stage by the searching policemen. He pulls out a gun and shoots at the detectives. Inadvertently, he shoots a patron who slumps over onto the lap of the woman next to him. The woman realizes what has happened, screams, and the audience runs for the exits, which allows Fry to escape with them.

Meanwhile, the climax of the film begins when Pat manages to escape from her captors. She was able to write a message and drop it out of the window of the skyscraper room in which she was being held. A number of cab drivers standing in a group on a New York City sidewalk retrieved the paper and read: "Help. In danger. Send police."[49] The men searched the skyline and saw a light reflected in a mirror in one of the windows of a building. Believing this to be a signal, they were able to locate and free Pat. When Fry escaped from the movie theatre, he took a cab downtown. Simultaneously, Kane was apprehended by the FBI; however, he is able to see and tell Pat to follow Fry. She complies and takes a cab in pursuit of him.

Fry exits the cab and boards a sightseeing boat bound for the Statue of Liberty. Pat follows him. The antagonist, heroine, and other passengers leave the boat at Bedloe Island. Pat calls the FBI and gives them details of Fry's whereabouts. She is admonished to detain Fry until FBI agents are able to arrest him. The FBI agents and Kane leave for Bedloe Island. Meanwhile, Pat tries to use her womanly charms to detain Fry. He is more interested in catching the returning boat to Manhattan Island. The following dialogue ends the subterfuge and establishes the truth between these two characters.

PAT

You've not being very nice to a lonely girl. You look as though you might be lonely, too.

FRY

Yeah. I got to catch that boat.

PAT

Fifteen minutes shouldn't make such a big difference, Mr. Fry!

FRY

Who are ya? Come on, quit stalling. Who are ya?

PAT

I think I told you—a working girl with a day off.

<pre>
                              FRY
Don't kid me! What are ya doing here?

                              PAT
It's rather a long story, Mr. Fry. It all started with an unknown blonde—an aircraft worker in an
airplane factory in Glendale, California.

                              FRY
I get it! Little Miss Liberty—carrying the torch. Why did you follow me?

                              PAT
Why do you think? Take a look down there. If you can't figure it out for yourself—they're coming
for you!⁵⁰
</pre>

The most politically significant dialogue in this scene is the discovery Fry
makes when he says, "I get it! Little Miss Liberty carrying the torch." At this
moment he perceives the real character of Pat, and the audience has an opportunity to perceive a significant trait in the character of Hitchcock through the
heroine. Like Fry, the audience gets it as well, and Hitchcock becomes Mr.
Liberty carrying the torch. The Statue of Liberty is one of the most prominent
symbols of freedom in the world; the light of the torch is used to discern truth.
Hitchcock is telling his audience, through their visual perception and symbolic
sensitivity, that the most sure foundation of freedom is truth. Moreover, for this
truth to be valid it must be an active value in the lives of American citizens.

At this point in the climactic sequence, Fry flees from the FBI and Kane, and
unintentionally drops his gun. Conflict occurs as Kane picks up the gun and
pursues Fry. A door opens and Kane comes through it. He is on the highest
observation deck of the Statue of Liberty—the torch is above his head. He moves
around to his left and sees Fry isolated. Fry has his back against the railing and
is startled by Kane's command, coupled with a motion of his gun, "Come on,
Fry!" Fear is present as Fry loses his balance and falls over the railing. Suspense
compounds as Kane runs to the place where Fry disappeared and sees the Nazi
saboteur clutching the hand of Liberty at the point between the thumb and index
finger. Fry's legs and body are supported by the weakening grasp of his hands.
Kane climbs over the railing to try to rescue Fry from his precarious position.
Kane carefully makes his way down and grasps Fry's sleeve to try and share the
weight of his dangling body. Meanwhile, the FBI have gone to get a rope to help
in the rescue. The constant sound of wind heightens the desperation of Fry's
situation, and the objective camera angles emphasize the apathy of the inanimate
Statue of Liberty. Hitchcock cuts to the part of Fry's sleeve that joins to the
shoulder of his coat. The threads are ripping out, causing an unexpected
complication. The visual rhythm of the parting threads is established and then
reinforced with different shots of the Statue, Kane, and Fry. Now each shot
represents the breaking of a thread and the imminent fall of Fry. This is another
touch of the meticulous master filmmaker. Fry's hands begin to slip, identifying

the dreadful alternative. The sleeve slowly slides over one of his hands. The subjective camera then shows Fry falling free and screaming as he moves away from Kane. A closeup shows Kane looking away and closing his eyes. Kane makes his way back to the platform and into the outstretched arms of Pat. The FBI are present to help Kane to safety and the film ends.

Criticism of *Saboteur*

The critics were not kind to *Saboteur*. Hitchcock himself thought Robert Cummings was not right for the part of the hero—"he was too undramatic, having what I call a 'comedy face,' and half the time you don't believe the situation."[51] Donald Spoto considered the scenario "episodic and uneven." He was also critical of character development, believing the leading figures to be lacking "essential color or interest because they are never examined interiorly."[52]

My major criticism of *Saboteur* concerns motivation. Barry Kane receives direct and indirect assistance from Mrs. Mason, a truck driver, a blind man, circus people, and Pat. Kane is a wanted man who has left the Glendale, California area, against the direction of the police authorities, to clear his name. Those who aid and abet a criminal such as Kane was believed to be are in jeopardy. There is nothing to recommend Kane's innocence to those who assist him, other than his personality. This is a flaw in credibility throughout the film. Although Hitchcock has done this to advance the idea that common people must trust and support one another, it is still a flaw that the analytical viewer will not be able to accept.

A secondary criticism is the creation of two main antagonists: Tobin and Fry. This split focus in characterization is a major weakness. The esthetic choice was governed by Hitchcock's political perception of two interrelated problems: sabotage and the Nazi infiltration of the America First Committee. Hitchcock addressed these real problems at the expense of a valid script. The esthetic flaw was that political truth needed to be more adequately integrated through the use of a single antagonist. Moreover, the escape of Tobin is an insult to the audience's value of justice. Perhaps Hitchcock wanted his audience to be responsible for solving this political problem.

As for the film's merits, I find the Statue of Liberty sequence to be the esthetic and ideological apex of *Saboteur*. A more thorough critical analysis of this sequence is needed here to reveal the expressionistic technique used by Hitchcock to express a strong anti-Nazi ideological message. Germany's contribution to the post-World War I era of film (1918–1925) was expressionism. Film elements of expressionism were strong diagonal lines, distorted and oversized sets, surreal lighting, distorted props, and heavy focus on abnormal plot and characters. The major creative purpose was to abstract and externalize the collective unconscious and conscious mind to show Germany's lack of balance due to social and economic upheaval.

It was in a cinematically innovative world, reflective of the need for a new government and social system, that Alfred Hitchcock spent part of his professional filmmaking apprenticeship in the Germany of the 1920s. Expressionistic films have their roots in art, and art was Hitchcock's basic approach to filmmaking. Hitchcock would come to view this artistic episode in his life as great fortune.

> Having started to write, I became involved with the German film industry, which in its day was the greatest—even greater, from an artistic standpoint, than Hollywood. I mean, they were making films like *Siegfried* and the *Ring* operas and all of Jannings' films. And I became tremendously influenced by them.
>
> My style was influenced by the German—angles of photography, the *visual ideas*. And it was the visual ideas that began to come to one very, very instinctively. There was no sound in those days. And in the film *The Lodger*, which was about Jack the Ripper, I even show him going out at night, shot from above a big staircase with a continuing handrail. And all you saw was a white hand going down. This, I would say, is almost oblique. Not to do the obvious. To avoid the cliché. And gradually—I suppose it's the religious training—the general theme because the triumph of good over evil. And that maintains itself even to this day, actually.[53]

The use of the Statue of Liberty in *Saboteur* was Hitchcock's responsibility. In addition, he personally designed all sets used in the picture.[54] Because of lighting difficulties, Hitchcock could not use the original statue itself, so he had a "frame-and-plaster reproduction of it built on the Universal lot where he lensed the closeups of both the exterior and interior."[55] Hitchcock's use of the statue is an expressionistic technique of a symbolically oversized set that expresses liberty and freedom. But more important, the Statue of Liberty reverses, or counterpoints, the intended ideology of the German expressionistic art form of film which called for a dictator, according to the cosmopolitan film analysis of Andrew Tudor[56] and Siegfried Kracauer.[57] Hitchcock has used the German art form of expressionism to undermine a basic tenet of Nazi ideology: the Fuhrer will lead the Aryan race to victory.

In *Saboteur*, the Nazi antagonist is defeated by the common man. What has been attacked by Tobin's secretive political group motivated by the alien Nazi ideology is the living value of freedom, which is one of the most basic values of a democratic people. Through the death of Fry, Hitchcock is telling his world audience that the Third Reich will eventually fall in a physical, political, and ideological sense as just retribution for its unjust war against the United States and her allies.

One other significant aspect of the Statue of Liberty is the torch. Symbolically, the light that emanates from this source recognizes that freedom and liberty have been established and will be valued among the people of this land. The light is also a symbol of hope to those who leave their homelands to live in the United States. Joseph Bornstein and Paul Milton believed that "a Hitler peace in Europe, even a voluntary integration of all conquered European peoples in the service of Germany, cannot be realized as long as a ray of hope beams toward Europe from the Statue of Liberty."[58] Nazi Germany had a counterpart of the Statue of Liberty flame: the Nazi sacred flame. A Nazi ritual was introduced in the summer of 1936, and it continued through World War II. Both the Hitler Youth (H.J.) and the S.S. shared in the guardianship of the sacred flame lighted atop Germany's highest mountain. On June 21, 1936 the Flame Speech was broadcast to millions of H.J. and S.S. personnel as confirmation that "here, where Germany is closest to the heavens . . . and devoted to the man whom [God] has sent us as our leader to honor and freedom, we pledge to Adolf Hitler to be the truest of the true."[59] Hitchcock, perhaps unknowingly, had ideologically established the Statue of Liberty flame in conflict with the Nazi German sacred flame. Through the victory of the American protagonist over the Nazi antagonist, he has implied that the sacred flame of Nazi Germany, like the life of Fry, will eventually be extinguished by the victorious Allied Powers, whose passion for freedom is symbolized by the flame of the Statue of Liberty. Hitchcock's implication became a historical fact.

Conclusion

Alfred Hitchcock's *Saboteur* is more than a vehicle of entertainment; it is a historical document that not only addresses the real problem of sabotage in the United States in 1941 and 1942, but also makes subliminal accusations against the Nazi infiltration of the America First Committee. *Saboteur* served as a source of feature film education for its audiences on a problem that may have seriously impeded the American War effort if it had not been solved by the Federal Bureau of Investigation. Not quite two months after the release of *Saboteur*, the Operation Pastorious agents were tried by military law. All eight were found guilty as charged and sentenced to death. The sentence of Dasch and Burger who betrayed the "Fatherland" was later commuted to thirty years imprisonment.[60] There is little doubt that Hitchcock's *Saboteur* was politically relevant.

The major thrust of Hitchcock's political ideology in *Saboteur*, however, is the preservation of freedom in the United States. His concern is pronounced through the use of the Statue of Liberty in the final sequence, where the major conflict between the protagonist and antagonist is settled. It allows for strong audience identification with the hero and animosity toward the villain. Hitchcock pointed out that "to have had the total involvement of the audience it should have been the hero who was in danger, not the villain, but the story demanded it otherwise."[61] The microcosmic victory of the hero gives the plot its major resolution of suspense, and at the same time, the climax is an ideological prophecy of the future victory of the United States over those nations seeking to jeopardize her sovereignty and freedom.

4

Lifeboat

Production: Kenneth MacGowan, 20th Century-Fox, 1943. *Director:* Alfred Hitchcock. *Scenario:* Jo Swerling, from a story by John Steinbeck. *Director of Photography:* Glen MacWilliams. *Special Effects:* Fred Sersen. *Sets:* James Basevi and Maurice Ransford. *Music:* Hugo Friedhofer; directed by Emil Newman. *Costumes:* Rene Hubert. *Editing:* Dorothy Spencer. *Sound Engineers:* Bernard Fredericks and Roger Heman. *Studio:* Fox, 1943. *Distributor:* 20th Century-Fox, 1943, 96 minutes. *Principal Actors:* Tallulah Bankhead (Constance Porter: "Connie"), William Bendix (Gus Smith), Walter Slezak (Willi, captain of the submarine), Mary Anderson (Alice Mackenzie), John Hodiak (John Kovac), Henry Hill (Charles J. Rittenhouse), Heather Angel (Mrs. Higgins), Hume Cronyn (Stanley Garett), Canada Lee (George Spencer: "Joe," the steward).[1]

Saboteur is a film with the continental United States as its overall set. Although the film had its technical and esthetic problems, it was welcomed as a source of encouragement to the waning hope of Americans who volunteered by the millions to fight the Nazis, whose blitzkrieg victories in Europe had almost proved them invincible. *Lifeboat* is different from *Saboteur*; unlike the cinematic journey across the United States in *Saboteur*, *Lifeboat*'s cinematic focus is a cosmopolitan cross-section of the war-torn lives of men and women in a lifeboat. *Lifeboat*'s dramatic format is much closer to realism than the melodramatic structure of *Saboteur*. Hitchcock's *Lifeboat* is an uncompromised microcosmic representation of the World War II situation. Although the film was not well received by reviewers and critics on both sides of the Atlantic, today it is a monument to the political integrity and realistic vision of a filmmaker who neither underestimated the military strength of Nazi Germany nor closed his eyes to the political weaknesses of the Allied Powers. *Lifeboat* premiered in New York City on January 12, 1944. In a mid-1960s interview Hitchcock established the historical period of this film as 1940–41, but his memory may have been dimmed in the interim of twenty-plus years.[2] The revised final script of *Lifeboat* (July 29, 1943) gives a hint of the film's time frame: "A packing case rises to the surface and drifts right under the lens, so near that we are able to read the black ink markings on it, which indicate that they are Red Cross supplies for the American Army in the United Kingdom."[3] The United States entered World War II on December

7, 1941, and the "American Army in the United Kingdom" was not established in any significant numbers until 1942-43. Furthermore, critics of *Lifeboat* interpreted its setting as contemporary with its release date. The film parallels World War II historical events that had happened up to its release. The esthetic spine of *Lifeboat* is its exceptional acting. Constance Porter (Tallulah Bankhead) is a calloused American newspaper reporter with a female chauvinistic value system. Miss Bankhead won the New York Film Critics Award for best actress of the year for her performance.[4] Kovac (John Hodiak) is a tough, two-fisted engine-room man from Chicago, with communism as his political frame of reference. Gus Smith (William Bendix) is a crew member from Brooklyn, and an exceptionally well-drawn character. The progression of his intoxicated state in one sequence—friendly, happy, melancholic, bellicose, and unconscious—is one of the best on film. Willi (Walter Slezak), the German U-boat commander, is a formidable foe. Alice Mackenzie (Mary Anderson) is a nurse with pacifist tendencies. Stanley Garett (Hume Cronyn), an Englishman, is the ship's navigation officer; he falls in love with Alice, and she with him. C. J. Rittenhouse (Henry Hull) is an American entrepreneur who likes to play poker. Mrs. Higgins (Heather Angel) is a psychotic woman who first drowns her baby and then herself. Her psychosis was induced by German air raids she experienced in England. George Spencer, called "Joe," is played by Canada Lee, a black actor who worked extensively on the New York City stage before making his screen debut in this Hitchcock film. Joe is a steward whose spiritual or religious qualities add redeeming hope to the plight of the other characters. Because of believable acting, *Lifeboat* is considered a film of dramatic worth today.[5] The political intent of *Lifeboat* began with Hitchcock. He stated, "the picture was my idea, a kind of microcosm of the war."[6] The characters reflect the world's prevalent political ideologies—democracy, Nazism, and communism. Using the dramatic mode of realism, Hitchcock dwarfed the international political situation of the time and placed it in a lifeboat, where he proceeded to give his political views of the European conflict in World War II.

The film begins with a passenger-carrying freighter being torpedoed by a U-boat. But before the freighter sinks, it hits the U-boat with a shell, which causes the U-boat to sink also. A German escapes from the U-boat and climbs into the freighter's lifeboat. He is the last to board, and the others discuss throwing him overboard to carry out immediate justice. He claims to be a crew member of the U-boat, not an officer, and he maintains self-control as the others argue about his fate, so he ends up staying on the lifeboat. Later he directs the boat on the course he intends, performs an operation on an injured crew member, and takes control of the lifeboat after a storm. While the others sleep, he pushes the injured American crew member overboard when the latter discovers the German has water. The others awaken, piece together the Nazi's crime, and beat him to death.

A German supply ship intercepts them, and it appears that the people on the lifeboat will spend the remainder of the war in a concentration camp. Fortunately, an Allied warship approaches and sinks the German supply ship. A young Nazi from the supply ship climbs aboard the lifeboat and pulls a pistol in self-defense. Joe disarms him, and the others muse about what should be done with the German as they wait in uplifted spirits to be rescued from their ordeal.

Thematically, *Lifeboat* strongly admonishes the major Allied powers—America, England, and Russia—to stop fighting among themselves, unite, and destroy the greatest military and ideological threat to their sovereignty, Nazi Germany. The primary focus is on the United States, which is represented by five characters as opposed to three for England and one each for Russia and Germany. The communist ideology of Russia is the foundation of Kovac's left-wing views; although he represents communism, he is still a member of American democracy. Nine of the ten major characters in *Lifeboat* are citizens of a democracy; it is within this context that we may understand Hitchcock's thematic statement:

> We wanted to show that at the moment there were two world forces confronting each other, the democracies and the Nazis, and while the democracies were completely disorganized, all of the Germans were clearly headed in the same direction. So here was a statement telling the democracies to put their differences aside temporarily and to gather their forces to concentrate on the common enemy, whose strength was precisely derived from a spirit of unity and of determination.[7]

Lifeboat and Internal Dissension in the United States and among the Allied Powers Concerning World War II

Lifeboat opens with the smokestack of a ship sinking beneath the surface of the sea. The camera pans across the ocean surface, revealing the floating residue of two ships, an American freighter and a German U-boat, both of which have sunk after doing battle with each other. Floating on the sea are a wicker basket, Red Cross supplies, a *New Yorker* magazine, an empty baby's bottle, Stephen Foster sheet music, a sailor's duffle bag, a poster of a pin-up girl with an attractive smile, and for stark contrast, a dead sailor with a shaved head. His body floats face down, and his life jacket identifies him as a German. The camera pans up to reveal a mist-shrouded horizon with a partially concealed lifeboat drifting toward the camera. What slightly puzzles and interests the audience is the one person sitting quietly in the lifeboat. Mrs. Constance Porter, Connie, is sitting in the lifeboat with a blasé expression on her face. Her immaculate appearance and expensive clothes imply that she is wealthy. She looks out over the water; her face registers excitement, and she grabs her 16mm motion picture camera, adjusts for dull weather lighting, and begins shooting pictures of a man (Kovac) swimming toward her. The man hesitates in the water, picks up a floating twenty-dollar bill, and continues to swim up and to climb into the boat.

In the shot where Kovac is swimming, Hitchcock uses slightly underdeveloped film and a hand-held camera to simulate the newsreel genre of filmmaking. During the first half of the twentieth century, newsreel journalism was a solid appendage to the film industry:

> The history of the newsfilm falls into three periods. The first began with the birth of the cinema itself, in 1895–96, for the very first programmes already included topical items. It ended around 1910 with the introduction of the first regular weekly newsreels. This period saw the experimental development of most of the basic techniques of news-communication by film, and it coincided with the newspaper revolution associated with the Harmsworth brothers. The second period, between 1910 and 1928, was the age of the silent newsreel, during which the structure of the elaborate international newsreel organizations was fully evolved and the newsreel's potential political significance foreshadowed, though its political impact was in fact severely restricted by the limitations inherent in a purely visual medium. The third period, the golden age of the newsreel, during which it emerged as a fully-fledged journalistic medium and as a potent form of political persuasion, began with the introduction of sound newsreels in 1927 and ended with the supplanting of cinema newsreels by television news in the course of the 1950s.[8]

The newsreel was and is accepted as reality or selected reality. Hitchcock was aware that his audience's visual understanding of World War II was closely linked to the newsreels they viewed along with regular feature films. With this awareness, he inserted the newsreel technique at the beginning of *Lifeboat* to visually inform his audience that this film is closer to "a slice of life" than to "a slice of cake."

The dialogue between Connie and Kovac shows a basic conflict that transcends Kovac's humanitarian concern and Connie's present lack of it; it reveals an ideological conflict between communism and democracy:

KOVAC

Those Nazi buzzards! A tinfish ain't enough—they've got to shell us, too.

CONNIE

(Holding up a tennis racket she has rescued from the sea.) Now I can perfect my backhand. Get that—it might come in handy.

KOVAC

(He reaches out and pulls in a wicker armchair. As he does this she sees something else that interests her and bends to pick it up.) It's a military hat of some sort . . . What are we worrying about this junk for? We'd better look around for some of the others before that U-boat surfaces again and sees us.

CONNIE

She won't surface; one of our shells got her.

KOVAC

Are you sure?

CONNIE

She was killed dead.

KOVAC

Did you see it?

CONNIE

All in here, my pet (*shows camera*).

KOVAC

(*He lifts his hand and points at her, almost as if making an accusation.*) You're Constance Porter. I heard you were aboard—so you took pictures, huh?

CONNIE

Nothing else but. And what pictures. Priceless . . . A little knot of people around one of the lifeboats—they looked kind of slow and heavy with their lifebelts on and terribly lonesome, darling, and then a shell hit the lifeboat and they all jumped overboard. I got a beautiful shot of the gun crew firing at the submarine—but the best of all was when I was in the lifeboat with Charcoal. I got the freighter going down, and one of the lifeboats caught in the suction and pulled under. I got some of the U-boat crew jumping overboard, and I—Look! There's a perfect touch! (*A section of wreckage from the freighter, featuring a baby bottle, half-full of milk, with nipple attached. She lets fall the military cap and reaches for her camera, but before she has a chance to use it Kovac reaches out with the tennis racquet and savagely strikes at the milk bottle. The milk from the broken bottle whitens a tiny area about it, then is blended with the sea.*) What did you do that for?

KOVAC

Why didn't you wait for the baby to float by and photograph that? (*As she stares at him, enraged, a sound drifts in out of the mist. They listen, and the faint cry for help is repeated. Mrs. Porter instantly raises her camera.*) Gangway! (*As he moves past her to reach for the steering oar, he accidentally hits the camera and knocks it out of her hand. It falls into the sea and is lost. Her face is contorted, she turns on Kovac who is working the oar to maneuver the boat toward the cry for help.*)

CONNIE

(*A scream of rage*) You stupid, clumsy—(*a lurch of the lifeboat, as Kovac swings it around, sends her down sharp on her backside at the bottom of the lifeboat, her nylon-clad legs, with one run, flying into the air. Almost hysterical with rage.*) Why didn't you look where you were going? Absolutely irreplaceable stuff, priceless, the best film I ever took—and it goes to the bottom of the sea!

KOVAC

That's better than going there yourself.[9]

One of the basic conflicts between communism and democracy is economic. As mentioned, the film opened with Connie sitting alone in the lifeboat decked out in her finery. Kovac's first comment is that she doesn't look like someone who has just been shipwrecked. On a broader level, the Russians have been fighting for their lives while the continental United States has gone virtually untouched in this world conflict. Unknown to them at their first meeting, Kovac and Connie both grew up on the south side of Chicago, the lower-class section of town. Kovac, a man "playing the communist," has assimilated left-wing ideology as his panacea to the economic problems of the United States.[10] Conversely, Connie has used intelligence, talent, and the capitalistic system to enter the upper class. Unfortunately, the economic dearth of her youth has caused her to make material objects more important than people. She makes the newsreel photographs more important than the lives of the shipwrecked victims struggling to survive. Kovac feels no remorse when he knocks her camera overboard because he despises her and other materialistic capitalists. Nevertheless, there is a flaw in Kovac's idealistic allegiance to communism. He has accepted the ideology without experiencing its application in real life. Both Kovac and Connie are victims of their weaknesses. In particular, Kovac is unaware that one of the mass killings of this century occurred in Soviet Russia. Stalin himself admitted to Churchill in 1942 that ten million farmers had been liquidated because according to communist standards they were too wealthy.[11] This fact far exceeds any internal political atrocities committed by a democracy. To relate this to the film, although Kovac perceives one of the weaknesses of the economic system of democracy (capitalism) in the materialistic character of Connie Porter, he does not reflect on the brutality of communism at this time.

Stanley Garett, an Englishman and the freighter's radio operator and navigator, is the next survivor to be taken aboard the lifeboat. He informs Kovac that he was unable to send an SOS because the first shell from the U-boat destroyed the radio compartment. They search for more survivors. Garett calls for a Miss Mackenzie, and for his efforts, he receives a faint reply from her in the distance. Three more people are taken aboard: Charles Rittenhouse, Gus Smith, and Alice Mackenzie—all Americans. It is obvious from Garett's concern for Alice Mackenzie, and hers for him, that they are in love. She is "truly representative of America as Stanley Garett is truly representative of Britain."[12] Like *Foreign Correspondent*, Hitchcock created a romance in *Lifeboat* between an American and an Englishman, only this time reversed the sexes. Still, the political symbolism of alliance is the same.

Those taken aboard the lifeboat quickly gravitate to others with similar values and concerns. C. J. Rittenhouse and Constance Porter discuss their good fortune at being alive and assess what personal belongings they were able to salvage from the ship. Gus, a likable down-to-earth sailor, has suffered a severe leg wound and is helped by nurse Mackenzie, Garett, and Kovac. The decimation of sailors' lives and American convoy ships by German U-boats was a bleak problem in 1942. U-boats were responsible for destroying a little over one thousand ships—almost three a day—in the North Atlantic and Arctic areas.[13] The year 1943 was an even greater success for the German U-boats inasmuch as their number in the Atlantic almost doubled (110 U-boats).[14] Toward the end of March, defeat stared the Allies in the face.[15]

After Gus has been put at ease as much as possible, Kovac has his first substantial communication with Rittenhouse, which results in Kovac rejecting money offered him by Rittenhouse. This rejection, like Kovac's previous rejection of Constance Porter, is ideologically based on the communist's disdain for capitalism.

> RITTENHOUSE
>
> The biggest pot of the game, but believe you me, I never even stopped to collect. The pot went to Davy Jones.
>
> KOVAC
>
> Not all of it. (*He takes from his pocket the slimy greenback he found in the sea and shows it.*) Here's twenty bucks Mr. Jones didn't get. (*He offers it to Rittenhouse.*)
>
> RITTENHOUSE
>
> It's yours.
>
> KOVAC
>
> It was floating in the water—
>
> RITTENHOUSE
>
> Salvage. Perfectly legitimate. I insist—Are you one of the crew, son?
>
> KOVAC
>
> Black gang. Oiler. The name's Kovac.
>
> RITTENHOUSE
>
> Rittenhouse.
>
> KOVAC
>
> Glad to— (*reaction*) Rittenhouse?
>
> RITTENHOUSE
>
> (*Jovially*) That's right.
>
> KOVAC
>
> C. J. Rittenhouse?
>
> RITTENHOUSE
>
> (*Rittenhouse's expression can only be described as demure. The great man is accustomed to such homage.*) C. J. Rittenhouse.
>
> CONNIE
>
> Junior.
>
> KOVAC
>
> Here— (*He thrusts the twenty-dollar bill into Rittenhouse's hand, and moves toward Gus.*) [16]

The examination and tentative treatment of Gus' leg wound is interrupted by a shout from someone outside the lifeboat. Those aboard struggle to see through the night mist. Constance Porter is the first to spot the black steward, Joe, who had helped her into the lifeboat and then jumped back into the sea when he heard a woman screaming for help. They row toward him. He swims toward the boat with Mrs. Higgins under one arm and a baby in his other hand held above his head. The passengers help them into the boat. Joe tells his rescuers that Mrs.

Higgins had been trying to drown herself and her baby; she succeeded with the infant. Apparently, she is psychotic. Compassionately, Connie takes off her fur coat and drapes it around Mrs. Higgins' shoulders. The latter snatches the dead infant from Mackenzie's arms and tries to nurse it. This sequence of pathos ends when Gus spots another survivor. Kovac and Rittenhouse help him into the boat. The audience deduces from the facial expressions of the people already in the lifeboat that this newest addition is totally unknown to them. Some of the mystery of his identity is dispelled when he thanks them in German.

With the introduction of the Nazi, Hitchcock has all the representatives for his allegory of the situation in Europe.

The Nazi becomes the source of the major conflict and suspense in the film. Minor conflict and rejection has already occurred beween the communist, Kovac, and the two capitalists, Constance Porter and Rittenhouse. Suspense builds as the audience realizes that minor conflicts among the characters who represent the Allies may blind and incapacitate them against the major enemy, the Nazi. The dialogue of the following sequence contains a minor level of conflict between the Allies and a major level between the Allies and the German:

THE GERMAN
Ich bin Ihnen sehr dankbar. Sie haben mein Leben gerettet. Es tut mir leid, dass wir Ihr Schiff versenken musten.

CONNIE
(*Apparently the only one of them who speaks German, now translates.*) He's very grateful to us for saving his life, and regrets very much the U-boat was compelled to sink our ship.

KOVAC
(*Grimly*) Ask him why they shelled our lifeboats.

CONNIE
Warum schiessen sie auf Rettungsboote?

THE GERMAN
Befehl des Kapitaens.

CONNIE
Those were the captain's orders.

STANLEY
If you ask me, he's the captain himself.

RITTENHOUSE
(*To Mrs. Porter*) Ask him if he's the captain.

CONNIE
(*To the German*) Sind Sie der Kapitaen des U-Boots?

THE GERMAN
Nein. Ich bin nur ein Mann—der Besatzung—kein Offizier.

CONNIE

He denies he's a captain or officer. He's just a crew member.

KOVAC

Crew member or skipper—he's German!

GUS

A guy can't help being a German if he's born a German, can he?

KOVAC

(*Fiercely*) Neither can a rattlesnake help being a rattlesnake if he's born a rattlesnake—that don't make him a nightingale. (*Savagely*) Get him out of here!

CONNIE

Don't be silly, darling—he can't very well get off in the middle of the ocean, now can he?

KOVAC

Throw him off.

RITTENHOUSE

Have you gone out of your mind?

KOVAC

Throw the Nazi buzzard overboard!

RITTENHOUSE

It's out of the question—it's against the law.

KOVAC

Whose law? We're on our own here. We can make our own law.

CONNIE

Now just a minute. This man was acting under orders. The freighter was an enemy ship. After all, we're at war—

KOVAC

(*Pointing at Mrs. Higgins*) Is that woman at war? Is her baby at war? (*To Connie*) Listen, how come you know the lingo so well? And how come when I climbed into this lifeboat, you were the only one in it?—all dressed up like you knew you were going some place?

CONNIE

I was going some place. I *was* going into a lifeboat. What is this? Are you insinuating—

KOVAC

You seem to be pretty anxious to stand up for your friend, here.

CONNIE

(*Shrill with rage*) What do you mean, *my friend*?

RITTENHOUSE

Now children, let's keep our shirts on.

KOVAC

I haven't got a shirt. (*Glares at Mrs. Porter*) Or a mink coat, either.

CONNIE

(*She glares back at him with interest. A dawning look of comprehension creeps into her eyes.*) Oh, I get it. A fellow traveler! I thought the Comintern was dissolved.

RITTENHOUSE

Now, children![17]

Rittenhouse and Constance Porter are against Kovac's intention of executing the Nazi. They seem instinctively to want to honor international law, not so much for the sake of the German as in the hope of preserving their own lives in case they are taken prisoners by the enemy, and even though the U-boat captain and crew shelled the freighter's lifeboats in direct violation of international law on the high seas. Constance's opposition to Kovac leads him to question her political allegiance. He implies that she is a Nazi agent who surreptitiously took part in the sinking of the freighter. But as the dialogue continues, Kovac is not the only one who wishes to execute the German.

RITTENHOUSE

We're all sort of fellow travelers here, in a mighty small boat on a mighty big ocean. And the more we quarrel and criticize and misunderstand each other, the bigger the ocean gets and the smaller the boat.

KOVAC

The boat's too small right now for me and this German.

RITTENHOUSE

Now look—I'm perfectly willing to leave it to the decision of the majority. That's the American way. . . . If we harm this man, we're guilty of the same tactics you hate him for. On the other hand, if we treat him with kindness and consideration, we may convert him to our way of thinking. That's the Christian way.

KOVAC

Okay. Now, me, I'm an American, too. I was born in Chicago. But my people are from Czechoslovakia. (*He turns to the German and almost spits the name in his face.*) Did you ever hear of *that* place? (*The German's face is inscrutable. Kovac turns to the others.*) I say, throw him overboard—and then stick around and watch him drown. And when he goes down, I'll dance a jig like Hitler did when France went down.

GUS

Me, too. (*Now they all look at him.*) Just for the record, I'm an American, myself. But I'm in a kind of a spot. My name is Schmidt, but I changed it to Smith. That's what I got against these guys more than anything else. They make me ashamed o' the name I was born with. I got a lot o' relatives in Germany. For all I know this guy may be one o' them. (*He looks at the German and delivers his verdict harshly.*) I say throw 'im to the sharks!

STANLEY

Now Gus. I don't say it wouldn't be a pleasure, mind you—we haven't got the right.

GUS

The right! What do you mean, the right!

STANLEY

Why, he's a prisoner of war. He's got to be treated as such. The way it's done is to hang onto him until we're picked up and hand him over to proper authorities. Until such time we represent the authorities. That's clear, isn't it? Do you see what I mean, Miss?

ALICE

(*Almost indifferently*) I don't understand any of it. (*Her eyes are on Mrs. Higgins.*) I don't understand people hurting each other or killing each other. I just don't understand it.

KOVAC

What are you doing in a uniform?

ALICE

I'm doing the only thing I can—trying to put them together again when they get hurt. As far as the German's concerned I—agree with Stanley.

CONNIE

So do I. I'll talk to the man—perhaps I can get some information from him—

KOVAC

(*Scornfully*) Material for your book?

CONNIE

(*Blithely*) Incidentally.

RITTENHOUSE

George?

KOVAC

What about you, Joe?

JOE

Do I get to vote, too? (*We don't know whether it's sarcasm or genuine surprise.*)

RITTENHOUSE

(*Taken aback*) Why, why certainly.

JOE

I guess I'd rather stay out of this.

RITTENHOUSE

(*To Mrs. Higgins*) How about you, sister?

MRS. HIGGINS

(*Casually*) My baby's dead.[18]

Kovac and Smith favor killing the German, but Garett argues the prisoner of war law, which they are bound to honor. Interestingly, the positions of Russia (Kovac), the United States (Smith), and England (Garett) were similar at the Teheran Conference (1943) between the leaders of these same three countries:

At Stalin's dinner party when the vodka began to take hold there was some merciless leg-pulling of Churchill by Stalin and Roosevelt. Uneasily, the Prime Minister sparred with humor and restraint—until Stalin suddenly grew serious and, in his quiet Georgian growl, said that after the

war the German General staff [50,000 officers and technicians] must be liquidated. . . .
Churchill, his mind only barely dulled by his consumption of champagne, responded very
sharply. He rose from the table and, pacing the dining room, retorted: "The British Parliament
and public will never tolerate mass executions."[19]

Churchill was later placated by Stalin and Roosevelt and they returned to the
business of the Conference.

Smith had changed his name to avoid being tainted by the nefarious action
of the Nazis. He had a good reason to do this. Nazi Germany expected American
citizens of German descent to form a political bloc in behalf of Hitler's world
ambitions.

The most notorious organization among Americans of German descent was
the American German Bund, which was officially organized by Fritz Kuhn on
March 29, 1936. Kuhn perceived himself as the American Fuhrer; however, he
and the Bund were subservient to the will of Hitler and Nazi Germany. This is
evident in the name of the organization, where "American" is used as an
adjective to modify German Bund. From 1936–39, the American German Bund
entered its golden era: *//*

When detractors suggested that he had few followers or that he had created paper organizations,
Kuhn pointed to a rally in Reading, Pennsylvania, where fifteen thousand had turned out, or to
one in New York City, where twenty-two thousand people had packed Madison Square Garden
to hear the American Fuhrer speak.[20]

The nemesis of Fritz Kuhn came in 1939. The financial books of the American
German Bund were seized by government officials in Yorkville, New York.
There was sufficient evidence in these records to prove that Kuhn had misap-
propriated funds. He was tried by jury, found guilty of "larceny and forgery,"[21]
and sentenced to two-and-a-half to five years in Sing Sing prison. The American
German Bund then dwindled into insignificance, even though there were five-
and-a-half million Germans or German descendants living on the North American
continent,[22] most of whom supported their respective governments—the United
States and Canada—and were politically chagrined by the American German
Bund's action and expectations. Hitchcock's character, Gus Smith, who is
embarrassed because he perceives his German name as a stigma, adequately
represents reality.

The next significant scene introduces some interesting religious concerns.
The communist and capitalist characters are unable to conduct the burial service
for Mrs. Higgins' baby. When Rittenhouse falters in his attempt to deliver the
twenty-third Psalm, Joe Spencer eloquently completes it is his richly resonant
voice.

KOVAC
Does anybody know the service for burial at sea? (*Nobody answers.*)

RITTENHOUSE

I suppose any prayer—will do. (*He thinks a moment, takes the cigar out of his mouth, then resumes.*) The Lord is my shepherd, I shall not want. He maketh me to lie down in green pastures—He— (*Rittenhouse has forgotten the rest of the words. Joe picks them up.*)

JOE

He leadeth me beside the still waters. He restoreth my soul. He leadeth me in the paths of righteousness for His name's sake. (*The sun is sinking below the rim of the horizon. The sea is darkening. The people in the boat are now pure silhouette.*) Yea, though I walk through the valley of the shadow of death, I will fear no evil, for Thou art with me. Thy rod and Thy staff, they comfort me. Surely goodness and mercy shall follow me all the days of my life and I will dwell in the house of the Lord forever. (*In her sleep, for the first time, Mrs. Higgins' face is peaceful. We hear a small splash.*)[23]

Kovac, a communist, is probably an atheist. Rittenhouse, on the other hand, is more concerned with the almighty dollar than with almighty God. Joe seems to be a deeply spiritual man. The Nazi's presence is an important part of the scene, because the audience begins to wonder what type of religious values, if any, would allow him to kill men, women, and children in lifeboats and feel no remorse. One suspects that in the minds and hearts of the German people, God and His commandments have been replaced by Hitler and his *Weltanschauung* (worldview).

Dr. Robert Ley, a Nazi leader known as the "Labour-front-Fuhrer," declared Hitler to be his religion and Nazism his faith and that students "should not seek to understand Hitler with their mere intellects but with their hearts, 'in religious faith.'"[24] Factories contained worship rooms where the symbols of the Nazi party were displayed.[25] There were those who perceived Hitler's *Weltanschauung* as the usurper of Christianity and God by placing itself above and beyond any religion or law through arrogating "unto itself the First Commandment."[26]

In 1941, Roosevelt warned citizens of the United States and the world of the Nazis' ruthlessness toward existing religions. He exposed the Nazis' plan to abolish all existing religions. There would be no clergy, no religious symbols— only an international Nazi church endorsing the words of *Mein Kampf* instead of the Bible.[27]

Hitler and the Third Reich allowed religion no sanctuary. However, the German people embraced the Nazi movement in the 1930s with a religious zeal. But Hitler either abolished or brought under his control communists, unions, political parties, army general staff and church alike. He offered a way of life that would alleviate problems in Germany that the socialists and communists could not eliminate because their approaches were inadequate:

The Nazis offered to the people the quickest and most radical way of relief from a situation of stress and insecurity. While the Socialists kept on talking vaguely in the name of peace and democracy, while the Communists promised a narrow class policy, the Nazis attacked the Versailles Treaty, promised economic autarky and employment. While the Socialists tied up the destiny of Germany with that of European democracy, and the Communists with that of Soviet Russia, the Nazis stirred up the feeling of pride of a heroic nation which is not only the master of its own destiny, but is called upon to master the world.[28]

The dictatorship organized by Adolf Hitler and the Nazi Party was all-encompassing. Hitler took on and accepted the stature of a god. Any act to protect or promote the growth of the Third Reich was sanctioned, and the edicts and actions of the Fuhrer became the collective ''will'' of the people. People pledged their allegiance not to the flag, or to God, but directly to Hitler.

Knowing this, we can understand the past and future actions of *Lifeboat*'s Nazi, Willi. What appears to be a religious void in his character is in effect a worship of Hitler and the Nazi ideology that permeated all German institutions.

After the burial scene, Mrs. Higgins wakes up, and when she realizes that the other crew members have buried her infant at sea, she tries to commit suicide by throwing herself into the sea. The others forcibly restrain her, place her in the wicker chair, and then tie her to it with a rope. That night, while the others sleep, she manages to partially untie herself and jump overboard. The next morning they find the rope attached to the boat, taut with the weight of her body. Kovac cuts the rope and the loose end disappears beneath the surface of the ocean. Rittenhouse feels responsible for the death of Mrs. Higgins because he fell asleep while on night watch.

It is not long before minor dissension again occurs between Kovac and Constance Porter. She asks him to fix the clasp on her diamond bracelet. He complies and takes the opportunity to comment on her work as a reporter:

KOVAC
Mrs. Porter, I've read a lot of your stuff. (*She looks up, pleased, but on guard.*) You want to know what's the matter with it?

CONNIE
(*Mrs. Porter's response comes with unexpected, deceptive mildness.*) No, do tell me.

KOVAC
You've been all over the world, and you've met all kinds of people—but you never write about them. You only write about yourself. You think the whole war's a show put on for you to cover, like a Broadway play, and if enough people die before the last act, maybe you might give it four stars. . . .

CONNIE
(*Tensely*) All right, Tovarich, now listen to me—[29]

America's democratic society emphasizes the rights of the individual; it is the purpose of the Bill of Rights to guarantee the civil rights of the individual.

Antithetically, the communistic system of government places supreme emphasis on the proletariat group. The individual exists for the group, not for himself. This is especially apparent in the plot structure of the major Russian films of the 1920s. Their climaxes come when the individual submerges into the group, which then collectively rises up against the Czar's regime. Kovac's criticism of Connie's writing style is more than a personal attack; it is an indictment against individuality and surpasses the complexity of her egocentricity. Connie's excessive focus on herself is odious to Kovac's communistic value system. But similarly, the nickname "Tovarich" that Connie gives Kovac is a direct ideological confrontation; she labels a communist a communist. The debate terminates when the lifeboat sail is set.

The next sequence combines minor and major contention over the course to be taken by the lifeboat. On the allegorical level, the contention concerns who will determine the ideological form and direction of the world. All those on board watch the billowing sail as a symbol of hope only to realize they are poorly prepared and ill-equipped to reach Bermuda, the sunken freighter's original destination. Without a compass they are hard pressed to come up with the correct direction. Stanley Garett, the freighter's navigation officer, points out a course which the German modifies and Kovac reverses as he declares himself captain of the lifeboat, even though by this time the German has unwittingly revealed himself as the U-boat captain. Connie and Rittenhouse are willing to give the job to the best qualified—the German—but Kovac insists they follow the direction Stanley points out. The rest support Kovac and for the time being dissension is silenced.

Allegorically, of course, the lifeboat is the world and the crew members are its inhabitants—the Allied Powers and the Nazis in particular. The competence of Rittenhouse (American capitalism) as a leader depends on his ability to make the correct directional decision, which will preserve the lives of his democratic constituents. Unfortunately, no one has a compass. Garett (British democracy) "thinks" he knows the right direction. Rittenhouse and Mrs. Porter are inclined to follow the nautical proficiency of the German captain. Unknown to all of them, the German has a compass and intends to take their "little world" in a Nazi direction. The two capitalists do not really care if Nazism becomes the dominant ideology, as long as they can continue to make profits through national and international trade and so maintain their high standards of living. Garett, Mackenzie, Smith, and Joe (American democracy) are passive or reluctant to accept leadership for the direction of the world. Kovac (Russian communism) is the exception—for two reasons: he is against following Rittenhouse and the Nazi. Russia was bitterly opposed to Nazi Germany because Germany had broken the Stalin-Hitler Pact (1939) when it attacked Russia on June 23, 1941.[30] Moreover, Kovac is of Czechoslovakian descent and bitterly remembers the successful

German invasion of that country in 1938. Communists in the United States and elsewhere have always opposed the democratic form of government because of its capitalistic-materialistic system. Interestingly, through the democratic support of the majority, Kovac takes control of the boat and follows the course set by Garett.

In the next scene, between Rittenhouse and Connie, Hitchcock continues to make a caustic comment about the materialism of the affluent Americans. Connie is complaining over the loss of her typewriter and Rittenhouse suggests she "quit grousing."

CONNIE

Why shouldn't I grouse? Little by little, I'm being stripped of all my earthly possessions. . . . First my jewelry, then my camera—I don't mind the loss of the camera so much, but the film in it . . . I get positively ill when I think about it!

RITTENHOUSE

(*From behind the newspaper.*) Remember the boom we had after the last war? (*He lowers the paper and speaks impressively.*) The boom we'll have after this one's over will make the other one look like a mild flurry.

CONNIE

Then my steamer rug goes—then my fur coat—and now my typewriter.[31]

Connie, however, is changing. As the film opened, she was alone and seemed unaffected by the war. Now she is beginning to feel its adversity through the loss of her worldly possessions and the death of the woman for whom she sacrificed her mink coat. Similarly, America took a position of isolationism at the beginning of the war, then became gradually involved by sending its wealth— losing it, in a sense—in the form of manufactured goods and agricultural products, to England and other allies.

But American citizens had a difficult time accepting Russia as a bona fide ally. After the Bolshevik revolution of 1917, the newspapers, politicians, and political scientists alike incessantly attacked the Soviet way of government and life. It was not until November 16, 1933 that the United States established diplomatic relations with Soviet Russia.[32] However, political relations with Russia remained cool throughout the 1930s. They went from bad to worse between 1939 and 1940 because of the Stalin-Hitler Non-Aggression Pact of August 23, 1939, Russia's occupation of eastern Poland, her assimilation of Lithuania, Latvia, and Estonia through setting up Russian bases in these Baltic states for their "protection," and Russia's attack, defeat, and occupation of Finland when she refused to allow Russia to establish bases in her borders.[33] Russia's overt imperialism was openly condemned by the United States.

Then the political tide turned: in 1941, Nazi Germany attacked Russia and Japan attacked the United States. Suddenly these two ideological enemies found themselves as shipmates in the Allied Powers' boat, both countries desiring self-preservation against Nazi world conquest. A distrust of Russia because of her disrespect for the territorial sovereignty of other countries led to a general distrust of Russians and anyone who succumbed to their communist ideology. This distrust is succinctly reflected in the following dialogue between Connie and Kovac.

                              CONNIE
(*Indignantly*) Say, where did you get that memo pad?

                              KOVAC
I borrowed it from you, to make a deck of cards.

                              CONNIE
You mean to say you opened my bag—

                              KOVAC
It was open. (*He tosses the remnants of the pad into her lap and addresses Rittenhouse.*) How about a little draw poker?

                         RITTENHOUSE
(*Eagerly*) Okie-doky!

                              KOVAC
(*To Connie*) Deal you in?

                              CONNIE
With the deck you made, darling?[34]

Kovac is a communist who, like his Russian mentors, takes what is accessible to him regardless of ownership rights. Rittenhouse, the businessman, does not mind playing Kovac's game if there is a possibility of making a profit. Connie, the newspaper reporter, has had first-hand experience with the Russians and knows they are corrupt. She implies that a man who harbors a corrupt ideology will make a corrupt deck of cards and play a dishonorable game, so she refuses his invitation. This negative statement about Russia and her diplomatic relations with the United States was not the type of political film statement the American government wished to be made at this time.

Historically, the United States was engaged in a most awesome and brutal war with a two-front theatre. England and America were vitally concerned that Russia not fall to the Nazi onslaught. Since the birth of Soviet Russia, the democratic nations had stood firmly against her. Now the Russian image had to be changed in the minds of the American people. For this purpose the "United States government asked Hollywood to make feature films with pro-Soviet themes."[35] Hollywood complied:

> The results included Sam Goldwyn's *North Star* (1943), MGM's *Song of Russia* (1943), and the official *Battle of Russia* (1943), part of Frank Capra's *Why We Fight* series made for the United States Army. The Warner Brothers contributed *Mission to Moscow*, a feature-length film glorifying Stalin, releasing it on April 30, 1943.[36]

Mission to Moscow was perhaps the greatest distortion of history in the films mentioned above. The government used this propaganda film "to wed the home-front citizen to official war aims." All of Hollywood's skills were used "to subvert an entertainment medium to sell a message in a risky and highly controversial fashion."[37] David Culbert comments that the historical weakness of the film highlights the main reason we should study it—to more clearly understand the motivation of government and Hollywood producers. *Mission to Moscow* in no way accurately presents what life was like in Russia during the late 1930s, "but it speaks volumes about what Warner Brothers and, through them, the Roosevelt administration wanted the American people to think about Russia in 1943 when the film was released."[38] *Mission to Moscow* was a vision sought by the government and supplied by Warner Brothers. It was an ideological and historical propagandistic placebo intended to mask historical truth with a distorted image of an ally. In short, the film was a lie. It portrayed Stalin as a benevolent political father whose purges in the 1930s were a matter of political justice. In truth, the purges were a matter of eliminating political and military dissidents who opposed the Stalin-dominated Russian state. John Dewey, an American philosopher and educator, attacked the film in a letter printed in the *New York Times* in which he held that *Mission to Moscow* was "the first instance in our country of totalitarian propaganda for mass consumption—a propaganda which falsifies history through distortion, omission, or pure invention of facts."[39] Arthur Pope, also a prominent scholar, came to the defense of the film "on the grounds that the purg trials really were a response to a Trotskyite conspiracy," adding that "in the middle of a war in which Russia was our ally, it was unseemly to argue over the content of the film."[40] Hitchcock's *Lifeboat* was released approximately nine months after *Mission to Moscow*. The characters of Connie and Kovac, through their conflict, represent the American press and Russia. Whereas *Mission to Moscow* distorted historical truth in its attempt to smooth over the dissension between two allies, *Lifeboat* honestly exposed it. *Mission to Moscow* has been relegated to the archives; *Lifeboat* is still screened today because it has that common spine which all film classics must possess: truth.

Among other things, Hitchcock wanted to truthfully present Nazi alleged mental and functional superiority. In one scene, the nurse, Mackenzie, is shocked by the spreading infection in Gus Smith's leg. Willi, the Nazi, examines the leg and diagnoses gangrene. An operation must be performed or Gus will die. After talking with the German, whom they have come to know as Willi, Connie tells the others that he is a surgeon by profession, that he has performed many amputations, and that he is willing to perform one on Gus. Alice Mackenzie first refuses to assist Willi because she has never even seen an amputation; however, she overcomes her fear and dutifully performs her work. Smith consumes a fifth of brandy as an anesthetic, and Willi operates successfully. The Nazi, a U-boat captain and a medical doctor, is a prime example of the German master race myth. Men like Willi, who accepted Nazi ideology, would father a new master race. Nazi ideological leaders—Chamberlain, Wagner, Rosenberg, and Hitler—wrote and taught that the German was racially superior to all other people. Jews were considered to be a contaminating virus, which had weakened the collective genetic structure of the Aryan race. This mythology of pride led Hitler and his followers to create laws and a foreign policy to exterminate the mentally deficient, Jews, and political dissidents.[41] They also formulated systematic aggression toward other nations as a means of world conquest and domination. Hitler's aim "envisaged world domination based on race and the plan for a new 'master race' forming a biologically bred elite which was intended to supplant the conservative leading groups in the ruling positions of the Reich."[42]

Understanding the master race myth helps us understand the forthcoming actions of Willi as he uses manipulation and subterfuge to take complete control of the lifeboat. Hitchcock employs all the elements of suspense as the plot moves toward the climax and resolution, and he continues to criticize the lack of unity between the Allies through dissension among the film characters.

The fact that Willi has performed a successful operation on Gus creates for him a new stature of competence and trust in the eyes of the other crewmembers. Furthermore, they know he was the captain of the U-boat, which presupposes excellent nautical ability. A correct course becomes essential to save Gus' life. Fear preys on the minds of the crew members, and because of the new trust they have in Willi, he is able to manipulate them to change the course of the lifeboat to one which he knows will eventually bring them in contact with a Nazi supply ship. Aware that Gus needs hospital treatment, Connie does all she can to persuade Willi to identify the correct course to Bermuda. He repeatedly feigns reluctance to accept the responsibility of making such a weighty decision. Connie persists and Willi finally admits they are on the wrong course. Kovac would do anything rather than follow the German's direction but seeing the anguish in Gus' eyes and the hostility in the eyes of the others, Kovac reluctantly agrees to change course.

In 1942, Joseph Bornstein and Paul Milton commented on the dissension among the Allies and called for a more cosmopolitan political awareness among Americans. Had the Allied Powers achieved the political discernment reflected in the following quotation, *Lifeboat* would have been a superfluous film.

> There is a long record of mistrust between us and England, the country which our history books have taught us—at an impressionable age—once oppressed us. We are predisposed to disbelieve all protestations of Russian, especially Communist, sincerity. And our British partners in turn cannot easily put faith in a people whom they regard as cocky and boastful, nor the Russians trust a nation they consider miserable slaves of capitalist oppression with imperialist designs. Added to this is the historical fact that "war by committee"—by coalition—has always been cumber-

some, difficult and irritating. We are waging war by committee now, and are paying the price in friction and lost opportunities. Each setback growing from disjointed co-operation adds more fuel to the Axis contention that we can't depend on our partners—nor they on us.[43]

What Bornstein and Milton, and Hitchcock, recognized was the need to differentiate between military and political purposes in the alliance. Each Allied country had to lay its political differences aside and join "the united aim of hitting the Axis wherever we can with weapons borne by men in any uniform."[44]

With Kovac's weary acquiescence to Willi's course, the plot of *Lifeboat* turns in favor of the Nazi, who has cunningly exerted his will to move the Allied crew members' microcosmic world toward his objective of rescue for himself and capture for the others. His secretive use of a compass allows him to direct the others toward his end. Nevertheless, the plot elements of recognition and reversal insure the eventual success of the other crew members. So far their world, the lifeboat, has been taken in two directions: the Russian's and the German's. The direction of the boat is corrected a third time through Garett's planetary knowledge. He knows they must head directly for the planet Mars if they are to land at Bermuda. After changing course according to Willi's direction, Garett realizes, once night falls, that they are sailing in the direction of Venus, since Mars is to the starboard side of their craft. He tells this to Mackenzie, and then changes the course to head for the reflected light of Mars and the island of Bermuda.

The following day, while the German sleeps, the Allied characters discuss possible deceit on the part of Willi. They agree that if he has a compass, he is guilty of attempted manslaughter because Gus' life is at stake and Willi has intentionally directed them away from Bermuda and the nearest hospital. They decide to have Joe "check" Willi for ownership of a compass. Joe carries out his mission and then gives a watch-like object he took from Willi to Kovac, who reveals that it is indeed a compass. Now they realize that Willi would have sacrificed Smith's life for his own freedom. Kovac is determined to execute the Nazi immediately; however, a sudden storm arises and they all struggle together to save the ship. Willi gives them commands in English, which they follow. Before this, he had spoken only in German and used facial expressions to suggest he knew no English so the others would be uninhibited in their communication. The sail is lost, along with the food and water, but the crew weathers the storm through Willi's expertise.

The fact that the German possesses superior knowledge and that Garett, an Englishman, was the first to detect Willi's real intentions has a parallel in history. The British were aware of the development of Enigma, a German machine capable of producing numerous ciphers "secure from even the most advanced cryptanalytical attack." Even if Enigma fell into Allied hands, there would be no benefit since it could not be operated without knowledge of the keying procedures.[45] Hitler trusted the use of Enigma completely, as did the head of Abwehr, Admiral Canaris.[46] Fortunately for the Allies, a top-secret weapon developed under the auspices of MI-6 and known as Ultra or "The Bomb" came into being for the "decryption of secret German written communications."[47]

The British were extremely anxious to have an Enigma machine. The break came in June of 1938. Sir Stewart Graham Menzies, department head of MI-6, received word that a certain Polish Jew, Richard Lewinski (an assumed name), wished to sell his knowledge of Enigma to MI-6. He had worked "as a mathematician and engineer at the factory in Berlin where Enigma was produced."[48] Now Lewinski was once again living in Poland because his Nazi hosts expelled him from Germany for religious reasons. Menzies called into his office Alfred Knox, England's most gifted cryptanalyst, and Alan Mathison Turing, a mathematical logician, both of whom were working for MI-6. Their boss gave them the assignment to travel to Warsaw to ascertain if Lewinski could produce the Enigma machine. They accepted the assignment and left for Poland.

When Knox and Turing arrived in Warsaw, they met with Lewinski and discussed the Enigma machine. After extensive conversations with him, in which the two MI-6 cryptanalysts were convinced he could produce Enigma, they returned to London and reported the good news to Menzies. In turn, Lewinski and his wife moved to Paris, where he reproduced Enigma. But of course, possession of the machine was of little value without a keying schedule. Turing had been "toying with the notion of a 'universal machine' . . . which, when supplied with suitable instructions, would imitate the behavior of another machine."[49]

Harold Keen, a top engineer in England, and twelve carefully selected men were put to work in the last quarter of 1938 on the Turing Universal Machine. A machine of this type had never been built.

> In complete secrecy—remnants of that secrecy were still being encountered in 1974—the machine took shape, and it was by no means as large as St. Paul's or the Capitol. It was a copper-colored cabinet some 8 feet tall and perhaps 8 feet wide at its base, shaped like an old-fashioned keyhole. And inside the cabinet was a piece of engineering which defied description. As Keen said, it was not a computer, and "there was no other machine like it. It was unique, built especially for his purpose. Neither was it a complex tabulating machine, which was sometimes used in cryptanalysis. What it did was to match the electrical circuits of Enigma. Its secret was in the internal wiring of [Enigma's] rotors, which 'The Bomb' sought to imitate."
>
> The machine was installed at Hut 3, a large Nissen hut under the trees in Bletchley's parkland, and the time soon came to begin operational trials by feeding Enigma intercepts to "The Bomb." These intercepts were simply obtained from the string of tall-pyloned wireless interception posts which the British government had established around the world. The post recorded all enemy, hostile and suspect wireless traffic and radioed it to Bletchley Park, where Enigma transmissions were identified, put on tape and fed into "The Bomb." If "The Bomb" could find the keys in which the transmissions had been ciphered, the cryptanalysts at Bletchley could then "unbutton" the messages.[50]

Turing's Universal Machine did work. The English now had a machine that allowed them to read the wireless mail of the Axis Powers. The creation of "The Bomb" was one of the best-kept secrets during and after the war. It was not until the early 1970s that Ultra became known to the world. Turing's "Bomb" began to function approximately seven months after Britain and Germany went to war: Turing's "Bomb" was renamed Ultra, and while the decoded messages were relatively unimportant, their significance was obvious.

> If "The Bomb" had penetrated Goering's traffic, how long would it be before it could decode the secret wireless communications of the other commanders of the German armed services, of Canaris and his secret intelligence service, of Hitler himself? . . . If Ultra lived up to its promise, it would surely become a weapon of great importance in the war against the Third Reich.[51]

To the members of the lifeboat Willi was as viable a weapon as Germany's Enigma. As he manned the tiller during the storm, he changed the direction of the boat for the fourth time. In this microcosmic sea-saw battle between the Nazi and the representatives of the Allied Powers, Willi exerted his will. The myth of the master race is once again reflected in the dialogue.

KOVAC
That's one for the book—your book—only when you write it, they won't believe you. Our enemy—our prisoner of war—and now we're his prisoners, and he's gauleiter of the boat, singing German lullabies to us while he rows us to his supply ship and a concentration camp. (*To the German*) Tell 'em, Willi, tell 'em how funny it is.

THE GERMAN
That isn't funny. That is logical. During the storm we were blown quite a bit off our course. Without a sail it would take us weeks to get to Bermuda.

RITTENHOUSE
Certainly. It's perfectly logical. The supply ship's our only chance.

KOVAC
You know how I feel about that—I'd rather take my chances with the sharks. But he'll never make it. Without food and water how long do you think he can keep rowing like this?

THE GERMAN
Long enough, Mr. Kovac, to reach my objective.

RITTENHOUSE
You're sure, Willi? (*To the others.*) Maybe one of us had better try to relieve you at the oars.

THE GERMAN
That is not necessary.

STANLEY
Maybe I can take over for a while.

THE GERMAN
I'll row.

ALICE
How can you keep rowing, Willi, hour after hour, when the rest of us can hardly lift an oar?

KOVAC
(*Sarcastically*) It's the master race—the Herrenvolk. Don't you know they can do anything?

RITTENHOUSE
I'm beginning to believe it.[52]

Willi is a stereotype of Hitler. His actions are in complete accordance with Nazi ideology of recreating a German Fatherland and fighting against "the delirium of democracy."[53]

In spite of the strong political conflict in the film suspense does not take a back row seat. The prevalent element of suspense at this time is the dreadful alternative. The free world audience realizes that if Willi achieves his main objective of contact with the Nazi supply ship, the pendulum will have swung irreconcilably in his direction. The audience identifies with the dreadful alternative of possible Nazi victory because if it really happened it would affect their own lives. The loss of democracy and its inherent freedoms was more than a fantasy for the audience; it was a reality they quietly and soberly considered when war reports favored Germany.

In the following sequences, suspense builds as the Allied characters resume fighting among themselves, taking them further from their main objective of defeating the Nazi German and, vicariously for the audience, Nazi Germany. A discussion on food between Rittenhouse, Kovac, and Willi grates on the nerves of Constance Porter, provoking her verbal attack on Rittenhouse and a physical and verbal attack on Kovac.

RITTENHOUSE'S VOICE
In the old days, there was a place in Boston—Young's Hotel—had the best restaurant in the world.

KOVAC
I'll bet it wasn't any better than Henrici's Coffee House in Chicago. Or Bookbinder's in Philly. That was food for you. (*Mrs. Porter's face is twitching with incipient hysteria.*)

THE GERMAN
In Munich there is a place called Lorber's. Their specialty is pot roast.

RITTENHOUSE
Pot roast? Young's used to have a menu of a hundred and fifty pages. (*He's unaware of the fact that Mrs. Porter is looking at him with loathing. He continues blithely.*) Yes, sir, one-hundred-and-fifty solid pages of eatments. Oh boy, and what eatments!

KOVAC
Did you ever eat in Antoine's in New Orleans?

RITTENHOUSE

Doesn't compare with Young's. You never saw such food in your life. (*The muscles of Mrs. Porter's face are twitching. She holds onto herself by dint of the greatest effort.*) Especially seafood—steamed clams with melted butter, and lobsters—lobsters à la Newberg, with a special white wine and sauce.

CONNIE

(*Furiously*) Ritt, shut up!

RITTENHOUSE

(*Surprised*) What's wrong?

CONNIE

Stop jabbering about food! (*She comes over, hysteria creeping into her voice.*) Isn't it enough that you lost all our supplies through your carelessness?

RITTENHOUSE

(*Injured*) Carelessness?

CONNIE

Yes, stupid, criminal carelessness!

RITTENHOUSE

It wasn't me. I wasn't in charge of the food. The commissary was Joe's job.

CONNIE

(*With rising hysteria.*) You dirty rat! Trying to shift the blame onto Joe!

JOE

Maybe it was my fault.

CONNIE

No, it wasn't! (*To Rittenhouse.*) If you'd had the brains of an ant you'd have taken care of it when you saw the storm coming.

RITTENHOUSE

(*Fearfully*) Connie, what's the matter with you?

KOVAC

She's all right. Just a little hungry. (*He looks at her and continues.*) What're you squawking about? When you write your book it'll make a swell chapter—how it feels to be starving—first person singular. Those are good things to write about—hunger and thirst—if you really come from back of the yards—(*She hits him across the face with all her might. He gets up and grabs her hand. She tears and claws at him with her free hand. Alice comes over with Stanley and they take hold of Mrs. Porter.*)

CONNIE

(*Wildly*) Kovac, why don't you kill Willi? Why don't you take your knife, as you said you would, and cut his throat? (*Shrieking*) I'll tell you why—you're not strong enough. He's made of iron and the rest of us are just flesh and blood—hungry flesh and blood—and thirsty! (*Suddenly she gives up struggling and sinks, sobbing, into Alice's arms. In the silence that follows, Rittenhouse and Kovac sit down to resume their poker game.*)[54]

The lack of unity among these three characters, who are native-born Americans, is unmistakable. This was true of Americans in general, then. Bornstein and Milton perceived several dissenting groups in 1942, including those who fail to see that economic isolationism is dead and that our country must hammer out a new politico-economic foreign policy; those who live in such daily terror of Communism that they would adopt another dictatorship in self-defense; those who damn an idea, a program or a person primarily because of Jewish origin; those who treat national minorities as "foreigners," and those of our national minorities who behave like foreigners; those who rake the raw wounds of racial discrimination; those among capital or labor who have lost hope of the other's good intentions and seek to persuade by force; those who rejoice in British and Russian defeats because their own acumen in distrusting their allies is thereby proven; those who, grown cynical about the spiritual capacity of the American people, have lost faith in its rebirth in travail.[55]

Connie's hysterical outbreak interrupts the poker game, in which Rittenhouse has repeatedly lost to Kovac. Although Rittenhouse's fortune is not in danger, his ego has taken a terrible beating. He tries to turn luck his way in the next sequence of major dissension among the Americans:

RITTENHOUSE

(*He has picked up a fourth deuce.*) Well, I guess I'll keep the pikers out. I'll bet five. (*Mrs. Porter, who has been leaning back apathetically, now sits up and takes notice. Kovac looks at Rittenhouse, then at his own hand—he has a full house.*)

KOVAC

Matched your kicker, eh?

RITTENHOUSE

(*Breathing hard.*) Five's the best. Going to see me!

KOVAC

And raise you five. (*He shoves over the matches. Rittenhouse looks at his cards again to make sure of what he has. Now he can't keep the satisfaction out of his voice.*)

RITTENHOUSE

Now you're talking my language. (*He shoves in his two remaining matches and draws aside eight to indicate the amount he's shy in the pot. Mrs. Porter is now watching with something approaching animation. The other kibitzers await Kovac's move. Kovac is studying Rittenhouse's face. He looks up at Mrs. Porter. She's watching him with a faint sneer on her lips. The sneer is what decides him.*)

KOVAC

I'll see your ten and raise you one. (*He shoves forth the matches. Rittenhouse now drops all pretense.*)

RITTENHOUSE

(*Gloatingly*) Kovac, this is the moment I've been waiting for. I've got you over a barrel. (*He puts his cards face down before him on the seat and leans forward.*) We'll do the bookkeeping later. I'm raising you all the chips you've got—plus all the money I owe you—(*Kovac hesitates. We get the feeling he's about to fold.*)

CONNIE

(*Deliberately goading*) Kovac, I think you've stepped out of your class this time.

KOVAC

I'll call you, Rittenhouse. What've you got?

RITTENHOUSE

(*As Rittenhouse reaches to pick up his cards a sharp gust of wind sweeps them off the seat and into the sea. Rittenhouse makes a terrific lunge after the fluttering cards, almost going overboard in his effort to save them. Then he turns to Kovac, his face working.*) That was my pot! You couldn't possibly beat me.

KOVAC

I have a full house.

RITTENHOUSE

I had four deuces.

KOVAC

How do I know you had four deuces?

RITTENHOUSE

You ought to know. You made the cards, didn't you? (*His voice grows shrill and ragged.*) And you marked them, too! They're crooked! And you're crooked! (*He suddenly lunges for Kovac's throat. The two men lurch about, struggling. Stanley runs over and tries to separate them.*)[56]

A sudden rain shower interrupts the fight between Rittenhouse and Kovac. The rain promises to alleviate their thirst, but unfortunately it ceases before a satisfactory amount can be collected.

According to John S. Gibson, a political scientist, periodic dissension among the constituents of a democracy is par for the course:

Fundamental to democracy is the idea that despite human differences, especially those of an economic nature, each man values the rights of others, and each joins in the protection and enhancement of the well-being of all. The American motto, occasionally forgotten, is *e pluribus unum*—unity through diversity. This simply means that, despite all the colorful political, economic, social, and religious differences in our society, we stand together on basic goals and democratic procedures. Consider how all our differences are tossed around in the heat and excitement of an American political campaign. But note how we close ranks after the election! Respect for diversity is indispensable to the democratic creed.[57]

"Unity through diversity" is a fine motto in view of the "melting pot" history of our country's population. The nations of the world contributed their people to the United States. For the most part, these immigrants enjoyed the political freedom and economic affluence which this country afforded them. However, the American communist was an exception to the motto of "unity through diversity." Hitchcock's Kovac may be a humanitarian, but he does not support the sovereignty of the United States government because of its economic system— he is not willing to close ranks. Hitchcock is careful to emphasize Kovac's attitude in *Lifeboat* as an internal weakness of ideological dissension in America. This situation in the lifeboat has a historical precedent. Robert Sherwood, a prominent American playwright and Roosevelt's biographer, reported an incident in February, 1940 where Roosevelt was booed and hissed by communists after he confronted them in these words with the illegality of their intention to overthrow the Republic of the United States:

It has been said that some of you are Communists. That is a very unpopular term these days. As Americans you have a legal and constitutional right to call yourselves Communists, those of you who do. You have a right peacefully and openly to advocate certain ideals of theoretical Communism; but as Americans you have not only a right but a sacred duty to confine your advocacy of changes in law to the methods prescribed by the Constitution of the United States— and you have no American right, by act or deed of any kind, to subvert the Government and the Constitution of this Nation.[58]

The following scene between Gus Smith and Willi, two characters of German origin, is filled with suspense and makes the political point that the virtue of Aryan blood is much less important than preserving the life and will of the Fuhrer. Gus tries to tell Stanley that Willi has water; however, Stanley simply assumes that Gus is delirious and after humoring him, goes to sleep. Willi then takes advantage of Gus' delirium to entice him to return to his girl, Rosie. After asking Gus to remember that his name is Schmidt, Willi brushes aside Gus' questions as to why Willi failed to share his water with the others and again suggesting Gus go off to Rosie, the German pushes Gus overboard. Gus' strangled cry for help wakens Stanley who hears "Willi— he's got—"[59] before Gus sinks below the surface of the sea.

Hitchcock includes all the elements of suspense in this tensely dramatic scene between Gus and Willi. The immediate conflict between these two men revolves around Willi's possession of a flask of water. Gus tries to tell Stanley Garett, but the latter falls asleep because he is physically exhausted. He is also drowsily aware of Gus' current tendency to hallucinate. Willi is the master antagonist because he has managed to conceal water from the others, who begin to perish from thirst. The suspense of the situation is compounded when Gus is isolated with Willi. The dreadful alternative is that Gus must alarm the others or face the murderer, Willi. The unexpected complication occurs when Willi pushes Gus overboard, and growing fear for the life of Gus is confirmed in the audience through the terror in his voice when he calls for his friend, Stanley. Following the murder of Gus, the audience is supposedly in the superior position because they are the only ones with a clear recollection that Willi has water. The remaining element—subjective camera—is used interchangeably when Willi and Gus talk with each other. Hitchcock implements all the elements of suspense in less than four pages of dialogue and simultaneously awakens his audience's sense of justice through the murder of Gus Smith.

In the next scene, Hitchcock reconciles their sense of justice through the climax of the film. The dialogue contains the plot elements of recognition and reversal, which, when they occur together, according to Aristotle's *Poetics*, render one of the more pleasing dramatic experiences for the audience.

RITTENHOUSE
(*Frightened*) Willi, what is it? What happened?

THE GERMAN
Schmidt went over the side.

STANLEY
He was calling my name. That's what woke me.

THE GERMAN
You can't imagine how painful it was to me all night long to watch him, turning about and suffering, and nothing I could do for him.

KOVAC
Why didn't you stop rowing?

THE GERMAN
Why should I?

STANLEY
To help him.

THE GERMAN
The best way to help him was to let him go. (*There is silence. They stare at him. Once again we get the feeling of isolation for the German. Suddenly he is no longer part of the group, but an individual alone, aloof, almost of a different species from the rest. He continues affably, like a school master explaining something to a group of not very bright pupils.*) I had no right to stop him, even if I wanted to. A poor cripple, dying of hunger and thirst—what good would life be to a man like that? (*He grows uneasy at the way the others are looking at him. Their silence is far more damning than words.*)

STANLEY
He was trying to tell me something. If I could only remember—

THE GERMAN
He's better off now, out of his troubles.

STANLEY
It was something about water. (*Suddenly Mrs. Porter and Kovac, by some telepathic current between them, get the same notion and look at each other. A hunted look creeps into the German's eyes as he watches them.*)

ALICE
He was in agony from thirst. I wanted to cry, but the tears wouldn't come.

CONNIE
No, how could they? (*To the German casually.*) If I remember rightly, tears are water with a trace of sodium chloride. (*His forehead is covered with beads of sweat.*) Isn't that so, Willi?

THE GERMAN
Ja.

KOVAC
What about sweat? (*Instinctively the German lifts his hand and with the back of it wipes the sweat off his brow.*) What's the chemical composition of sweat?

CONNIE
Water, with a trace of something or other.

STANLEY
Now I remember—Gus said that Willi had some water.

JOE'S VOICE

Yes, right under his shirt. (*Next to the German, Joe is holding up Mrs. Porter's flask, with an inch or so of water in it. Obviously he has just purloined it from the German.*) Right under his shirt—(*The German reaches up and grabs Joe's wrist. They struggle. The flask falls and breaks. The others look down with mute anguish at the broken flask, with its precious fluid wasted, and then, slowly, they turn their gaze at the German, with a silent, overwhelming hostility. The German shows no sign of either fear or guilt.*)

THE GERMAN

Quite so. (*Still they stare, wordless, as if the strangling hate in their hearts has stricken them dumb.*) I took the precaution of filling the flask from the water beaker before the storm—just in case of emergency. (*There's a striking contrast between the quiet, reasonable talk and the aura of hatred that hovers about the group, like something visible and palpable. The German continues in a calm, rational manner.*) And I had food tablets and energy pills, too. Everybody on a U-boat has them. You should be grateful to me for having the foresight to think of such things. To survive one must have a plan. (*Their eyes are fixed upon the German as upon a loathsome reptile, creeping up on them.*) There's nothing to worry about—soon we'll reach the supply ship—and then we'll have food and water. It's too bad Schmidt couldn't have waited. (*The camera is now on Alice's face and we can hardly recognize it for the hate which has transfigured it. Strangely enough it is Alice who, with an animal cry, is the first to hurl herself at the German. Alice's attack is like a trigger that releases in them the same uncontrollable desire to kill. Now they all leap at the German.*)[60]

The Nazi is executed through the concerted efforts of the other crew members. This satisfies their, and the audience's, wounded sense of justice.

In retrospect, it was Garett's intelligence which brought about the downfall of the German. Likewise, it was the intelligence gathered through Britain's Ultra system which made victory possible for the Allied powers in the Battle of the Atlantic. Knox and Turing's contribution to World War II triumph cannot be overestimated. "Because Ultra compromised German intelligence, the German U-boat fleet was defeated."[61]

Following the execution of the Nazi, the other crew members, except Constance Porter, quickly slip into a defeatist state of mind. Connie has been stripped of all but one of her worldly treasures—a diamond bracelet. Her altruism comes through in the succeeding dialogue.

CONNIE

We haven't got energy pills, but the ocean's full of them—millions of fish swimming around! Why don't we catch some?

RITTENHOUSE

We tried it. We have no bait. (*Mrs. Porter hesitates, then looks at her hand with the diamond bracelet.*)

CONNIE

Sure we have! (*She rips the bracelet off and holds it aloft.*) Bait, by Cartier! (*They stare at her dumbfounded.*)

KOVAC

Are you kidding?

CONNIE

Kidding, my foot—I'm starving! Well, what're you waiting around for? Where's the fish line? (*They all look around. Kovac spots Joe's line and bends to pick it up. Mrs. Porter thrusts the bracelet into his hand.*) Bait your line, chum! (*Kovac starts to fix the bracelet to the end of the line. The whole atmosphere in the boat has changed magically. The mere promise of food has lifted their spirits extravagantly. They crowd around Kovac, all jabbering at once.*)

RITTENHOUSE

Not only food, but oil! We can squeeze the fish for the oil! It's better than water.

CONNIE

I can recommend the bait. I should know—I bit on it myself.

ALICE

I've never eaten raw fish before.

STANLEY

Oh, I have many times—it's good.[62]

Constance Porter's sacrifice of her wealth for her friends symbolizes the United States' willingness to expend her wealth during World War II to insure the victory of the Allied powers. As President Truman said, "The United States contributed $341,000,000,000 toward winning World War II. This is an investment in world freedom and world peace."[63]

The "war" in the lifeboat has ended in victory for the Allied characters. Now that the allegorical conflict has ended, Hitchcock returns the crew to the world war through the introduction of the Nazi supply ship that Willi had been trying to reach. Joe is the first to see the ship and makes a matter-of-fact announcement of its presence. Connie's bracelet, which is still being used as fish bait, is lost in the ensuing excitement. The crew members watch as the ship approaches. A lifeboat is lowered from the ship and it moves in their direction. When it has come about halfway toward them, a signal is sent from the Nazi ship to its lifeboat, which then begins to return to the supply ship.

STANLEY

(*Unbelievingly*) They're not going to pick us us.

RITTENHOUSE

That's impossible! They can't leave us here like this! Why—why—it's inhuman. (*The small boat has now turned around completely and is rowing back toward the supply ship.*) In fact, it's a violation of international law. (*Angrily*) What're you going to do, Kovac?

KOVAC

Sue them.[64]

A distinct boom is heard from the horizon behind the Allied lifeboat, and a geyser of water erupts between the Nazi ship and her lifeboat. The next shell is from an Allied warship hits and destroys the Nazi lifeboat. The Nazi supply ship barely misses the Allied lifeboat in its haste to escape the shelling by the warship. The supply ship clears the lifeboat but is struck by the shells of the Allied ship and goes down rapidly, leaving the lifeboat in suddenly stilled water strewn with debris. The crew members have witnessed this sea battle in wordless awe. They shake off the close call with death and turn their attention to the warship, which is approaching them and should shortly reach them. For the first time in the film, there is carefree and lighthearted communication between the characters.

Their jubilation is interrupted when a German from the supply ship struggles to climb into the lifeboat. They instinctively help him in. Almost immediately Rittenhouse becomes aggressive.

THE GERMAN SAILOR

(*Gasps*) Danke Schoen. (*They look at each other speechless. Alice bends over the German sailor.*)

ALICE

He's hurt—his arm—let's get his coat off. (*Mrs. Porter and Joe help Alice to get the boy's coat off. Kovac and Rittenhouse look at each other and their gesture indicates: "Well this is the last straw!" Rittenhouse, observing their reaction, visibly inflates with anger.*)

RITTENHOUSE

Hey—wait a minute. Have you forgotten about Willi, already? (*They look at him astonished.*)

CONNIE

But, Ritt, this is different. The kid's wounded.

RITTENHOUSE

Throw him back!

CONNIE

(*Indignantly*) Don't be silly, darling, he's utterly helpless—only a baby. (*Rittenhouse suddenly takes a panicky step back. As the two women turn to look behind them, they see ratlike panic in his eyes. The German is pointing a gun at them. They are so stunned they seem not to be aware of the menace of the gun in the German boy's shaking hand. Their reaction is more astonishment than fright.*)

KOVAC

The baby has a toy.

JOE

(*Scowling*) I should've frisked him.

RITTENHOUSE

You see? You can't treat them like human beings. You've got to exterminate them. (*Mrs. Porter suddenly spits out a word and her voice is that of a Prussian sergeant. Joe's hand shoots out and grabs the wrist that holds the gun; twists and the gun falls at Mrs. Porter's feet. She picks it up as Rittenhouse starts toward the German boy, his intent obviously homicidal. Kovac grabs him and holds him back.*)

KOVAC

Easy, Ritt, he'll be taken care of. (*The German boy has been looking at them and now he speaks.*)

GERMAN SAILOR

Werden Sie mich nicht umbringen? [Aren't you going to kill me?] (*Mrs. Porter looks at the gun in her hand and throws it overboard. Already Alice has started to roll up the boy's sleeve to examine the wounded arm.*)

ALICE

I'll have to tie this up till the ship's doctor takes care of it. (*Shame-facedly, Rittenhouse takes off his belt and hands it to Alice, who goes to work fixing up the injured arm, assisted by Joe. Mrs. Porter stands at the side of the boat; Kovac, Stanley and Rittenhouse watch. All their enmity for the German they killed is changed into almost excessive consideration for the German who has just tried to kill them.*)[65]

In this final sequence of the film, Rittenhouse is determined to kill the young Nazi but is dissuaded by the others. This almost parallels President Roosevelt's demand for unconditional surrender of Nazi Germany at the Casablanca Conference in January 1943. The difference is that dissension is immediately quelled and forgiveness and assistance finally control Allied character action in this last microcosmic sequence.

Criticism of *Lifeboat*

Lifeboat met with much positive and negative criticism, but few critics gave it both. One critic is disappointed at the lack of psychological truth: "unless of course *Lifeboat* is meant to be an allegory in which case it is much too deep for me."[66] Some critics see a film burdened with clichés and characters "exaggeratedly stereotypical."[67] As did others, Bosley Crowther misinterprets Hitchcock's characterization of the Nazi. Crowther is unable to conceive that Hitchcock deliberately created a "Superman" ideal in the character of Willi.[68] David Lardner more accurately assesses Hitchcock's characterization of the German. Others would wish to see an enemy "which is described as ignorant and blundering when it patently is not. The people we are fighting should be consistently represented as smart, resourceful, lovely to look at, and complete heels."[69] Richard Winnington denies that Willi's "superior" competence and resourcefulness cast a slur on democracy and adds that "a Nazi surgeon U-boat commander with a secret supply of food tablets, water and compass would make a formidable companion in any lifeboat." Winnington praises Hitchcock's portrait of the Nazi and considers it "good and timely propaganda."[70] Harris commended Hitchcock's use of set, noting that "it succeeded in depicting the war in microcosm without overworking the symbolism."[71] From another perspective, Jon Tuska notes how well the film "sustains interest no matter how confined its visual scope . . . and its skepticism, however mild, about the human race again at war with itself; no one is innocent and guilt for inhumanity and brutality is shared by all the characters." He adds that "if anything Hitchcock did not go far enough."[72]

Conclusion

In conclusion, Hitchcock creates suspense on two interdependent levels in *Lifeboat*: minor ideological conflicts between the "Allied" characters, and the major conflict between them and the Nazis, Willi and the young sailor, in the last sequence of the film. As in *Foreign Correspondent* and *Saboteur*, the director uses the ten elements of suspense for both entertainment and a political purpose.

The political purpose in *Lifeboat* is to help the audience recognize the danger of dissension among the Allies. In life in 1944, as in the film, the minor conflict between communism and capitalism had to be momentarily shelved so the major conflict, Nazi aggression, could be resolved. In the film, the execution of Willi was the meting out of justice for his murder of Gus Smith. For Hitchcock, this indicated his approval of the Allied Powers' efforts to win World War II.

The limited acting space made it difficult to accentuate the theme of espionage, but it is present in *Lifeboat*. Conversations between Willi and Constance Porter were always a cat-and-mouse game with political purpose. Joe Spencer secretively removed Willi's compass on a microcosmic reconnaisance mission. But above all, Garett's realization that the lifeboat was not headed for Bermuda paralleled England's Enigma broadcasts to ascertain her real direction in the war. Her carefully guarded Ultra intelligence secret permitted the Allied Powers to win the Battle of the Atlantic and ultimately World War II in Europe.

Lifeboat is a classic because of its sustained dramatic tension and truthful condensation of political facts. According to one commentator, "Hitchcock was in trouble in some quarters for making the Nazi the most cunning, resourceful, and powerful character, and it was suggested that he had fallen victim to the [Nazi] ideology."[73] However, no one criticized the Master of Suspense for telling the truth, as he knew it, of the World War II situation. I completely agree with Jon Tuska's statement: "I sometimes think that Hitchcock's films are disparaged . . . because of the unsettling truth in his representation."[74] Hitchcock had not fallen prey to Nazi ideology. If he were guilty of anything, it was of originating and directing a "rougher and severer" film for the "soul's health," to borrow Plato's words.[75] Hitchcock was concerned more with the survival of the democratic world community than with the praise of film critics.

5

Notorious

Production: Alfred Hitchcock, R.K.O., 1946. *Associate Producer*: Barbara Keon. *Director*: Alfred Hitchcock. *Scenario*: Ben Hecht, from a theme by Hitchcock. *Director of Photography*: Ted Tetzlaff, A.S.C. *Special Effects*: Vernon L. Walker and Paul Eagler, A.S.C. *Sets*: Albert S. D'Agostino, Carrol Clark, Darrell Silvera and Claude Carpenter. *Costumes*: Edith Head. *Music*: Roy Webb; conducted by Constantin Balaleinikoff. *Editing*: Theron Warth. *Sound Engineers*: John Tribby and Clem Portman. *Assistant Director*: William Dorfman. *Studio*: R.K.O. *Distributor*: R.K.O., 1946, 101 minutes. *Principal Actors*: Ingrid Bergman (Alicia Huberman), Cary Grant (Devlin), Claude Rains (Alexander Sebastian), Louis Calhern (Paul Prescott), Leopoldine Konstantin (Mrs. Sebastian), Reinhold Schunzel (Doctor Anderson), and Moroni Olsen, Ivan Triesault, Alexis Minotis, Eberhardt Krumschmidt, Fay Baker, Ricardo Costa, Lenore Ulric, Ramon Nomar, Peter von Zerneck, Sir Charles Mandl, Wally Brown.[1]

Notorious is a historical document revealing Alfred Hitchcock as a prescient director. He showed social and scientific astuteness by making a film with uranium—the vital element in an atomic bomb—the object of conflict between Nazi German subversives and U.S. agents in post-World War II South America.

In 1944, Alfred Hitchcock and scriptwriter Ben Hecht traveled to the California Institute of Technology at Pasadena to talk with Dr. Millikan, a well-known American scientist, who was aware of the research that would culminate in the development of the atomic bomb. The two filmmakers were ushered into Dr. Millikan's office where all shook hands. The three men sat down and Hitchcock asked his first question: "How big is an atom bomb?"[2] Dr. Millikan quickly blurted out: "Do you want to be arrested? Do you want me to be arrested, too?"[3] The famous scientist soon regained his composure, however, and spent the next hour trying to convince Hitchcock and Hecht how impossible it would be to make an atom bomb and even more absurd to base a motion picture on the concept. Hitchcock and Hecht left Dr. Millikan's office with no answer to Hitchcock's original question. The Cal Tech scientist reported this incident to the proper Federal authorities, and Hitchcock was under surveillance by the FBI for the next three months.[4]

Hitchcock was undaunted by Dr. Millikan's pessimism. He knew from other sources that Dr. Millikan's remarks confirmed the future importance of uranium.

A writer friend of mine [Russell Maloney] had told me that scientists were working on a secret project some place in New Mexico. It was so secret that once they went into the plant, they never emerged again. I was also aware that the Germans were conducting experiments with heavy water in Norway. So these clues brought me to . . . uranium.[5]

History has proven Hitchcock right on both counts. Nazi Germany had an intense interest in Norway's heavy water. Moreover, the secretive work in New Mexico was indeed a reality. William L. Laurence, a scientific reporter for the *New York Times*, was the journalist chosen by the government to write about the researching, building, testing, and ultimate delivering of the atomic bomb. He affirms Hitchcock's mention of the nuclear research conducted at Los Alamos, New Mexico.

By the summer of 1945 the vast majority of the scientists had lived with their families at Los Alamos for about two and a half years. As far as the world knew, they had vanished completely, lost without a trace. Arriving at the place and finding them all there gave one the sensation of discovering a lost world. The mountains and canyons and the mesas provided the perfect setting for such a world.[6]

Hitchcock, certain he had a good film script, was determined to use uranium ore as the object or macguffin from which the ideological conflict between FBI agents and Nazi subversives would surface.[7]

There was one problem, however, David O. Selznick was skeptical about the use of uranium in a film he intended to produce.

But Selznick could not be convinced, and shortly afterwards he sold the whole package, script, stars and Hitchcock, to RKO for $800,000 and 50 percent of the profits. As Hitch, who then took over as producer as well, remarked, this was very silly of him, for if he had had confidence in the picture and stuck with it he could have had all the profits, over $8 million.[8]

Notorious was shot and edited in 1945, and then released in 1946. The atomic bomb and uranium were, by then, household words.

Notorious opened in New York City on May 18, 1946 and quickly became a commercial and critical success.[9] The film begins in a federal courtroom in the state of Florida. A Nazi agent is sentenced to prison for his spy activity in the United States. His daughter, Alicia Huberman (Ingrid Bergman), although not a part of her father's conspiracy, suffers guilt and self-hatred. She tries to escape the stigma of her past through an endless round of wild parties and promiscuous affairs. Devlin (Cary Grant), an FBI agent, approaches her with a proposal that she accept a secret mission. At first she refuses, then reluctantly accepts and takes a plane to Rio de Janeiro with Devlin and other FBI agents. Devlin and Alicia fall in love, but he does not trust her because of her earlier indiscretions. Alicia's secret mission is to renew a relationship with one of her father's pro-Nazi friends, Alex Sebastian (Claude Rains). She is to report on Sebastian's activities and a small group of Nazi refugee scientists who reside at his estate. Because of an unrequited love affair between Alex and Alicia, it is easy for her to regain his attention and confidence. The major complication arises when Alex wishes to marry Alicia. The heroine hopes that Devlin will object, and when he does not, she marries Sebastian.

Alicia becomes the mistress of the Nazi estate despite the antagonism of her mother-in-law, Madame Sebastian (Leopoldine Konstantin). Devlin has persuaded Alicia to procure a key to the wine cellar in the basement of the house. During a party for friends of the newly-married couple, Devlin and Alicia explore the wine cellar and discover a mysterious ore concealed in wine bottles. They obtain a sample, and the ore is later found to be uranium. The following morning Sebastian becomes aware that his wife is an American agent. After consulting with his mother, they decide to administer small doses of poison to Alicia, so that her death will appear to be from natural causes. This tactic will protect them from the other desperate Nazis in their household who would kill them for introducing an American agent into their cabal. Devlin becomes anxious when Alicia fails to make her periodic reports to him. After receiving the consent of his superior, Devlin goes into the Sebastian home to discover that Alicia is seriously ill. She informs him that she has been poisoned by the Sebastians. He admits his love for her and then helps her out of her bedroom. Devlin's intention is to get Alicia into his car and take her to the nearest hospital. He is accosted by the Sebastians. But these two Nazis are helpless to prevent Devlin from achieving his objective, for they realize they are being watched by their Nazi colleagues on the main floor of the house. Devlin and Alicia drive away, and the film ends with Sebastian being called back into his home by the Nazis, who have become suspicious of Alicia's exit with Devlin.[10]

Notorious and the Development of the Atomic Bomb

In the opening scene of *Notorious*, a federal court judge in Miami, Florida, sentences John Huberman, an American citizen and Nazi spy, to twenty years in a Federal penitentiary for the crime of treason against the United States. Just before the judge passes sentence, Huberman makes a statement: "I have something to say. You can put me away, but you can't put away what's going to happen to you and to this whole country—next time. Next time we are going to . . ."[11] Huberman's threatening declaration is interrupted by another man, who perhaps realizes that Huberman's emotional words will only serve to alienate the judge further and reduce chances for an early parole. Huberman uses the pronoun "we" in his threat against the judge and whole country. So even though he is incarcerated, the word "we" implies other Nazis who still intend to try to destroy the United States—the Third Reich's nemesis. Hitchcock is telling his audience through a defeated individual enemy of democracy that other Nazis exist who still intend to harm the United States. This is the inciting moment in the film. The audience now wants to know who and where these Nazis are.

Alicia Huberman, the convicted man's daughter, is accosted by reporters, who besiege her with questions. Bewildered, she does not respond as she leaves. The scene ends when the camera pans to two detectives as one admonishes the other to "Let us know if she tries to leave town."[12]

The second expository sequence takes place in Alicia's home during a party. Her movement and dialogue quickly indicate to the audience that she is partially inebriated and is probably living a debauched life. At this time she meets Devlin (Cary Grant). When the party ends, Alicia and Devlin go for a ride in her car. A policeman stops them because Alicia has been speeding. Devlin avoids a fine when he shows his FBI identification to the policeman. After the officer leaves them, Alicia verbally and physically attacks Devlin because she realizes he is a Federal officer. When she fails to respond to his ultimatum to drive her car home, Devlin knocks her out with a quick short punch and takes her home.

The following morning, Devlin offers Alicia work with the government as a secret agent in Rio de Janeiro. She refuses it. Devlin then forces her to listen to a record that the FBI surreptitiously made of a conversation between herself and her father:

DEVLIN

We've had your bungalow wired for three months. Conversation . . . between John Huberman and daughter, Alicia, six-thirty p.m., January the ninth, nineteen forty-six, at Miami Beach, Florida. Some of the evidence that wasn't used at the trial.

ALICIA

I don't want to hear that.

DEVLIN

Relax, hard-boiled, and listen.

HUBERMAN

There is for us, both of us, a mint of money in it, Alicia.

ALICIA

I told you before Christmas I wouldn't do it.

HUBERMAN

You don't use your judgment. You can have anything that you want. The work is easy.

ALICIA

I'm not listening, father.

HUMBERMAN

This is not your country, is it?

ALICIA

My mother was born here. We have American citizenship.

HUMBERMAN

Where is your judgment? In your feelings you are German! You've got to listen to me. You don't know what we stand for!

ALICIA

I know what you stand for. You and your murdering swine. I've hated you ever since I found out.

HUBERMAN

My daughter, don't talk to me like that!

ALICIA

Stay on your side of the table!

HUBERMAN

Alicia—put your voice down.

ALICIA

I hate you all—and I love this country. Do you understand that? I love it. I'll see you all hang before I raise a finger against it. Now, go on—get out of here, or, so help me, I'll turn you in. Don't ever come near me or speak to me again of your rotten schemes.[13]

Alicia has a choice. She can accept the job offered by Devlin, or she can take a Caribbean cruise with a wealthy man who has become enchanted with her beauty. In a more sober state than she was the night before, she now yearns to love and be loved—rather than to be bought. Alicia also desires to exonerate her character from the stigma of her father's treason through service to her country. Furthermore, she is attracted to Devlin. For these reasons Alicia changes her mind and accepts the job. The creation of such complex characterization and psychological truth in the expository sequences of this film mark the excellence in film structure by Hitchcock and his scriptwriter, Ben Hecht.

Shortly after Alicia gets her assignment, she and Devlin embark on a plane bound for Rio de Janeiro. Paul Prescott (Louis Calhern), an FBI employee and Devlin's superior, passes on information to Devlin concerning John Huberman. Alicia's curiosity motivates questions about their future work, but Devlin has no answer for her. However, he has news of her father.

DEVLIN

He died this morning.

ALICIA

Oh. How?

DEVLIN

A poison capsule.

ALICIA

He did it himself?

DEVLIN

Yes. In his cell. Sorry.

ALICIA

I don't know why I should feel so bad. When he told me a few years ago, what he was, everything went to pot. I didn't care what happened to me. But now I remember how nice he once was— how nice we both were. Very nice. It's a curious feeling. As if something had happened to me, and not to him. You see, I don't have to hate him anymore, or myself.[14]

Although these two film characters are not aware of their real mission, it will involve the prevention of post-war Nazi German subversives from using uranium to make atomic bombs for use against the free world. There is a historical parallel between the plane trip and mission of the characters in *Notorious*.

On June 17, 1942, Winston Churchill sat in the co-pilot's seat of a plane bound for the United States and a rendezvous with President Roosevelt. The political business on the agenda for their meeting "may have been the most important mission of World War II."[15] Churchill was trying to work out a mutual commitment of Allied operations in 1942–43. However, another singular matter kept invading his thoughts at this time: "It was the question of 'Tube Alloys,' which was our code-word for what afterward became the atomic bomb."[16] Churchill was reunited with his personal friend and colleague, Franklin D. Roosevelt, at Hyde Park, New York, where the President was delighted to give his guest an automobile tour of the Roosevelt estate.

The next day these two men broached the subject of the atomic bomb. "The Germans were believed to be ahead of both the United States and Britain, and it was considered vital that they should not be the first to bring atomic weapons into the field of battle."[17] Progressive intelligence reports of Nazi German action in the atomic bomb race intensified the Allied Powers' need for immediate counteraction.

Churchill and Roosevelt were also acutely aware of the Allied intelligence reports from agents in Norway that Germany had twice ordered Norsk Hydro to increase its production of heavy water. In May 1940, immediately following the fall of Norway, Germany had ordered Norsk Hydro to increase its heavy water production to 3,000 pounds a year. In February 1942, it was learned that Germany had demanded a further increase to 10,000 pounds a year. Since the Nazis had already placed an embargo on the export of uranium ore from Czechoslovakia, and since American and British physicists were in agreement that, given a large enough pile of uranium imbedded in a sufficient amount of heavy water, a self-sustained, chain-reacting pile could be made to operate, Churchill and Roosevelt had no choice but to assume that they and Hitler were in a race for possession of a weapon powerful enough to determine the fate of the free world.

In general terms, Churchill and Roosevelt agreed that Britain and the United States should pool their information and concentrate the work of British and American scientists in the United States and Canada.[18]

The Nazis were thought to have at least a two-year lead in the atomic bomb race. The Allied Powers knew they would have to do something fast to neutralize this lead in atomic bomb research. English and Norwegian secret agents and military officials accepted the dangerous mission of stopping the Nazis' production and movement of heavy water from Norway to Germany. The history of this suspenseful espionage and sabotage episode will be given as the plot of *Notorious* unfolds in this chapter.

Hitchcock, always the economist in film structure, uses three short scenes to show Devlin's emotional restraint toward Alicia, the termination of that restraint, and a romantic sharing of their love. The essential dialogue of each scene is given to show the changes in their relationship.

ALICIA

Why don't you give that copper's brain of yours a rest? Every time you look at me, I can see it running over its slogans, once a crook, always a crook. Once a tramp, always a tramp. Go on, you can hold my hand. I won't blackmail you for it afterwards. Scared?

DEVLIN

I've always been scared of women. But I get over it.

ALICIA

And now you're scared of yourself. You're afraid you'll fall in love with me.

DEVLIN

That wouldn't be hard.

ALICIA

Careful. Careful.

DEVLIN

You enjoy making fun of me, don't you?

ALICIA

No, Dev, I'm making fun of myself. I'm pretending I'm a very nice unspoiled child whose heart is full of daisies and buttercups.

DEVLIN

Nice day-dream. Then what?[19]

Three lap dissolves are used to establish Devlin and Alicia on a hilltop overlooking Rio de Janeiro. In the ensuing dialogue, Alicia explains to Devlin why he will not believe in her:

ALICIA

I know why you won't, Dev. You're sore. You're sore because you've fallen for the little drunk you tailed in Miami and you don't like it! It makes you sick all over, doesn't it? People will laugh at you . . . the invincible Devlin, in love with someone who isn't worth even wasting the words on! Poor Dev—in love with a no-good gal. It must be awful . . . I'm sorry . . . (*He grabs her— kisses her.*)[20]

The next love scene between Devlin and Alicia is one of the most intimate in the film. It is also one of the best balanced examples of the love-versus-duty theme in the character of Devlin; however, he manages to break away gently from the affection and charm of Alicia to meet his superior, Prescott. At the beginning of this scene, Alicia offers to cook supper for them both. It's not that she likes to cook, she simply wants to be alone with Devlin. Devlin likes the idea and says so but needs to check with his hotel for any messages. Alicia responds: "Do you have to?"

DEVLIN

I have to. (*They stop—Devlin picks up phone—she talks—they kiss.*)

ALICIA

This is a very strange love affair.

DEVLIN

What?

ALICIA

Maybe the fact that you don't love me. (*He talks on phone—they kiss.*)

DEVLIN

Hello. Palace Hotel? Fala-Ingles [sic]? [Do you speak English] This is T.R. Devlin. Are there any messages for me? (*They talk—kissing*) When I don't love you I'll let you know.

ALICIA

But you haven't said anything.

DEVLIN

Actions speak louder than words. (*He talks on phone.*) There is? Good. Read it to me, please. (*He puts the phone down—talks—as they kiss*) Prescott wants me over right away.

ALICIA

Did he say what about?

DEVLIN

No.

ALICIA

Maybe it's our assignment.

DEVLIN

Probably. (*Alicia clings to him.*) Do you want me to bring anything back with me?

ALICIA

Yes. What about a nice bottle of wine to celebrate?

DEVLIN

What time shall I be back? What time do you want me back?

ALICIA

Seven o'clock.

DEVLIN

Good-bye.

ALICIA

Good-bye.[21]

The next two scenes reveal Alicia's mission as agreed upon by the American and Brazilian authorities, and Devlin's reaction to it. After several concerns are brought up about Alicia's suitability for the mission the men conclude it is essential that contact be made with Alexander Sebastian, leader of the German scientists, and who better to do that than Alicia Huberman, with whom Sebastian had once been in love. It becomes apparent that Devlin really has no knowledge of Alicia's mission.

PRESCOTT

No, we haven't discussed it with him at all. But I can set your mind at rest about her.

BARBOSA

Are you sure . . . of her political side?

PRESCOTT

Oh, oh yes.

BARBOSA

Well, there is nothing to be lost if we proceed as you advise.

PRESCOTT

Oh, that's fine. I'll give Devlin his instructions right away.[22]

Devlin plays a scene with FBI agents Prescott and Beardsley, in which he is informed of Alicia's mission. The two men are amazed when Devlin first objects on moral grounds, then switches to a secondary premise, lack of intelligence experience on her part, to defend his position further. Because of Alicia's questionable background and her previous relationship with Alex Sebastian, known to Devlin's colleagues, Devlin finds himself unable to admit his love for Alicia Huberman. Once again love is victimized by his pride.

DEVLIN

She's never trained for that kind of work. They'll see through her.

PRESCOTT

Miss Huberman was chosen not only because her father gives her an ideal background, but because Sebastian knows her—Oh, yes, he was once in love with her.

DEVLIN

Oh, I didn't know that.

BEARDSLEY

I don't know why we're arguing about petty things like this. We've got important work to do. Sebastian's house is a cover up. We've got to get Miss Huberman inside that house, and find out what's going on there!

PRESCOTT
Yes, that's right. I think you'd better go back to Miss Huberman and explain to her what she has to do.

DEVLIN
I . . . uh . . .

PRESCOTT
What is it?

DEVLIN
Nothing, sir.

PRESCOTT
I thought you were going to say something.

DEVLIN
How is the meeting to be arranged?

PRESCOTT
Oh, well, we've discussed that. I think the riding club would be the best place. Sebastian usually rides there in the morning. So the rest is up to you and Miss Huberman. Okay, Devlin, that's all.[23]

Hitchcock's film *Notorious* implies that Nazi ideology has infiltrated Brazil. The film's implication is corroborated in world history from the 1930s to the present, in Brazil, as well as other countries in South and Central America. The United States government had an active interest in these countries, for it hoped to prevent the spread of Nazi ideology and stop possible conquest attempts by Nazi Germany. Extensive German settlement before the outbreak of World War II allowed the Nazis open channels of communication with their *"Volksge Nossen* (racial comrades)." German schools were an attractive target for Nazi infiltration. By the mid 1930s, 62 schools were established in Chile, 70 in Argentina, 50 in Paraguay, and 1,300 in Brazil. Many immigrants were "what we might call actively German, at least in a cultural sense."[24] So it is not surprising that this area of the world became a haven for Nazi war criminals who sought sanctuary from the Allied Powers' post-World War II judiciary system. In 1940, President Roosevelt appointed Nelson Rockefeller Coordinator of Inter-American Affairs. This was America's first major thrust of becoming involved in South American propaganda and Rockefeller "launched an exchange of persons program . . . and opened offices . . . to cultivate opinion leaders and sponsor libraries and jointly operated binational cultural centers."[25] The FBI's major charge was to thwart the work of resident Abwehr directors in Central and South America as well as break up large scale smuggling of platinum and industrial diamonds from Colombia and Venezuela to the Fatherland.[26] It was left mainly to holocaust victims who worked out of the Jewish Documentation Center to trace the whereabouts of Nazi war criminals. Many of them are known to be free and living in South America.[27] Hitchcock's feature film substantiates Nazi German ideological and refugee invasion of Latin American countries. Although the plot incident involving uranium in *Notorious* has no place in South or Central American history, living Nazi refugees in South America are a reminder of the injustices originating in World War II. From the perspective of the film, Devlin now has the dubious task of explaining to Alicia the details of her espionage mission.

Devlin enters Alicia's apartment in a mental and emotional state of conflict. This time there is no balance between the basic elements of the love-versus-duty theme. Pride forces Devlin to deny his love for Alicia. Devlin must show devotion to duty and complete avoidance of love. But Devlin also desires to hurt Alicia, because the present situation necessarily denies him the object of his love. Alicia is jubilant when Devlin returns but is quick to see that he is troubled. Devlin doesn't want to say anything until after dinner; Alicia insists.

ALICIA

No, now. Look, I'll make it easy for you. The time has come when you must tell me that you have a wife and two adorable children, and this madness between us can't go on any longer.

DEVLIN

I bet you've heard that line often enough.

ALICIA

Right below the belt every time. That isn't fair, Dev.

DEVLIN

Skip it. We have other things to talk about. We've got a job!

ALICIA

Oh, so there is a job!

DEVLIN

You a . . . remember a man named Sebastian?

ALICIA

Alex Sebastian?

DEVLIN

Yes.

ALICIA

One of my father's friends. Yes.

DEVLIN

He had quite a crush on you.

ALICIA

I wasn't very responsive.

DEVLIN

Well, he's here, the head of a large German business concern.

ALICIA

His family always had money.

DEVLIN

He's part of the combine that built up the German war machine. He hopes to keep on going.

ALICIA

Something big?

DEVLIN

It has all the earmarks of something big. We have to contact him.

ALICIA

Go on, let's have all of it.

DEVLIN

You're meeting him tomorrow. The rest is up to you. You go to work on him, and land him.

ALICIA

Mata Hari. She makes love for the papers.

DEVLIN

There are no papers. You land him. Find out what's going on inside his house, what the group around him is up to, and report to us.[28]

Alicia is at a loss to fathom the reasons for the complete absence of affection from Devlin. She accuses Devlin of knowing about the job all the time and is crushed that he made no attempt to exonerate "the new Miss Huberman" and relieve her from being submitted to so ugly a fate. Devlin is not amused and when Alicia asks if he wants her to take the job Devlin leaves it entirely up to her. He will give her no hint as to his feelings.

ALICIA

Not a peep, eh? Darling, what you didn't tell them, tell me. That you believe I'm nice and that I love you, and that I'll never change back.

DEVLIN

I'm waiting for your answer.

ALICIA

What a little pal you are! Never believing me, hm? Not a word of faith. Just down the drain with Alicia, that's where she belongs? When do I go to work for Uncle Sam?

DEVLIN

Tomorrow morning.

ALICIA

Oh, we shouldn't have had this out here. It's all cold now. What are you looking for?

DEVLIN

I had a bottle of champagne. I must have left it somewhere.[29]

The bottle of champagne is a foreshadowing device Hitchcock uses to close the scene. Devlin had in fact left the champagne in Prescott's office, and Hitchcock used a shot of it as a closing image. The audience is not aware why he highlights this particular object, but as the plot progresses it becomes of paramount importance in the structuring of suspense and as the macguffin. The wine bottle becomes the macguffin in *Notorius* when it is used as a container for uranium ore. There is an important historical connection between uranium used in the first self-sustaining nuclear reactor and the contents of a wine bottle shared among scientists at this monumental occasion. Everything seemed normal at the . University of Chicago on December 2, 1942. Busy students passed the west stands of Stagg Field Stadium, as they had so many times before. Many of them knew of the squash courts below the west stands, frequently used by the academic community. A few months before, however, the gates leading to the squash court doors had been locked. Even the president and trustees of the University were not aware of what was happening in this area of campus.[30] All they knew was the government needed it for World War II purposes. Years would pass before they found out that this normal winter day marked "the birth of atomic energy in a controlled reaction with slow neutrons" in a primitive nuclear reactor.[31]

Enrico Fermi and ten other noted scientists were busy trying to build "the first self-sustained chain-reacting uranium pile ever made,"[32] which would lead to the birth of the atomic bomb. Fermi had been head of this group of scientists directed by General Groves of the Manhattan Project. On December 2, 1942 history was made: atomic power was a reality.[33]

> Immediately, Wigner stepped forward and handed Fermi a bottle of Chianti. Fermi, delighted, uncorked the bottle and somebody produced paper cups for everyone. Fermi poured a little wine in each cup, and they all drank to success. "And let's hope that we are the *first* to succeed!" one scientist exclaimed pessimistically, thinking of Hitler's physicists. After the bottle was empty, all witnesses of the first chain reaction autographed its straw basket.[34]

Slow fission was a reality. Now these scientists and others would begin experimentation on an unprecedented scale to try to discover fast fission, or the atomic bomb. Although there is no evidence that Hitchcock had knowledge of this successful self-sustaining chain reaction at the University of Chicago and the use of the contents of a wine bottle in celebrating the event, it is important for us to be aware of the developmental stages of the atomic bomb as they relate to the building of suspense within the plot of *Notorious*. The wine bottle, symbol of success in the real world of nuclear research, becomes the microcosmic macguffin of Hitchcock's plot.

Alicia consents to enter the "underworld" of the Nazi refugees. Death will be the penalty if she fails to convince her hosts of her total allegiance to Nazi ideology and scientific research. Her impending and willing descent into this political subterranean sphere is synonymous with a descent into hell. This theme is present in other Hitchcock films:

> It is symptomatic that the most obvious legacy of Hitchcock's Jesuit education should be the lingering fascination with Hell and damnation, often concretised in the detail of the films. When Uncle Charlie arrives in Santa Rosa (*Shadow of a Doubt*), the character is thereafter repeatedly shown with smoke hanging around him from his cigarettes; when Bruno pursues Miriam through

the Tunnel of Love (*Strangers on a Train*) his boat is named Pluto; when Marion Crane tells Norman Bates [*Psycho*] that she "thought she must have gotten off the right road," he replies that "Nobody ever comes here unless they've done that." It is to these "damned" characters (ambiguously lost souls or devils) that Hitchcock's strongest interest gravitates, giving us some of the most vividly realized performances in his films; one looks in vain for any compensating intimation of Heaven.[35]

Notorious may be added to Wood's list of "Hell and damnation" films. Alicia's entrance into a world where she will be compelled to discard her political rights and moral values to preserve the secrecy of her mission and life is like a journey into Dante's Inferno, minus the traditional guide. The use of uranium ore as the object upon which the plot turns and suspense is generated is also a potential atomic bomb in the mind of the audience, representative of the fury of hell's fire.

The purpose of the immediate sequences is to permit Alicia to renew her acquaintance with Alex Sebastian and become an accepted part of his household. Devlin and Alicia locate Sebastian at an equestrian club. He is riding with a woman. To precipitate an encounter between Alex and Alicia, it is decided to use the subterfuge of Alicia on a runaway horse. Her horse charges past the Sebastian party; Alex, perceiving the possible danger, quickly rides up and stops Alicia's horse. A distant subjective shot from Devlin's point of view is given of Alicia and Sebastian talking. A love triangle now forms between Sebastian, Alicia, and Devlin. This triangle, coupled with the future triangle of Madame Sebastian, Sebastian, and Alicia, will account for most of the dramatic tension and suspense in the remainder of the film. The contrived meeting between Alicia and Sebastian gives Sebastian the opportunity to arrange a future rendezvous.

Such a meeting takes place at a restaurant, where they order drinks and share conversation as a prelude to dinner. The scene is one of manipulation—Alicia flatters Sebastian by telling him that he looks younger than the last time she saw him in Washington. Her positive support of his youthful appearance and her denial of an interest in any other man motivates Sebastian to invite her to his home for dinner the following evening. What is significant about their conversation is Alicia's mentioning Washington as the last place they saw each other. It is logical to assume through this dialogue that Alex Sebastian, John Huberman, and Alicia were in Washington in 1942. Both men worked for the Nazis, for which John Huberman was eventually sent to jail, while Alex Sebastian managed to escape justice. The chapter on *Saboteur* and the following quotation historically affirm the reality of enemy agents at work in the United States.

Between 1940 and 1943 the number of "defense matters" [of which espionage was one category] reported to the Bureau increased almost twenty-fold, to more than 200,000. That this was a serious business and not just panic is evidenced by the fact that up to the end of 1945, 102 enemy agents were convicted under the espionage statute or its equivalent under military law alone.[36]

Enemy agent activity in the United States suggested in *Notorious* and validated in recorded history was a serious problem for the Allied Powers; it necessitated top security in the Allied Powers' atomic bomb project and counteraction espionage, sabotage, and conventional bombing of key targets to stop the efforts of Germany in building an atomic bomb. No one knew exactly where the Nazis were in their nuclear research. The get-the-job-done manner of General Groves, a construction engineer and director of the Manhattan Project, was necessary if America was to overcome the obstacles of time and production to offset the alleged lead of the enemy in the atomic bomb race.

Germany had invaded Norway in 1940 and quickly conquered all outward resistance. One of the Nazis' first actions was to take control of the Norsk Hydrogen Electrolysis plant at Vemork, the only plant in the world then capable of producing heavy water. It was believed that uranium submerged in heavy water would create a self-sustaining nuclear reaction. Nazi Germany's efforts were being closely watched by England's MI-6 and Denmark's "Princes"— two secret service organizations. In October 1941 the "Princes" informed MI-6 that Niels Bohr, a prominent Danish physicist, believed Germany was engaged in the construction of an atomic bomb.[37] The situation was considered critical and an espionage reconnaissance mission was planned. An exiled Norwegian secret agent by the name of Skinnerland was parachuted onto the Hardanger Plateau above Rjukan where the heavy water plant was located. Skinnerland learned from Jomar Brun, chief engineer of the plant, that the Nazis had increased the production of heavy water, all of which was to be sent to Germany. This information and detailed microphotographs of photographs of the plant, as well as drawings of the surrounding countryside, were procured and smuggled to Stockholm in a toothpaste tube. The tube eventually reached London where the contents were perused by MI-6 and the Joint Intelligence Committee. MI-6 recommended immediate sabotage of the heavy water plant and JIC concurred. "Operation Freshman" was the result. Despite the work of Brun and Skinnerland, Operation Freshman failed. Freshman teams of saboteurs crash-landed in heavy weather. German ski patrols immediately killed the injured while the rest were first interrogated and then shot even though they were in British army uniform. The Germans were quick to realize the intent of the assault and hastily strengthened defenses around the plant.[38] The outlook for the Allies was bleak.

Life was no less bleak for Alicia, now exiled in Latin America. The next scene in *Notorious*, played between Prescott, Devlin and Alicia, is obligatory and serves to further the separation between Alicia and Devlin. Most of the dialogue is between Prescott and Alicia. Prescott helps her put on the jewels she will wear when she goes to the dinner party at Sebastian's home that evening. Prescott admonishes her to avoid asking questions at the party, because she may arouse suspicion and put her life in jeopardy. Her mission is one of observation. Also, she is to memorize the names of all the Germans she meets so the FBI can run a check on their World War II status in Germany to see if any of them are wanted for war crimes. Just before Alicia leaves for her date, Prescott directs Devlin and Alicia to avoid each other for the next couple of days in case Sebastian's agents are watching her.

The dinner party sequence begins when the butler, Joseph, admits Alicia into the Sebastian home. Madame Sebastian, a discerning woman who already dislikes Alicia because of the romantic interest her son has for her, descends the staircase and approaches Alicia, who is a threat to Madame Sebastian's control of her son's life and the household. Her intelligence, perception and social savoir faire, as well as her willingness to commit murder, make her a master antagonist. Madame Sebastian greets Alicia and immediately points out Alicia's resemblance to her father. After expressing a few niceties, Madame Sebastian asks Alicia why she failed to testify at her father's trial.

ALICIA
He didn't want me to. He refused to let his lawyers call me on the stand.

MADAME
I wonder why.

ALEX
Hello—Alicia. I am so glad. You met my mother.

ALICIA
Yes, we just met.

ALEX
You didn't meet Alicia when we were in Washington four years ago, did you, Mother? I don't know where you were at that time.

MADAME
Alex, I think we should join our other guests.[39]

In this scene, Alex Sebastian is the mediator between the two women. He takes Alicia's hand and kisses it. Madame realizes her son is enamoured of Alicia and has completely forgotten the unanswered question of why Alicia did not testify at her father's trial. When Madame senses Alex might inadvertently reveal something that compromises her background, she diverts them by suggesting they join the other guests. The checkered floor on which they walk suggests a mental chess game where Alicia and Madame fight for supremacy as Queen, while Sebastian as the King floats along in a bubble of romantic love; the conflicting ideologies of Nazism and democracy supply the most basic reason for the life-and-death earnestness of the game of wits between the two women in this and following sequences.

The beginning of the scene is novel in structure; it rests on the suspense principle of the subjective camera, which forces the audience to accept the plight of Alicia Huberman. The camera and the audience become Alicia. The dialogue and the use of the prolonged subjective camera make the audience feel the anxiety Alicia experiences in meeting the Germans. The interesting cinematic point is that Hitchcock does not use any cut-away shots to lessen the tension of meeting the previously distant and depersonalized Nazi enemy in the standard World War II films. Now the enemy is personal, close, and constant. The subjective technique would tend to unnerve the politically aware audience when it is "bombarded" with the enemy. Each Nazi is formally introduced to Alicia. Again, niceties are exchanged and all is pleasant until Madame Sebastian cuts short Alex's introduction of Dr. Anderson—the guest of honor.[40]

In an interview with Hitchcock, Charles Samuels extolled Hitchcock's use of the subjective camera. Hitchcock responded to this by explaining what he was trying to accomplish:

> You obtain your best results, I think, by creating sharp intrusions of the subjective in an otherwise objective narrative. For example, I'd instance the change to subjective camera angle in *Notorious* when Ingrid Bergman has to meet all of her [future] husband's Nazi friends and convince them she's a Nazi, too. By making the camera her eyes, you convey the intensity of the threat.
>
> Yes. I wanted to say visually, "Here is Ingrid in the lions' den; now look at each lion!"[41]

The Sebastian party now moves into the dining room. Alicia is one of the first guests to sit down at the dinner table. This permits her to view the others as they take their places. Emil Hupka and Sebastian move to their seats on the opposite side of the table from Alicia. She has a clear view of them. There is a wine display case against the far wall. Suddenly, Hupka gets excited over one of the wine bottles. He gestures frantically toward Sebastian about a certain bottle and is quickly quieted by him. The dialogue between these two men is inaudible in the film because of music and other conversation, but it does appear in the script.

HUPKA

Alex, that bottle does not belong here. Somebody remove it, quick!

ALEX

You are mistaken.

HUPKA

That label![42]

Although Alicia could not hear their spoken words, she is very much aware of a definite significance attached to the wine bottle. This is the second foreshadowing its importance. The scene ends with conversation about future speed advances in transoceanic travel.

After dinner, the German scientists meet in a room to discuss the blundering of Emil Hupka. These men are afraid Hupka will cause too much curiosity among people not involved in their scientific cabal, and this will inevitably lead to exposure of their nuclear research. The men come to a consensus to kill Hupka.

MATHIS

I'm afraid, gentlemen, that something must be done about Emil.

ANDERSON

I don't know. It was an understandable slip. The man was tired.

ROSSNER

But it was a very dangerous slip.

KNERR

It is not the first one. There have been several lapses before. There will be more.

ANDERSON

That's bad—that's very bad.

MATHIS

I think gentlemen, that you can leave it to me to find some way. When you drive up to Petropolis the road winds quite a bit. It is very high. It has some very awkward turns. I am sure I will not have any difficulty in getting Emil to give me a lift in his car. It is quite a trick to jump clear. I will just have to be careful, that is all. I turned my ankle the last time.[43]

Hupka has not measured up to the myth of the superiority of the Aryan race. Among this remnant of men from the fallen Third Reich, Hupka is to be eliminated because he has jeopardized the life of everyone in the group. Furthermore, there are no individual rights for those who use the Nazi ideology as their frame of reference for society. Raymond Murphy, in a direct comparison of National Socialism with the rights of democracy, explains the reasons for this absence of individual rights:

> The concept of personal liberties of the individual as opposed to the authority of the state had to disappear; it is not to be reconciled with the principle of the nationalistic Reich. There can no longer be any question of a private sphere, free of state influence, which is sacred and untouchable before the political unity. The constitution of the nationalistic Reich is therefore not based upon a system of inborn and inalienable rights of the individual.[44]

The elimination of Hupka by his fellow Nazis has a clear effect on the suspense generated in the audience. Hupka's murder at the hands of these men has, in a collective sense, brought into play the "mind of the murderer" suspense element. The future presence of Alicia and Devlin in Sebastian's home will engender greater suspense, because we will see these two American agents surrounded by Nazis who are capable of murder. In addition, the suspense will increase among members of the audience if one or both of these agents should engage in spy activities while in the Sebastian home. The penalty for being caught in an act of espionage will be death. The Hupka incident is an obligatory sequence necessary to generate and increase the suspense value of *Notorious*.

In a short scene, Madame Sebastian tries to plant doubt in Sebastian's mind concerning the loyalty of Alicia because of her extended absence from their home:

                    MADAME
Miss Huberman has been gone a long time.

                    ALEX
Mother, is it necessary for you to always address Alicia as Miss Huberman? I do wish you could be a little more cordial to her.

                    MADAME
Really? I thought I was behaving very well. Has she been complaining about me?

                    ALEX
No.

                    MADAME
I am grateful.

                    ALEX
You might smile at her.

                    MADAME
Wouldn't it be a little too much if we both grinned at her like idiots?

                    ALEX
Please, Mother, I want to enjoy myself.

                    MADAME
Is it so boring to sit with me alone?

                    ALEX
Not at all, not at all . . . [45]

Madame has not trusted Alicia since hearing that she did not testify at her father's trial. Furthermore, she kept Alicia from sitting next to Anderson, a German scientist, during the first dinner party, where she might use her womanly charm to extract information from him. The third incident with her son is an attempt to develop eventual estrangement between him and Alicia. These actions and future ones will qualify Madame as the master antagonist.

When Alicia and Devlin next meet—at a Rio racetrack—Alicia passes on information to Devlin about the Nazis she met at Sebastian's dinner party. She mentions Hupka's reaction to the wine bottle, whose contents they drank. Hupka has not been seen by Alicia since the evening of the party; this confirms his death for the audience and gives them a reason for anxiety over the life of the heroine. The dialogue then turns to the personal relationship between Alicia and Sebastian. Alicia tells Devlin that he can add Sebastian's name to her "list of playmates." Devlin reacts coldly and reminds Alicia of her remarks "about being a new woman." Alicia reminds him that he knew what she was doing and that he could have stopped her "with one word" instead of throwing Sebastian at her. Devlin will have none of this.

DEVLIN

I threw you at nobody.

ALICIA

Didn't you tell me to go ahead?

DEVLIN

A man doesn't tell a woman what to do. A woman tells herself. You almost had me believing in that little hokey-pokey miracle of yours—that a woman like you could ever change her spots.

ALICIA

Oh, you rotten . . .

DEVLIN

That's why I didn't try to stop you. The answer had to come from you.

ALICIA

I see, some kind of love test.

DEVLIN

That's right.

ALICIA

Oh, you never believed in me anyway, so what's the difference.

DEVLIN

Lucky for both of us I didn't. It wouldn't have been pretty, if I'd believed in you.

DEVLIN—OFF

If I'd figured, she'd never be able to go through with it. She's been made over by love.

ALICIA

If you only once had said that you love me. Oh, Dev . . .

DEVLIN

Listen, you've chalked up another boyfriend, that's all. No harm done.

ALICIA

I hate you!

DEVLIN

There's no occasion to. You're doing good work. Number ten's out in front.

DEVLIN—OFF

Looks as if Sebastian knows how to pick 'em.

ALICIA

Is that all you've got to say to me?

DEVLIN

Dry your eyes, baby. It's out of character. Except keep on your toes. It's a tough job we're on.
Snap out of it. Here comes dream-boat.

ALICIA

Oh, hello, Alex, it was so exciting! A beautiful horse! You remember Mr. Devlin, Alex.

ALEX

How do you do.

DEVLIN

Hello. Alicia tells me you had a bet down on number ten. Sorry I didn't get the tip earlier. So
long.

ALICIA

See you some time, Dev.[46]

Alicia and Devlin both suffer from wounded pride, which motivates their
dialogue. The conversation between them solidifies personal conflict. The
estrangement separates Alicia and Devlin, making her more vulnerable to the
Nazis.

It is helpful to analyze the conflict between the protagonists to lend greater
suspense as the plot develops. Alicia tells Devlin of her involvement with
Sebastian because, psychologically, she wants to test his love for her and hurt
him at the same time. Alicia is angry at her father and Devlin for the pain these
two men she loves have caused her. John Huberman generated an estrangement
in his daughter through the social stigma of his treason, which she was forced to
share. Devlin compounds the estrangement through his lack of commitment to
her moral worth, and by his allowing her to prostitute herself in the riptide of two
conflicting political ideologies. Alicia had previously remarked to Devlin, "I'm
pretending I'm a very nice, unspoiled child whose heart is full of daisies and
buttercups."[47] Alicia is a woman-girl. Devlin is expected to reinforce her moral
reformation among the world of men the way a father protects and supports his
daughter's innocence. Alicia wants Devlin to take the place of the father who
failed her; however, Devlin is in a business that will mean his death if he cannot
trust the integrity of his colleagues.

Alicia continues the sequence with Sebastian, the third part of the romantic
triangle. Instead of watching the race, he uses his binoculars to watch Alicia and
Devlin. Sebastian suspects she is in love with Devlin.

ALEX

I watched you. I thought maybe you are in love with him.

ALICIA

Don't talk like that. I detest him.

ALEX

Really? He's very good looking.

ALICIA

Alex, I've told you before Mr. Devlin doesn't mean a thing to me.

ALEX

I'd like to be convinced. Would you—maybe care to convince me, Alicia, that Mr. Devlin means nothing to you?[48]

Sebastian wants Alicia to marry him; then he will be convinced that she does not love Devlin. The proposal dumbfounds Alicia. She pays a visit to Prescott and the other agents to seek their advice. Devlin is present. His personal pride shows through his professional decorum as he comments that Alicia's marriage to Sebastian would be a "useful idea"[49] and then goes on to ask what inspired the proposal, believing Sebastian's motivation to be Alicia's expression of love for him. Prescott and his colleagues consider the marriage a perfect arrangement.

The marriage of Alicia to Sebastian will give her free access to the entire household. Such a condition will also give her ample opportunity to ascertain the main research objective of the Nazi scientists. Prescott, Barbosa and Beardsley, who began this sequence before Alicia made her entrance, give the audience a compelling reason these agents want her as a permanent member of the Sebastian household.

PRESCOTT

You'll be pleased to hear, Senor Barbosa, that our little theatrical plan is working. We've got hold of something concrete for a change.

BARBOSA

I'm delighted, gentlemen. What is it?

PRESCOTT

Professor Wilhelm Otto Renzler is working here in Brazil.

BEARDSLEY

One of Germany's scientific wizards.

BARBOSA

I didn't know he was here!

PRESCOTT

Oh, yes. He's living and experimenting in Sebastian's house. They call him Dr. Anderson.[50]

While, in the world of *Notorious*, Dr. Anderson is experimenting with uranium in Sebastian's house, in the real world of Allied espionage the follow-up to the unsuccessful Operation Freshman is being planned. The Gunnerside mission of 1943 involved the training of six saboteurs carefully chosen from the Royal Norwegian Army who would meet up with the "Swallows" party—four men who were an advance party to Operation Freshman—and together make an assault on the Norsk Hydro heavy water plant at Vemork. Following Brun's instructions, the men entered the plant, laid charges on the cells producing the heavy water, and escaped during the confusion that followed the total destruction of almost a ton of heavy water.[51]

The British thought it would be at least two years before the Germans could start producing heavy water again but by the end of 1943 production recommenced. The American high command then sent the 8th Air Force on an air raid assault of the Vemork plant. The power system next to the plant sustained sufficient damage to stop production. Goering then decided to evacuate the plant and rebuild it in Germany. Hydroelectric power was so limited in Germany that this intelligence caused no undue alarm among the Allied forces. However, the fourteen tons of heavy water the Germans intended to transport to Germany worried the Allies, because it would greatly accelerate their research in the construction of a nuclear reactor. Einer Skinnerland and Knut Haukelid, two agents who took part in the successful Gunnerside mission, were still in Norway. They were ordered by MI-6 to destroy this stock of heavy water.[52] Their efforts also relate to plot development in *Notorious.*

In the Sebastian household, Madame has become estranged toward her son and Alicia, as seen in the following two scenes. In the first scene, Madame is against the marriage of her son and Alicia. Madame, lacking faith in Alicia's love for Sebastian, insinuates that their marriage is one of financial convenience for the young woman. Sebastian is blunt in his communication with his mother after she questions Alicia's motivation.

ALEX
You know, all these carping questions are merely the expression of your own jealousy, just as you've always been jealous of any woman I have ever shown any interest in. In this case, there is nothing more to discuss!

MADAME
You mean, then, that you are going ahead with this marriage?

ALEX
I mean, that the wedding will be next week. It will be private. We shall both be pleased to have you present, if you wish.[53]

We next see Sebastian and Alicia after their marriage, having returned home following a short honeymoon. The low lighting of the empty main floor permeates the visual atmosphere with alienation. Joseph, the butler, informs the newlyweds that Madame Sebastian sent the housekeeper to bed. Sebastian apologizes to his wife for the gloomy homecoming. Tired, Alicia retires upstairs.

Both scenes manifest Madame Sebastian as the antagonist. She has previously smothered her son's attempts to lead his own life. She is one of the most self-centered characters among the many antagonists in Hitchcock's films. Her guarded self and lack of spontaneity make the home empty, void of warmth and love. This complements the visual atmosphere of the second scene.

There is an interesting similarity between Hitchcock's female antagonist and Hitler. Although Hitler was not alive at the release date of the film (1946), his Nazi ideology and political objectives were alive in the fictional character of Madame Sebastian. Madame Sebastian embodies the Fuhrer principle:

> Hitler possesses all power (what primitive man calls "mania" or magical potency) which may be delegated to others but which may also be withdrawn at the leader's wish or whim. This is a new form of the theory of the divine right to rule. This in itself gives rise to "leader-anxiety," such as fear of arbitrary dismissal by an immediate superior without appeal, to say nothing of other more serious implications. Linked up to this is the long-established German thesis that the state is master, not the servant, of the people.[54]

Madame Sebastian also represents Nazi Germany's desire to control Brazil:

> In conversations with Rauschning during the years 1932–1934, the Fuhrer expressed goals for Nazi activity in North and South America fully as incredible as those he had earlier sketched for German expansion into Eastern Europe. If Latin America was to develop, the vigorous leadership of Germany would be required and on this subject Hitler waxed prolific a few months after he came to power. He was especially interested in Brazil, which he was convinced was ripe for revolution and which he vowed to transform, within a few decades or even years, from "a corrupt mestizo state into a German dominion."
>
> "We shall create a new Germany there," he cried. "We shall find everything we need there."[55]

Another scene from *Notorious* shows Alicia investigating the closets of the house. As she inspects the house in her role as its new mistress, she discovers several locked doors. She goes to her husband for the keys. Sebastian has to procure them from his mother before he can give them to Alicia. As soon as Sebastian gives the keys to Alicia, she is able to open the closet doors, but when she eventually tries to open the wine cellar door, she discovers she does not have a key for it. Joseph, the butler, tells her that only Sebastian has the key to this particular door.

During Alicia's inspection of her new home an important scene is played between Dr. Anderson and Sebastian. Anderson misses Hupka's talent as a metallurgist, while Sebastian considers the new man, Gleichen, to be as good. Wishing to end the conversation on a more positive note, Anderson discloses that his work is over and that he has been successful. The appearance of Alicia to request the closet key ends the dialogue between these men.

Aware of Allied fears that Nazi Germany would be the first nation in the world to develop an atomic bomb, Hitchcock purposely gives the audience pieces of the puzzle on the state of Nazi research to keep their interest as *Notorious* progresses, but he withholds the major piece of the puzzle—uranium ore—so that he may use it later to build a major sequence of suspense and romance around the hero and heroine.

Another scene brings us one step closer to Hitchcock's use of uranium. It is an obligatory scene between Alicia and Devlin, employing the suspense element of the audience's superior position. Devlin commissions Alicia to steal Sebastian's wine cellar key. Then he tells her to influence Sebastian to have a party. Devlin is to be invited, given the key by Alicia, and left to investigate the contents of the cellar. The attempt to procure the key is suspenseful and, if successful, will establish the suspense of the subsequent major sequence at the party.

The scene occurs in the Sebastians' bedroom. Alex is off-camera talking to Alicia, who is intent on borrowing the wine cellar key. She picks up a set of keys, removes the crucial one and replaces the rest. Just as she began picking up the keys, Sebastian started talking to her from the bathroom, startling both Alicia and the audience. No sooner does she have the key in her left hand than Sebastian walks into the room. He continues his conversation as he takes Alicia's hands in his. Always the romantic, Sebastian opens her right hand and kisses her palm. When he starts to open her left hand, Alicia throws her arms around him, transfers the key to her right hand and drops it, kicking it away under a chair.

This short scene has many elements of suspense. The basic ideological conflict—Nazism versus democracy—has been hidden from the husband. The suspenseful conflict generates a form of refined anxiety in the audience, sustained through the dramatic tension of Alicia and Sebastian's relationship. Alicia's love for Sebastian is a ruse. Sebastian is a master antagonist because he has managed to survive the Nazi's defeat in World War II. Fortunately for the heroine, his excellent powers of analysis and perception have been blinded by his love for her. Compounded suspense occurs when Sebastian enters the room while Alicia still has the key in her hand. The dreadful alternative is that Sebastian must not become aware of the key in Alicia's hand, or her life will be in immediate peril. The audience is in a superior position because of the information gathered from the closet sequence with Joseph, when Alicia learns that Sebastian has the key; and from the previous scene with Devlin, when she is told to get the key. The unexpected complication takes place when Sebastian starts to kiss the hand holding the key. Hitchcock uses the subjective camera intermittently while Alicia is in the process of approaching the dressing table and taking the key from the chain. Alicia is isolated in the bedroom. Fear occurs because of the possibility of discovery that she has the key and because of what might consequently be done by a man with the mind of a murderer.

However, something is missing from this scene: Alicia does not speak. Her silence illustrates Hitchcock's capacity to use cinematography to tell a story, an ability he learned in his professional apprenticeship in the silent era of the 1920s. Sebastian is the sole contributor of dialogue. Consequently, the suspense created is accomplished through visual means. Alicia's silence makes her actions and person that much more forceful, yet vulnerable. Words are often used to direct and establish distance between people. Hitchcock denies her this power, which in turn causes the audience to fear that Sebastian will become worried about Alicia's lack of communication. Her silence will motivate him to investigate, and this progressively augments suspense within the audience, because Sebastian may realize his wife is a spy.

Devlin is admitted to the Sebastian home and promptly asks to see Alicia. She greets Devlin, who kisses her hand, and in the process gives him the key to the wine cellar. The following dialogue establishes the objects that will generate suspense in the audience:

DEVLIN

This isn't going to be easy.

ALICIA

Why?

DEVLIN

He's quite sensitive about you. He's going to watch us like a hawk.

ALICIA

Yes, he's rather jealous of anybody who . . .

DEVLIN

Where'd you get the key—off his chain?

ALICIA

Yes.

DEVLIN

Let's hope the liquor doesn't run out and start him down the cellar for . . . more.

ALICIA

Oh, I hadn't thought of that.

DEVLIN

It's quite a point.[56]

While Devlin socializes with one of the guests, Alicia goes to check on the supply of wine behind the serving table.

ALICIA

Joseph.

JOSEPH

Madame?

ALICIA

Do you think you have enough champagne to last for the rest of the evening?

JOSEPH

I don't know, Madame. I hope so.[57]

The nine bottles on ice represent the fuse that could ignite Sebastian if he goes to the wine cellar for more champagne and either finds Devlin and Alicia intent on their investigation, or gets to the cellar door, only to find his key is missing. Alicia tells Devlin to go into the garden and wait for her. Devlin passes the wine table on his way out and notices that there are seven bottles left. He and Alicia meet outside, and after pointing out the wine cellar door, Alicia posts herself at the back door of the house as a lookout while Devlin investigates the wine cellar. An insert shot of the wine bottles shows only five remaining. Devlin goes straight to the wine bottles and begins to peruse them. As he checks the wine sheets, he unintentionally knocks over a bottle of wine, causing it to break. The noise of the bottle shattering brings Alicia quickly into the room.

DEVLIN

Look, vintage sand! We've got to leave things as we found them. Help me find a bottle with the same label as these others.

ALICIA

It isn't really sand, is it?

DEVLIN

It's some kind of metal ore.[58]

Devlin collects a sample of the ore and places it in an envelope. A second insert shot shows three bottles left on the upstairs wine table. In the cellar, Alicia waits nervously as Devlin finishes up his business. They start to leave the wine cellar by the back door when they see Sebastian coming down the interior basement stairs. Because Sebastian has already seen them, Devlin persuades Alicia to let him kiss her so that Sebastian will get the impression they are lovers. After their embrace, Alicia is to push Devlin away and pretend that he is drunk. Sebastian approaches them and accuses Alicia of loving Devlin. As Alicia utters a denial, Devlin answers Sebastian:

DEVLIN

For what it's worth, as an apology, your wife is telling the truth. I knew her before you, loved her before you, but I wasn't as lucky as you. Sorry, Alicia.

ALICIA

Please go!

DEVLIN

Good night.

ALICIA

Alex, don't be foolish. I . . . I came down here because he threatened to make a scene unless
I'd see him alone.

ALEX

He kissed you.

ALICIA

I . . . couldn't stop him; I tried.

ALEX

We'll talk about it later. Your guests are upstairs. Will you please go to them.[59]

Later, Alex starts to return to the wine cellar when he notices the key is
missing from his chain. Now he has reason and possible proof to suspect his wife
of infidelity in their marriage and betrayal of his political purposes. The
following short scene between Alicia and Alex is a ruse on his part.

ALICIA

I'm sorry about what happened, Alex.

ALEX

Oh, my dear . . . I shall never forgive myself for behaving like a stupid schoolboy.

ALICIA

Then you believe me?

ALEX

Of course, it isn't even worth mentioning again.

ALICIA

Thank you. Are you coming up?

ALEX

Not for a little while. Dr. Anderson is waiting for me in the study. Sleep well. It was a very
successful party.

ALICIA

Good night, then.

ALEX

Good night.

ALICIA

Thanks for being so nice.[60]

We know that Alex Sebastian does not believe his wife because of the grim
expression on his face at the end of the scene and his subsequent investigation.
There are twin beds in the Sebastian bedroom. Alicia is supposedly asleep.
Sebastian places his keys on the dressing table and retires to his bed. He remains
awake all night. At six A.M. he rises and goes to the dressing table to find the wine
cellar key on his key chain. In the next shot, Alex is in the wine cellar
investigating the bottles. He finds a broken wine bottle and uranium ore

underneath the wine rack. This event introduces the suspense elements of recognition and reversal—recognition by Sebastian of his wife's true political allegiance, and reversal of his feelings for her from love to murderous hate.

Alex takes the problem of Alicia to his mother. He tells her that Alicia is an American agent. Sebastian's immediate fear is that his Nazi colleagues will find out and kill him for indirectly betraying them. The Sebastians decide to poison Alicia slowly, so that it will appear she becomes progressively ill before finally dying.

Mother and son are determined not only to maintain their power but advance it; just so was the German high command and with the same source of power—uranium. The Germans had every intention of moving the heavy water in Norway to Germany for atomic bomb research. It was the task of the Allies to pick up where the Gunnerside mission left off and prevent the shipping of heavy water to Germany.

Einer Skinnerland and Knut Haukelid, two Allied secret agents, were assigned to destroy the shipment of heavy water. They decided that a direct attack on the Vemork plant was out of the question. Haukelid went to Alf Larsen, manager of production at Norsk Hydro, to find out the most fortuitous time to destroy the shipment. Aware of the transit route of the heavy water, Larsen told Haukelid that the only possible sabotage period would be when the heavy water was placed on the rail-ferry and transported across Lake Tinnsjo. The lake was 1300 feet deep at one point, and the sinking of the ferry there would make the heavy water irretrievable. The following records the suspenseful historical events:

> At 11 P.M. on February 19, the night before the consignment was to arrive, Haukelid and two of his men went down to the quay and boarded the *Hydro*; the boat was alongside overnight and her crew was having a party. There were no German guards aboard, but there were Norwegian watchmen. One of them stopped Haukelid and his companions as they entered the passenger saloon, but Haukelid explained that they were on the run from the Gestapo and asked for his help. The watchman showed them the door into the bilges, and Haukelid went down with one of his men, leaving the other to guard the door. Once in the bilges, they made their way along the flat bottom to the bow, and there, deep in filthy water, they laid the charge with an electric detonator and timed the fuse. By 4 A.M. that morning the job was finished, and Haukelid and his men left the *Hydro*. If all went well, at 10:45 the following morning the *Hydro* and its cargo would be on the bottom of Lake Tinnsjo.

> At 8 A.M. that Sunday—February 20, 1944—the ferry train left the Rjukan sidings with two wagons laden with drums containing the heavy water. Guards were posted at 30-yard intervals on either side of the track, and the Fieseler Storchs flew overhead. The train itself was guarded by SS men, and Muggenthaler rode on the locomotive. By 10 A.M. the wagons had been anchored to the *Hydro*'s decks, and the ferry set out on schedule with fifty-three people aboard. Then, exactly at 10:45 A.M., the ferry shuddered under the impact of a violent "knock." The exploding *plastique* ripped a hole in the *Hydro*, and it began to settle by the bow. Seconds later, the railway wagons broke loose and plunged through the bow doors into the depths of Lake Tinnsjo. Within five minutes the *Hydro* had sunk, with the loss of twenty-six passengers and

crew, all of whom were drowned. Only three of the heavy water containers were ever salvaged.[61]

The loss of the heavy water ended Nazi Germany's hope to develop an atomic bomb before the Allies did. Dr. Kurt Diebner, a prominent scientist in Nazi Germany, stated that the elimination of German heavy water production in Norway was "the main factor in our failure to achieve a self-sustaining atomic reactor before the war ended."[62] Germany failed in her atomic bomb attempt, and as will be seen, the antagonists in *Notorious* also fail in their attempt to kill Alicia, who has helped to expose their clandestine atomic bomb research.

In order to leave the house, Alicia uses the excuse that she wants to go into town to pick up some books. Her real mission is to meet with Prescott. At their meeting, she is told that Devlin has been reassigned to Spain. There is a definite feeling of loss in Alicia's voice as she receives this news. Prescott also identifies the metal ore taken from the wine cellar.

PRESCOTT

I think you can be very proud of yourself, Mrs. Sebastian. That sand that Devlin brought in shows uranium ore. So now we know what we're driving at. And your job from now on will be to try to help us find out where that sand comes from. The location of the uranium deposit is of vast importance and we're putting quite a few people on it. But I think you'll be of great help.

ALICIA

All right.[63]

The uranium connection has been made. The audience is aware of the paramount importance of uranium ore to the atomic bomb. This information increases the suspense value of the film. Through the audience's knowledge of the use of uranium, and their willing suspension of disbelief, they perceive an immediate and urgent need to have the Nazi nuclear research stopped.

Another factor is introduced to increase suspense: Alicia complains to Prescott about headaches, and the light in his office bothers her eyes. These subjective symptoms lead the audience to conclude that the antagonists have begun to poison Alicia. She leaves Prescott's office as he admonishes her to stay out of the sun. A short scene at home shows her becoming worse as Sebastian offers his sympathy. Another scene, this time with Devlin, increases the audience's tension as he diagnoses the deterioration of Alicia's physical condition as due to too much alcohol. She leaves him to return home. Both Prescott and Devlin have underestimated the Nazis' ability to detect a secret agent in their midst.

Fortunately, the Axis Powers underestimated the unity of purpose and commitment of the Allied Powers to invent the atomic bomb. Dr. Rolland Perry recounts what happened at 5:30 A.M. on July 16, 1945 at Alamogordo, New Mexico:

First we saw the intense flash of light at the top of the tower where the bomb was situated. This was a 100 foot tower and the flash of light was very intense, and very quickly after that the shock waves from the bomb struck the ground and we saw a great cloud of dust spread out from the base of the tower. Then suddenly this movement reversed and as the intense heat of the bomb heated the atmosphere it began to rise and it pulled in all this dust that been thrown out at the base, pulled all that into the rising column. The thing that struck me shortly after this, as the cloud rose into the atmosphere, was the very striking colors that appeared in the atmosphere. I recognized this as being quite unusual, something that one seldom sees in any other situation and it turned out to be the molecular spectra from ionized nitrogen in the atmosphere that gave off these peculiar shades of color on the outside of the column. . . . [64]

The theory of the atomic bomb had become an awesome reality. President Truman made the decision to use the bomb against Japan. The other two major Axis Powers, Germany and Italy, already had been defeated. Although the use of the atomic bomb would result in unprecedented devastation and loss of life, the decision to use it would actually save American and Japanese lives. In *Notorious*, however, the life of an individual, in the dramatic sense, has been placed in peril: Alicia Sebastian.

The heroine is at home and in the society of Anderson, Madame Sebastian and her husband. Madame Sebastian suggests that Alicia take a cruise with her, perhaps to Spain. Alicia demurs on the grounds that she always gets seasick. Anderson, innocent of the Sebastian's attempt to murder Alicia, invites her to go into the mountains with him. When he starts to tell her where he plans to work in the mountains, Sebastian changes the subject. The audience has been in a superior position to the plight of Alicia. Anxiety is increased in the audience and complicated through Alicia's continued presence in the Sebastian home, and her lack of knowledge that she is being slowly poisoned. Hitchcock allows Alicia to share the audience's knowledge that she is being poisoned, to increase the strength of audience-heroine identification:

ALEX

Would you care for some more brandy, Otto?

ANDERSON

No—no, thank you. I . . . never drink more than one brandy, and even this is sometimes too much. I'll just finish my . . . coffee.

MADAME

No—no, that is not your cup.

ALEX

But that is Alicia's . . . (*Alicia looks startled.*)[65]

Alicia is now aware that her husband and mother-in-law are in league to murder her. Hitchcock emphasizes the poisoned drink through use of an excessively large coffee cup. As a tool of expressionism, it externalizes the new psychological significance of the growth of fear of death in Alicia. She excuses herself and tries to get to her room to make a phone call for help. Unfortunately, she falls down and is taken upstairs against her wishes. Sebastian, in his cunning, has the phone removed from their bedroom to ensure his wife's uninterrupted rest. Anderson says that he will call an excellent doctor to aid Alicia's recovery.

Hitchcock has tightened the screw of suspense. Even though he has made Alicia aware of her precarious plight, he has removed her ability to walk and to communicate her problem because the drug impedes her physical mobility, while the removal of the phone prevents contact with her FBI colleagues. Now her death is imminent.

The three scenes—parlor revelation, fainting spell, and bedroom incarceration—collectively make up the suspenseful obligatory sequence that necessitates the hero's action to save the heroine. The audience is exasperated, because they know Devlin thinks Alicia is merely drinking to escape her problems. This obligatory sequence is filled with the elements of suspense. Conflict occurs between Alicia and the Sebastians, who have proved themselves master antagonists through duping Prescott and Devlin, then isolating Alicia so they can destroy her. The dreadful alternative is that Alicia must escape or die. The audience, in the superior position before the sequence begins, now shares it with Alicia. The unexpected complication is the incarceration of Alicia and denial of her communication with the outside world. The subjective camera is used effectively when the audience is forced into Alicia's mind to look at the oversized cup containing the poison, and again just before Alicia faints as the camera revolves and there is a macabre play of light and shadow. The possible death of Alicia generates fear in the audience, while the mind of the murderer is harmoniously unified in the persons of Madame and Alex Sebastian. Hitchcock uses this obligatory sequence as a foundation for the subsequent climax and resolution of *Notorious*.

In the next scene, Devlin is seen sitting on a park bench waiting for Alicia. There is a dissolve to Alicia's bedroom, where we see her in bed. The camera pans to the left, where we see Madame Sebastian keeping a vigil over her son's wife. Another dissolve shows Devlin pacing back and forth in front of the park bench, visibly nervous. Another dissolve presents the audience with a verbal scene between Prescott and Devlin—the previous three shots have been silent. Devlin has not seeen Alicia for five days. Furthermore, after reflecting on Alicia's hangover, he concludes she is sick, not suffering from the residual effects of alcohol. He therefore intends to visit the Sebastian family to check on Alicia's well-being. Prescott, although disinclined to allow Devlin to visit the Sebastians, gives his permission.

The remainder of the plot is a suspenseful sequence of climax and resolution. Devlin is admitted into the Sebastian home by Joseph, who informs him that Mr. Sebastian is in the study with some business associates and has requested not to be disturbed. He also informs Devlin that Mrs. Sebastian has been seriously ill for a week. Joseph, deciding to tell Sebastian that he has a guest, enters the study for that purpose. As Joseph exits, the camera lingers in the study, and we learn that Anderson has been followed by an unknown man during the week. The next camera shot cuts to Devlin sitting on a bench, waiting for Sebastian. A short time later, Devlin goes upstairs and enters a room he believes to be Alicia's bedroom. The suspense intensifies, for now the hero and heroine are subject to death at the hands of the Sebastians. Finding Alicia in her bed, Devlin begins to question her.

DEVLIN

What's wrong with you, Alicia?

ALICIA

Oh, Dev . . .

DEVLIN

What is it, dear? What's wrong with you?

ALICIA

They're poisoning me . . . I couldn't get away. I tried, but I was too weak.

DEVLIN

How long?

ALICIA

Since the party. Alex and his mother found out.

DEVLIN

Come on—try to sit up. Sit up! I've got to get you out of here.

ALICIA

I thought you had gone.

DEVLIN

No, I had to see you once and speak my piece. I was getting out because I love you. I couldn't bear seeing you and him together.

ALICIA

You love me. Why didn't you tell me before?

DEVLIN

I know. But I couldn't see straight or think straight. I was a fat-headed guy full of pain. It tore me up not having you.

ALICIA

Oh, you love me . . . You love me . . .

DEVLIN

Yes—long ago. All the time. Since the beginning . . . [66]

There are three dramatic factors in this scene between Alicia and Devlin: recognition, reversal, and reconciliation. The hero recognizes that Alicia has almost lost her life in service to her country. Simultaneously, he reverses his opinion of her and is now determined to reverse the fate intended for Alicia by the master antagonists by taking her to a hospital for medical attention. The reconciliation is brought about when Devlin admits his love to Alicia, giving the audience yet another reason for wanting to see the hero and heroine escape from the Nazis. They leave the bedroom and start to walk down the stairs, only to be accosted by Sebastian and then his mother. As they continue to descend, Sebastian's colleagues come out from the study on the main floor to find out what is happening. This situation presents a triangle of conflict and concern. The Nazis at the bottom of the stairs want Alicia to receive medical attention. Sebastian, however, is caught in a dilemma. He doesn't want his companions to realize that he is married to an American agent; such knowledge would mean certain death for him and his mother. The conflict leads to Sebastian's indecision. Madame Sebastian will be the one to break the mental deadlock, culminating in the climax and resolution of the film.

ALEX

What is this? What are you doing, Alicia? What is this, Mr. Devlin?

DEVLIN

I'm taking her to a hospital and get the poison out of her.

ALEX

Poison?

DEVLIN

How would you like your friends downstairs to know? They have yet to be told.

ALEX

I'm taking her back to her room.

ALICIA

No, Dev . . .

DEVLIN

It'll raise quite a rumpus if you try.

MADAME

Alex . . . He knows?

ALEX

Yes.

ANDERSON

What is happening, Alex?

MADAME

Alicia . . .

ANDERSON

She is worse?

MADAME

Yes.

ALICIA

Go on . . .

DEVLIN

All right, dear. We're going—we're going. You haven't forgotten what they did to Emil . . . have you, Sebastian?

MADAME

Help him . . . Alex.

DEVLIN

I'm glad you have a head on you, Madame.

ALEX

I'm not afraid to die.

DEVLIN

You've got your chance here and now. Tell them who she is.

ANDERSON

Do you need any help, Alex?

DEVLIN

No—we can handle her.

ANDERSON

Where are you taking her?

DEVLIN

You answer that one, Sebastian.

MADAME

To the hospital. Alex, talk to them—quick!

ANDERSON

I'm glad she is going. You should not have waited so long, Alex.

DEVLIN

Well, what am I going to do? Start shooting? Hold on darling. You've only got about twenty yards to go.

ROSSNER

What happened, Alex?

ALEX

Hmmm? Oh . . . she collapsed. Mr. Devlin heard her scream when he was waiting for me. Come on, Alicia.

DEVLIN

Yes, I telephoned the hospital . . . as soon as I saw how she was.

MADAME

You have a car . . . Mr. Devlin?

DEVLIN

Out in front.

MADAME

Your hat, Alex.

MATHIS

You are going with them, Madame?

MADAME

No. Alex will call me up. I'll wait here.

ANDERSON

Poor Alicia.

DEVLIN

How do you feel?

ALICIA

A bit dizzy.

DEVLIN

Take some deep breaths.

ALEX

Now just a minute. I must sit with her.

DEVLIN

No room . . . Sebastian.

ALEX

You must take me! They're watching me!

DEVLIN

That's your headache.

ALEX

Please take me with you! Please . . . please . . . please.

ROSSNER

There is no telephone in her room to call the hospital.

MATHIS

Alex, will you come in, please? I wish to talk to you.[67]

Hitchcock has used all the elements of suspense in the final sequence of *Notorious*. Conflict is internal in the character of Alex Sebastian and simultaneously external between him and the two American agents. The master antagonist is Alex Sebastian. His mother, however, places more stock in personal survival, which allows the hero and heroine to escape. The dreadful alternative is confronted by the American agents and the master antagonists. The element of audience in the superior position is partially true. Although the four characters descending the stairs share the same plot knowledge with the audience, the Nazi scientists who come out of the study to find out what is happening do not have full knowledge of the situation. This leads to double anxiety for the audience, yet it provides the logical way of escape for the protagonists. The unexpected complication occurs when the scientists come out of the study to observe the actions of the protagonists and antagonists. If Sebastian informs his colleagues of the truth, it will mean the death of all four of them. The suspense of the situation is magnified through use of the subjective camera shot. In an earlier scene, Hitchcock used the subjective shot to force the audience to meet the Nazi scientists face to face. He wanted to place the audience in the lions' den, along with the heroine. Fear is created through the subjective camera descending the staircase, he slowly takes the audience into the lions' den with both the heroine and hero. The possibility that Sebastian will reveal their real identity represents the apex of suspense in the film. Isolation has been the plight of the two American agents since Devlin was admitted into the Sebastian home at the beginning of the last sequence. Because of the earlier Emil Hupka sequence, we know that collectively the Nazi scientists have the mind of the murderer. In the last two successive sequences—obligatory and climactic—Hitchcock has managed to use all the elements of suspense.

As the protagonists in *Notorious* were successful in their major objective to stop the Nazis from developing an atomic bomb, so were the men and women of the Manhattan Project successful in the development of an atomic bomb to end World War II in Japan. The historical events were as suspenseful as any Hitchcock film. General Groves was dining at the Army-Navy Club in Washington, D.C., when he received a phone call at 6:30 P.M. on August 6, 1945, informing him that the plane carrying the atomic bomb to Hiroshima had left on schedule. Now the suspense of the situation began to mount for Groves and his colleagues, because of the enormous cost involved in producing the bomb, the type of bomb actually used, and the communication process involved in transmitting the outcome of the operation.

The Manhattan Project cost a total of $2,191,000,000.[68] If the bomb did not perform according to plan, Groves and the other project leaders would face a Congressional investigation of unprecedented magnitude.

The bomb headed for Hiroshima was a gun-assembly method bomb:

> In the gun-assembly method, a subcritical mass of uranium-235 (the projectile) is fired down a cannon barrel into another subcritical mass of U-235 (the target), which is placed in front of the muzzle. Both gun and target are encased in the bomb. When projectile and target contact, they form a critical mass which explodes.
>
> If firing is not fast enough, the neutrons emitted by the projectile will begin interacting with the target *before* the contact and *before* the mass has become critical. In this case, a pre-detonation occurs.[69]

The major concern was that this bomb had never been tested. There was simply not enough U-235 for two bombs. The bomb at Alamogordo, New Mexico, was a plutonium implosion-type bomb. A uranium bomb was on its way to Hiroshima which cost approximately one billion dollars, and no one knew whether or not it would explode. Groves knew that if the bomb did not explode, there definitely would be a political explosion in Washington. Few men would have had the courage to give the order to drop an untested bomb. President Truman and General Groves had the courage.

The third reason for suspense involved a breakdown in communication. The method of relaying the success or failure of the operation was top secret. Unfortunately, there was an abnormally extended lapse of time before Groves received a communiqué on the matter. Groves explained that: "Messages to me had always been sent over an Air Force top-secret channel which went from Tinian to Guam to Washington. On this occasion the message left Tinian and then somehow was put on an Army channel. This went to Manila and from there to Washington. Why, I have never learned."[70] Finally, he received the long-awaited news: "Results clearcut, successful in all respects. Visible effects greater than New Mexico tests. Conditions normal in airplane following delivery."[71] The aircraft crew had been hand picked and specially trained, and they had top security clearance. None of them had seen a detonation of an atomic bomb. The following is an excerpt from the Captain's Log:

> It is 8:50. Not long now, folks.
>
> As we are approaching our primary, Ferebee, van Kirk, and Stiborik are coming into their own, while the Colonel and I are standing by and giving the boys what they want.
>
> At this point Captain Lewis jotted down: "There will be a short intermission (in the diary) while we bomb our target."
>
> The next entry read:
>
> "My God!"[72]

It is indeed a foregone conclusion that a great deal of suspense surrounded the development and deployment of the atomic bomb. Moreover, the general agreement among historians is that the atomic bomb ended World War II. Unlike the Axis Powers, however, the Allied Powers wished to use atomic energy as a means of achieving peace swiftly. Dr. Perry recalls that those engaged in the development of the bomb at Alamogordo hoped their work would "bring a cessation to the military operations and perhaps be the end of conflict in the future." All concerned were aware of the devastation the bomb could cause but "in terms of moral consideration we felt that it would not be worse to annihilate a group of people in one city by that method than to do the same thing by a more prolonged method by using conventional military weapons."[73] The unconditional surrender by Japan on September 2, 1945 fulfilled the hopes of men and women who, like Hitchcock, wished democracy to be a never-ending legacy.

Criticism of *Notorious*

There was general agreement among film critics and historians that Alfred Hitchcock's *Notorious* deserved positive acclaim. Bosley Crowther declared *Notorious*

> A superior film, for Mr. Hecht has written and Mr. Hitchcock has directed in brilliant style a romantic melodrama which is just about as thrilling as they come—velvet smooth in dramatic action, sharp and sure in its characters and heavily charged with the intensity of warm emotional appeal. As a matter of fact, the distinction of *Notorious* as a film is the remarkable blend of love story with expert "thriller" that it represents.[74]

James Agee was enthusiastic in his praise of Hitchcock's use of the subjective camera as one of the characters, noting that "few people try it and Hitchcock is the only living man I can think of who knows just when and how to."[75] Harris and Lasky highlight specific scenes in their praise of Hitchcock's ability to create suspense "where suspense is built magnificently as the champagne slowly disappears."[76] Robin Wood considers *Notorious* to be one of Hitchcock's best films, particularly regarding "the sensitivity and insight with which the Grant-Bergman relationship is developed."[77] Donald Spoto affirms the film's "immediate appeal," adding that "the complexity of its villainous characters raises unsettling questions about fundamental psychology."[78] Robert Sklar's final word is praise indeed: "In the early postwar years, Hollywood made a number of films rightly regarded as classics, among them Hitchcock's *Notorious*."[79]

Conclusion

Although the plot of *Notorious* is the development of an atomic bomb by refugee Nazi scientists in post-World War II Brazil, Hitchcock based the film on real political knowledge of a heavy water plant in Norway and a top secret plant in New Mexico. The clandestine race and conflict between Nazi Germany and the Allied Powers to develop an atomic bomb provided an excellent social and political vehicle from which Hitchcock fashioned a film filled with espionage, political ideology, suspense, and romance.

Espionage is the main professional duty of the hero and heroine in *Notorious*. The infiltration of the Sebastian home, discovery of uranium ore, and the climactic freeing of the protagonists from the Nazi antagonists are the high points in the film. In 1946, audiences viewing *Notorious* knew the reality of the atomic bomb and the devastation it caused in Japan. The solution to World War II may have generated more tension than the war itself. Moreover, the audiences were also aware of the scientific prowess of the Nazi Germans and their twelve-year rise and fall that resulted in the loss of many millions of lives. These two spheres of awareness—atomic bomb and Nazi Germans—on the part of the audience, coupled with the espionage activities of the *Notorious* protagonists, provide a film whose dramatic tension and suspense guarantee it a place among film classics.

6

Conclusion

Let me begin by summarizing the answers to questions I posed in the preface of this book.

During the course of World War II, the Axis and Allies carried out acts of espionage and sabotage which Hitchcock represented in specific films. Hitchcock's interest and knowledge in such affairs, together with his desire as activist to aid the Allies' war effort through his creative film talent, led him in the 1940s to make the four films we have examined.

Foreign Correspondent (1940) pits an American newspaper reporter against German espionage agents who seek to destroy peace in Europe. In this film, German agents succeed in their plot in 1939—paralleling events in the war itself—but the American reporter succeeds in uncovering their conspiracy and printing it for the world to read. The film shows Nazi Germany's interest in undermining peace in Europe through espionage and eventual military aggression. It implies that espionage was perpetrated in England, Holland, and the United States. However, this was only the tip of the espionage iceberg. The German *Auslandorganisation* (Foreign Organization) was a massive secret agent network directed by Rudolph Hess. "From humble beginnings in Hamburg it came to administer, by 1934, some 350 groups abroad; three years later, its head office in Berlin employed 700 people, who looked after 28,000 party members abroad, plus 23,000 organized merchant seamen."[1] Raymond Murphy notes that

> German agents were busy throughout the world in ferreting out the natural, political, social, and economic cleavages in various countries and in broadening them in order to create internal confusion and uncertainty. Control was covertly obtained over influential newspapers and periodicals and their editorial policies shaped in such a way to further Nazi ends.[2]

The fifth column was very much alive.

Hess's network was a direct result of the geopolitical theories of Dr. Haushofer, a professor at Munich University, who had actually taught Rudolph Hess in graduate school. Haushofer believed, and Hitler agreed, that the military security of Germany depended on her domination of middle Europe. However, Hitler's ambitions exceeded the classroom theories of Haushofer. Hermann

Rauschning, a political friend of Hitler who eventually fled Nazi Germany to reside in the United States, recalls a conversation about *Lebensraum* [living space] he had with Hitler in 1934. Hitler's concern was for "space . . . to make us independent of every possible political grouping and alliance. In the East, we must have the mastery as far as the Caucasus. . . . In the West we need the French coast. We need Flanders and Holland. Above all we need Sweden."[3] By 1942, most of the territory Hitler had mentioned was under the military control of Nazi Germany. In 1940 *Foreign Correspondent* represented a small but significant part of the espionage problem in the western world.

Saboteur (1942) focuses on sabotage in the United States by both Nazis and Nazi sympathizers. This was a real problem that hampered the United States efforts to supply war materials to the other Allied Powers. In the film, airplane factories, dams and naval yards were major targets for enemy sabotage.

The Nazi Abwehr organization, under Admiral Canaris, and the American German Bund, under Fritz Kuhn, were involved in espionage and sabotage in the United States. Canaris was responsible for Operation Pastorious—a sabotage mission against aluminum plants to indirectly frustrate airplane manufacturing in America. Fritz Kuhn was the American Nazi Fuhrer of the late 1930s. In the summers of this period, he had German-American youth sent to Hitler youth camps in Germany where they were indoctrinated with Nazi ideology resulting in allegiance to Hitler. These young men returned to the United States in the early fall having been turned against their country—a result of mental sabotage.

The America First Committee, an organization with an isolationist charter, opposed the United States entry into World War II. Some of its members proved to be either Nazis or at least influenced by Nazi doctrine. In *Saboteur*, Hitchcock represented this treasonous element of American society in the persons and activities of Charles Tobin and Mrs. Van Sutton. Although there is no direct evidence of it in the film, Frank Fry, saboteur, had all the trappings of an Abwehr agent.

Lifeboat (1943), because of its tight allegorical structure, contains compressed examples of espionage and sabotage: Willi, the Nazi U-boat captain, leads the Allied characters to believe that he speaks no English, allowing him to gather intelligence at will; the Allied characters direct Joe to use his skills as a pick-pocket to determine if Willi has been deceiving them and actually possesses a compass. Willi's deceit is confirmed, and only a storm at sea diverts the protagonists from killing him. Among the characters representing the Allied Powers, Kovac perpetrates sabotage against Connie because of the ideological conflict between communism and capitalism. His destruction of much of her personal wealth is motivated by his hatred of a class society that exploits the labors of the proletariat. However, the most important sabotage centers around the direction of the lifeboat—the world. Willi uses his compass and his superior cunning to outwit the Allied characters and sets a course to rendezvous with a

German supply ship instead of to reach the island of Bermuda. Espionage and sabotage result directly from the conflicting ideologies and microcosmic warfare among the film's characters.

In the *Lifeboat* war, the capacity to discern between the truth and falsehood of Willi's statements will make the Allied characters victorious. Similarly, the Allied Powers' invention and use of the Ultra machine to break the German Enigma machine's communication code eventually gave victory to the Allied Powers.

Notorious (1946) is a chess game of romance and espionage. Hitchcock masterfully interweaves the two factors of love and war to achieve an excellent film. Espionage is initiated and maintained through the relationship and marriage of Alicia Huberman and Alex Sebastian. The major incident of espionage centers around the uranium ore—Hitchcock's macguffin—stored in the Sebastian wine cellar. In 1944, the *Notorious* film script was ahead of its time. In 1946, after the development and use of the atomic bomb, the film was a success.

The use of uranium in *Notorious* resulted from Hitchcock's awareness of atomic bomb research in Norway and the United States. The Nazis' efforts to make and transfer heavy water from Norway to Germany met with Allied resistance through espionage, bombing, and sabotage missions. Roosevelt and Churchill feared that Nazi Germany would be the first country to develop an atomic bomb and would consequently win the war and establish a world-wide dictatorship under the Axis Powers. Fortunately, Germany failed to develop an atomic bomb. The Allied Powers won the conventional war in Europe and used the atomic bomb in Japan to end World War II in Asia.

Foreign Correspondent, *Saboteur*, *Lifeboat*, and *Notorious* are filled with incidents of espionage and sabotage that parallel actual events of the World War II era. Hitchcock relied on his audience's exposure to such events through newsreel, radio, and newspapers, to create a sense of *déja vu*. The films analyzed in this book derive their impetus and importance from the political clashes of nations whose conflicts escalated to engulf and reshape the world.

Let me refer now to the second question I raised in the preface concerning how Hitchcock advocated his political ideology in the four films discussed and how his ideology underscored that of the United States. Hitchcock's World War II-oriented films manifest and support a democratic political ideology on both national and international levels. For the most part, the protagonists in these films are characters with democratic values who are, or become, committed to destroying the spread of Nazi ideology in the United States and other nations of the world. The protagonists provide a role model for the World War II audience; the antagonists represent Nazi ideology. The films parallel the historical profile of United States foreign policy during the World War II years as it passed through the phases of isolationism and interventionism to internationalism.

Foreign Correspondent's main character, Huntley Haverstock, discovers and affirms his own political identity as he uncovers the news story about Nazi agents who kidnap and torture a Dutch ambassador engaged in the struggle for peace in Europe. The denial of physical and mental freedom through the kidnapping and drugging of the Dutch diplomat makes Haverstock aware of his democratic heritage. But then his own "life, liberty, and pursuit of happiness" are threatened when the Nazis try to kill him because of his evidence of their undercover actions. Now the hero accepts his personal responsibility to extend his ideology on an international level by confronting and opposing Nazi ideology in every way open to him. Haverstock ends the film with a radio broadcast plea to America to unite and rearm herself to support the Allied nations in their struggle against the Third Reich.

The foreign policy of the United States at the release of *Foreign Correspondent* was in transition from isolationism to interventionism. From England, Haverstock calls for military supplies and men from the United States to help fight the Nazis; his appeal is a direct invitation to enter World War II on the side of the Allied Powers. Through this film, Hitchcock advanced democratic ideology by calling for America to accept responsibility for the preservation of democracy on a world level. Through the theatrical process of identification, he made the audience equally responsible. It becomes apparent why isolationist senators included *Foreign Correspondent* among forty-nine other films they cited in accusing Hollywood filmmakers, in 1941, of influencing the foreign policy of the United States toward internationalism. In Hitchcock's case they were right.

Saboteur is a political vehicle Hitchcock used to give the American people insight of saboteurs and traitors—major internal obstacles the United States faced in her attempt to wage a successful war. The film depicts treason among wealthy citizens from both rural and urban areas of America who are in league with saboteurs capable of destroying war-time industrial production. Hitchcock was bold enough to show one of his own countrymen, Stephen Fisher, as treasonous in *Foreign Correspondent*, and he did not hesitate to represent similar Americans in *Saboteur*. After all, the United States' success in the war effort would directly determine England's. Furthermore, the political apathy of American citizens was a significant threat to the sovereignty of the United States. Hitchcock makes this apparent in the New York City mansion sequence when guests fail to respond to the protagonists' admonitions to recognize subversive activity within their group.

Hitchcock's political ideology in *Saboteur* is democratic. This even takes precedence over the law, as in the circus truck scene where a majority vote is taken to decide the fate of Barry Kane. However, Hitchcock covers himself in this disregard for police authority later in the plot when the police are implicated as part of the Nazi-inspired corruption. The final sequence in *Saboteur* promotes the democratic common man as victorious hero over the Nazi saboteur. Besides advancing democratic ideology on the American home front, Hitchcock subtly advances it on the international level. Treason and Nazi sabotage were dominant factors in the fall of European countries. Hitchcock his telling his international audience that the United States will be victorious against such tactics and will continue to support Allied nations economically and militarily to withstand the Nazi onslaught. The democratic ideology in Hitchcock's *Saboteur* was in harmony with that of the United States. Although America was fighting a two-front war, the first priority of the Allied Powers was to defeat Nazi Germany.

In *Saboteur*, Barry Kane is assisted by the FBI in his final successful conflict with the antagonist, Frank Fry. Likewise, the FBI was instrumental in protecting the internal democratic integrity of this country through tracking down and prosecuting any suspected or reported incidents of espionage and sabotage. Such reports led to over one hundred trials and convictions of men and women who were judged to be enemies of the United States.

But the intelligence agencies of the two major military organizations of the United States—Army and Navy—and the Federal Bureau of Investigation did not have the capacity to gather sufficient global intelligence. Roosevelt and retired Colonel "Wild Bill" Donovan met to discuss the problem. The ability of the United States to use its superior production power—Hitchcock's major concern in *Saboteur*—to help win World War II would not be possible without greater intelligence of the enemies' war intentions in the United States and among other Allied Powers. Donovan suggested a centralized clearing agency for all intelligence, and Roosevelt agreed. As a result, the Office of Strategic Services was established to protect the national and international interests of the United States and her allies. The OSS had as many as 22,000 men and women working for it in the United States and abroad. It and other intelligence agencies played a significant role in making good Hitchcock's implied promise in *Saboteur* that the United States would not fail the other Allied nations in their struggle against Nazi Germany.

Lifeboat is Hitchcock's political allegory of major ideological conflicts on both national and international levels. The national conflicts among the Americans prevent them from cleanly facing the main conflict with the Nazi, who uses the other characters' conflicts, nautical ignorance, and irresponsibility to gain temporary control of the lifeboat.

This representation of conflicting ideologies among the Allies makes *Lifeboat* one of the more honest historical documents of World War II. Hitchcock used this film to warn the United States that Nazi Germany represented a united entity, whereas she and her two major military allies, England and Russia, did not because of ideological and procedural differences. After seeing the film, critics felt that Hitchcock himself had fallen victim to Nazi ideology. Although he uses *Lifeboat* to show the Allied Powers the weakness created by their dissension, he supports democratic ideology and the Allied Powers' major objective to win the war. The democratic powers are victorious in the microcosmic war against the Nazi, Willi, and the Allied warship is victorious over the Nazi supply ship.

Lifeboat's message was in harmony with the freedom guaranteed by United States democracy but at odds with the country's image of herself and her allies in the 1940s. For instance, democratic England was an acceptable ally when America entered World War II, whereas communist Russia was not. The Office of War Information, a U.S. government agency concerned with positive propaganda, had used its influence in Hollywood during the early World War II period to have films made which gave a positive view of America and her allies. A number of films were made to show Russia in harmony with our war objectives and worthy of the trust of the United States. The Truman Committee began an investigation of OWI's excessive expenditures, and in 1943 the OWI lost its political clout through a Congressional withdrawal of funding; therefore, there was no government process to censor or alter *Lifeboat* in 1944.

In *Notorious*, Hitchcock defends American democracy on an international level. The film concerns American agents who stop Nazi refugees from developing nuclear weapons in Brazil which would then be used against the United States. It also reemphasizes the need to maintain peace through vigilant intelligence in Europe. Hitchcock's message is a direct antithesis to the pre-World War II foreign policy of isolationism. Had he placed the Nazi subterfuge in the United States, the American and international audience may have wondered about the breadth of his political concerns. By locating Nazis working on an atomic bomb in South America and by mentioning future espionage in continental Europe, Hitchcock directly repudiates the isolationist policy previously adopted by the United States and warns that another such policy is untenable in the atomic age.

Notorious presents the United States as a responsible nation that safeguards and preserves democratic ideology at home and abroad through active vigilance and necessary action against her enemies. The United States, through her involvement in Europe, possession of the atomic bomb, and great industrial production power, had a solid foundation for a foreign policy of internationalism. Hitchcock's *Notorious* was in harmony with this new political position of American responsibility to police the world. Furthermore, the use of American security agents with the cooperation of a foreign government, Brazil, to stop the proliferation of nuclear weapons foreshadows the anxiety of the atomic age and the disarmament conferences between nations to attempt to control these weapons of instant holocaust. In this regard, Hitchcock was current and even prophetic regarding the United States foreign policy of internationalism to protect democracy.

Hitchcock's politically-oriented films of the World War II era supported and advanced democratic ideology for the United States and for the world. *Foreign Correspondent* asked the U.S. to arm herself and join the fight with the Allied Powers against Nazi Germany. This eventually occurred. *Saboteur* warned

American citizens of Nazi ideological infiltration and acts of sabotage in their country. The film also promised the world that liberty and freedom would prevail, sponsored by American democracy, and that Nazi Germany would fall. Again the United States made good the promise. *Lifeboat* showed the need for the Allied Powers to avoid wasting time and energy in a cul de sac of dissension and to unite in defeating their common enemy, Nazi Germany. This country and her Allies finally managed to unite in a winning effort against the enemy, as the symbolic Allied characters did in *Lifeboat*. *Notorious* is an example of America's efforts to protect democracy abroad. The United States in 1946 was a leading world power. The monitoring of foreign political events affecting her democratic sovereignty was therefore a necessity. Hitchcock's *Foreign Correspondent*, *Saboteur*, *Lifeboat*, and *Notorious* are representational records of history. However, when these films were released they were vanguards for American democratic ideology, which was extended and defended beyond our borders through a foreign policy in rapid transition from isolationism and interventionism to internationalism in the turbulent years of World War II and its aftermath.

Finally, I would like to refer to the third question raised in the preface, namely how Hitchcock created and resolved suspense in his political films. In each film we have examined suspense elements that have paralleled some aspect of the real political suspense in the world during the 1940s. Hitchcock's major theme and personal concern in these films was the suspense involving the preservation of world freedom.

Foreign Correspondent's suspense is created through the adventures of a newspaper reporter who struggles to uncover Nazi subterfuge in the kidnapping of a European diplomat. The audience wonders if Huntley Haverstock will survive the treachery of his Nazi antagonists in order to learn the real story and have it printed. The resolution occurs when Haverstock manages to communicate his story to his newspaper.

Hitchcock was experiencing great suspense in his life at the beginning of World War II as the sovereignty and democracy of England were in great peril. The radio broadcast plea by Huntley Haverstock to the United States at the end of the film leaves the resolution of Hitchcock's personal suspense to American economic and military support of Britain and her allies. Haverstock's plea, "America, hang onto your lights. They're the only lights in the world," could be reworded as Hitchcock's plea, "hold onto your freedom, America. It is the only freedom in the world." Hitchcock wants the United States to recognize that world freedom is under siege and that the resolution of the anxiety over freedom demands a foreign policy of defensive and aggressive internationalism including war against the tyranny of Nazi Germany.

Saboteur manifests the political anxiety Hitchcock was experiencing at the time. Fifth-column conflicts in the plot of *Saboteur* were realities in the political fabric of America, and Hitchcock had seen such tactics lead to the downfall of

European nations. The film focuses on the suspense generated by the apathy and lack of allegiance to democracy among the American people at the onset of World War II. Barry Kane and Patricia Martin, the protagonists, fight against police, Nazi saboteurs, and treasonous wealthy Americans who have embraced Nazi ideology. The audience experiences suspense in their desire for the protagonists to stop the hydra-headed antagonist. The resolution is partially realized when Frank Fry, a Nazi saboteur, falls to his death in the final sequence of the film. However, Charles Tobin and Mrs. Van Sutton, two film characters who support Nazi ideology and sabotage, are never arrested. This leaves the thinking audience politically uneasy and reminds them of the parallel problems of treasonous activity of both American citizens and aliens in the United States. Through this incomplete resolution, Hitchcock shifts the responsibility of resolution from the film to the lives of his audience. He is telling them this situation is a reality in their political environment and that they must replace apathy with political action and vigilance in order to survive.

Lifeboat continues the problems explored in *Saboteur*, with this major difference: *Saboteur* examined the internal problems threatening American democracy, and *Lifeboat* exposes the international ideological problems among the Allied Powers which were then frustrating the main objective of defeating Nazi Germany. The main suspense in *Lifeboat* comes through the increasing fear that the Nazi will reach the German supply ship. Two climaxes in the film answer justice and terminate suspense, namely the execution of Willi and the sinking of the supply ship.

The film realistically addresses the Allied audience's fear of losing world freedom. Hitchcock suggests that nations espousing democracy will prevail if they put aside their national and international ideological conflicts. Moreover, they must not underestimate the military strength and ideological dedication of the Nazi Germans. Such a blunt message did not endear Hitchcock to certain critics. But *Lifeboat* is more than a feature film; it is a representational record of history and ideology made by a filmmaker who would not compromise his political vision of the real problems that the Allies would have to resolve to win World War II.

The suspense in *Notorious* is centered on two FBI agents, Devlin and Alicia, who travel to Rio de Janeiro in 1946 to police the activities of Nazi spies and scientists—a refugee remnant of Hitler's Third Reich. The mission places their intertwined professional and romantic lives in peril from the moment Alicia agrees to accept the assignment. Machinations of murderous Nazis and the eventual disclosure of their atomic bomb research are plot complications which increase suspense for the audience through their identification with the protagonists and foreknowledge of the ultimate weapon of World War II: the atomic bomb.

Notorious represents the suspense resulting from the United States' commitment to an international foreign policy following World War II. The atomic age of anxiety resulted from the Allied Powers' development and use of the atomic bomb to end the war. A major fear among Americans was that another country might develop a similar weapon. Hitchcock simply coupled the new international tension related to the atomic bomb with the old fear of the Nazis.

Hitchcock's democratic ideology is historically recorded in *Foreign Correspondent*, *Saboteur*, *Lifeboat*, and *Notorious*, which are film documents of world politics and history. The continuous political spine of suspense in these films is whether freedom, sponsored by democracy, will prevail in the United States and the world. Although Hitchcock, as activist, experienced the anxiety of America's vicissitudes of isolationism and ideological conflict during the World War II era, he never lost faith in this country's democratic objective to help purge the world of Nazi tyranny through supporting the war effort and post-war internationalism to reestablish and maintain world peace and freedom.

Notes

Chapter 1

1. John Russell Taylor, *Hitch: The Life and Work of Alfred Hitchcock* (Boston: Faber and Faber Limited, 1978), p. 2.

2. Ibid., p. 31.

3. Richard Schickel, *The Men Who Made the Movies* (New York: Atheneum, 1975), p. 275.

4. Robert A. Harris and Michael S. Lasky, *The Films of Alfred Hitchcock* (Secaucus, N.J.: The Citadel Press, 1977), p. 5.

5. François Truffaut, *Hitchcock* (New York: Simon and Schuster, 1967), p. 90.

6. Ibid., pp. 17–18.

7. Ibid., p. 18.

8. Ibid.

9. Taylor, *Hitch*, p. 35.

10. Ibid., p. 33.

11. Ibid., p. 34.

12. Ibid., pp. 35–36.

13. Truffaut, *Hitchcock*, p. 90.

14. Harris and Lasky, *Films of Alfred Hitchcock*, p. 6.

15. Donald Spoto, *The Art of Alfred Hitchcock* (New York: Hopkinson and Blake, n.d.), p. 3.

16. Taylor, *Hitch*, pp. 46–47.

17. Ibid., pp. 56–57.

18. Truffaut, *Hitchcock*, p. 21.

19. Taylor, *Hitch*, p. 61.

20. Ibid., pp. 63–64.

21. Truffaut, *Hitchcock*, p. 26.

22. Taylor, *Hitch*, p. 68.

23. Truffaut, *Hitchcock*, p. 31.

24. Taylor, *Hitch*, pp. 71–72.

25. Maurice Yacowar, *Hitchcock's British Films* (Hamden, Connecticut: Archon Books, 1977), p. 31.

26. Taylor, *Hitch*, p. 78.

27. Ibid., p. 40.

28. Gavin Lambert, "Hitchcock and the Art of Suspense," *American Film* 4 (January–February 1976), p. 18.

29. Peter Bogdanovich, *The Cinema of Alfred Hitchcock* (New York: The Museum of Modern Art, 1963), p. 4.

30. Truffaut, *Hitchcock*, p. 31.

31. Ibid., pp. 31–32.

32. Fort Gerard Buckle, *The Mind and the Film* (New York: Arno Press and the New York Times, 1970), p. xiv.

33. Bob Thomas, *Directors in Action* (New York: Bobbs-Merrill, 1973), p. 28.

34. Bogdanovich, *Cinema of Alfred Hitchcock*, p. 4.

35. Kenneth W. Leish, *Cinema* (New York: Newsweek Books, 1974), p. 65.

36. Yacowar, *Hitchcock's British Films*, p. 288.

37. Ibid.

38. Truffaut, *Hitchcock*, p. 47.

39. Ibid.

40. Ibid.

41. Taylor, *Hitch*, p. 101.

42. Ibid., p. 102.

43. Lawrence Hammond, *Thriller Movies* (London: Octopus Books, 1974), p. 41.

44. Andrew Tudor, *Image and Influence: Studies in the Sociology of Film* (London: George Allen & Unwin, 1974), p. 114.

45. Wells Root, *Writing the Script* (New York: Holt, Rinehart and Winston, 1979), p. 52.

46. Ibid.

47. Ibid., p. 53.

48. Ibid.

49. Ibid., p. 54.

50. Ian Cameron, ed., "Suspense and Meaning," *Movie Reader* (New York: Praeger Publishers, 1972), p. 30.

51. Pete Martin, "Alfred Hitchcock: Pete Martin Calls on Hitchcock," *Film Makers on Film Making*, ed. Harry M. Geduld (Bloomington: Indiana University Press, 1967), p. 129.

52. Root, *Writing Script*, p. 56.

53. William S. Pechter, *Twenty-four Times a Second* (New York: Harper & Row, 1971), p. 181.

54. Charles Thomas Samuels, *Encountering Directors* (New York: G.P. Putnam's Sons, 1972), p. 233.

55. Gordon Gow, *Suspense in the Cinema* (London: A. Zwemmer, 1968), p. 25.

56. Ibid., p. 58.

57. Ibid., p. 73.

58. Taylor, *Hitch*, pp. 123–124.

59. Charles Bennett and Alma Reville, *The Thirty-nine Steps*, Production: Michael Balcon, Gaumont British, 1935 (film soundtrack).

60. Ibid.

61. Yacowar, *Hitchcock's British Films*, p. 182.

62. *Steps*, film soundtrack.

63. Ibid.

64. Taylor, *Hitch*, p. 131.

65. Harris and Lasky, *Films of Alfred Hitchcock*, p. 68.

66. Sydney Gilliatt, Frank Laundner, and Alma Reville, *The Lady Vanishes*, Production: Edward Black, Gainsborough Pictures, 1938 (film soundtrack).

67. Ibid.

68. Ibid.

69. Yacowar, *Hitchcock's British Films*, p. 244.

70. *Lady*, film soundtrack.

71. Leif Furhammar and Folke Isaksson, *Politics and Film*, trans. Kersti French (New York: Praeger Publishers, 1971), p. 139.

72. Truffaut, *Hitchcock*, pp. 60–61.

73. Yacowar, *Hitchcock's British Films*, p. 182.

74. Spoto, *Art*, pp. 40–41.

75. Ibid., p. 53.

76. Roger Manvell, *Films and the Second World War* (New York: A.S. Barnes and Company, 1974), p. 13.

77. Spoto, *Art*, p. 55.

78. Yacowar, *Hitchcock's British Films*, p. 244.

79. Ibid., p. 247.

80. Ibid.

81. Colin Cross, *Adolf Hitler* (London: Hodder and Stoughton, 1973), pp. 272–273.

82. Miss Davis, head of the library at the British Film Institute in August, 1979, when asked what the general political feeling was like in London when British Prime Minister Neville Chamberlain was negotiating with Hitler at the Munich conference, said it was like a dark cloud over London. The people of Britain were full of fear that they would get into a war with Nazi Germany without adequate armaments and munitions.

83. Cross, *Hitler*, p. 273.

84. Irving Thalberg, "The Modern Photoplay [1929]," *Film and Society*, ed. Richard Dyer MacCann (New York: Charles Scribner's Sons, 1964), p. 45.

85. Furhammar and Isaksson, *Politics and Film*, p. 139.

86. Arthur Jacobs, "Foreign Policy and Cinema," *Sight & Sound* 15, p. 102.

87. Taylor, *Hitch*, pp. 126–127.

88. Ibid., p. 127.

89. Alfred Hitchcock, "'Stodgy' British Pictures," *Film Weekly*, British Film Institute, Slide 1, Column 2, p. 14.

90. Truffaut, *Hitchcock*, p. 71.

91. Hitchcock, "'Stodgy' British Pictures," p. 14.

92. Ibid.

93. Ibid.

94. Truffaut, *Hitchcock*, p. 59.

95. Taylor, *Hitch*, p. 130.

96. Alfred Hitchcock, "Directing," *Focus on Hitchcock*, ed. Albert LaValley (Englewood Cliffs, N.J.: Prentice-Hall, 1972), p. 39.

97. Siegfried Kracauer, *From Caligari to Hitler* (Princeton: Princeton University Press, 1947), p. 134.

98. Ibid., p. 135.

99. Charles Higham and Joel Greenberg, *The Celluloid Muse: Hollywood Directors Speak* (London: Angus & Robertson, 1969), pp. 86–87.

100. Alfred Hitchcock, *The Times*, 23 June 1969, British Film Institute microfiche.

101. Rudy Behlmer, ed., *Memo from David O. Selznick* (New York: The Viking Press, 1972), pp. 257–258.

102. Ibid., p. 276.

103. Ibid., pp. 277–278.

104. Ibid., p. 278.

105. Taylor, *Hitch*, p. 157.

106. Ibid., p. 158.

107. Ibid.

108. Huw Wheldon, "Alfred Hitchcock on His Films," *The Listener* (August 6, 1964), p. 190.

109. Philip Dynia, "Alfred Hitchcock and the Ghost of Thomas Hobbes," *Cinema Journal* 15, no. 2 (Spring 1976), p. 28.

110. James Monaco, "The Cinema and Its Double: Alfred Hitchcock," *The Canadian Film Magazine*, p. 8.

111. Taylor, *Hitch*, p. 19.

112. Monaco, "The Cinema and Its Double," p. 8.

Chapter 2

1. Truffaut, *Hitchcock*, p. 248.

2. Charles Bennett et al., *Foreign Correspondent*, Production: Walter Wanger, United Artists, 1940 (film soundtrack).

3. Ibid.

4. Curt Riess, *Total Espionage* (New York: G.P. Putnam's Sons, 1941), p. 15.

5. *Foreign*, film soundtrack.

6. Ibid.

7. Ibid.

8. Leroy N. Rieselbach, *The Roots of Isolationism* (New York: Bobbs-Merrill, 1966), p. 9.

9. Thomas Jefferson, *Democracy* (New York: Greenwood Press, 1939), p. 204.

10. Dexter Perkins, *A History of the Monroe Doctrine* (Boston: Little, Brown and Company, 1963), p. 391.

11. Manfred Jonas, *Isolationism in America, 1935–1941* (New York: Cornell University Press, 1966), p. 12.

12. Ibid., p. 20.

13. Carleton Allen, *Democracy and the Individual* (New York: Books for Libraries Press, 1972), pp. 35–36.

14. Rita James Simon, *Public Opinion in America: 1936–1970* (Chicago: Rand McNally College Publishing Company, 1974), p. 125.

15. Ibid.

16. Harris and Lasky, *Films of Alfred Hitchcock*, p. 98.

17. *Foreign*, film soundtrack.

18. Ibid.

19. Ibid.

20. Walter Johnson, *The Battle Against Isolation* (Chicago: University of Chicago Press, 1944), p. 30.

21. *Foreign*, film soundtrack.

22. Spoto, *Art*, pp. 106–107.

23. *Foreign*, film soundtrack.

24. Ibid.

25. Ibid.

26. Martin, "Pete Martin Calls on Hitchcock," p. 131.

27. *Foreign*, film soundtrack.

28. Ibid.

29. Ibid.

30. Gordon Gow, *Suspense in the Cinema*, p. 25.

31. Hitchcock, "Directing," p. 35.

32. *Foreign*, film soundtrack.

33. Raymond E. Murphy, Francis B. Stevens, Howard Thuers and Joseph M. Roland, *National Socialism* (Washington: United States Printing Office, 1943), p. III. The book was "prepared by competent officials of the Department of State from studies of German official records. . . . and confidential reports and information obtained by representatives of the Department of State . . . " over a period of several years. "Source material has been carefully analyzed, and only that known to be reliable and accurate has been used."

34. Ibid., p. 132.

35. Ibid., p. 133.

36. Ibid., p. 136.

37. Ibid., p. 133.

38. *Foreign*, film soundtrack.

39. Ibid.

40. George R. Poage, "The Age of the Aryan: A Study of Political Religion" (Ph.D. dissertation, State University of Iowa, 1954), p. 55.

41. Edward G. McGrath, *Is American Democracy Exportable?* (Beverly Hills: The Glencoe Press, 1968), p. 9.

42. *Foreign*, film soundtrack.

43. Ibid.

44. Ibid.

45. Johnson, *Battle Against Isolation*, p. 14.

46. Julius W. Pratt, *A History of the United States Foreign Policy*, 2nd ed. (Englewood Cliffs, N.J.: Prentice-Hall, Inc., 1965), pp. 390–391.

47. Ibid., p. 390.

48. Margaret Thorp, *America at the Movies* (New Haven: Yale University Press, 1939), pp. 274–276.

49. Ibid., p. 273.

50. *Foreign*, film soundtrack.

51. Ernst Nolte, *Three Faces of Fascism* (New York: The New American Library, 1965), p. 441.

52. Ibid., p. 443.

53. Marquess of Lothian, "Text of Address of the Marquess of Lothian, December 11, 1940," *International Conciliation: Documents for the Year 1941* (New York: Carnegie Endowment for International Peace, 1941), p. 16.

54. Ibid., p. 18.

55. *Foreign*, film soundtrack.

56. Joe Morella, Edward Z. Epstein, and John Griggs, *The Films of World War II* (Secaucus, N.J.: The Citadel Press, 1973), p. 37.

57. Chester E. Eisinger, ed., *The 1940s: Profile of a Nation in Crisis* (New York: Doubleday & Company, 1969), p. 4.

58. Manvell, *Films and Second World War*, p. 35.

59. Gerald Pratley, "Alfred Hitchcock's Working Credo," *Films in Review* 3, no. 10 (Dec. 1952), p. 501.

60. Dynia, "Hitchcock and the Ghost," p. 32.

61. Morella, Epstein and Griggs, *The Films of World War II*, p. 38.

62. Ibid.

63. Ibid.

64. Leo Rosten, "Movies and Propaganda," in *Film and Society*, ed., Richard Dyer MacCann (New York: Charles Scribner's Sons, 1964), p. 79.

65. U.S. Congress, Senate, Committees on Interstate Commerce, *Propaganda in Motion Pictures*, Hearings before a Subcommittee of the Committee on Interstate Commerce on S. Res. 152, 77 Cong., 1st sess., 1942, p. 20.

66. Ken D. Jones and Arthur F. McClure, *Hollywood at War* (New Jersey: A. S. Barnes and Co., 1973), p. 16.

67. U.S. Congress, "Propaganda in Pictures," p. 25.

68. Ibid., p. 323.

69. Ibid., p. 20. (Wendell L. Wilkie)

70. Ibid., p. 21.

71. Ibid., p. 338. (Harry M. Warner)

72. Ibid., p. 339.

73. Ibid.

74. Ibid., p. 411. (Darryl F. Zanuck)

75. Taylor, *Hitch*, p. 183.

Chapter 3

1. Truffaut, *Hitchcock*, p. 248.

2. Taylor, *Hitch*, p. 178.

3. Peter Viertel, Joan Harrison and Dorothy Parker, *Saboteur*, Production: Frank Lloyd and Jack H. Skirball, Universal, 1942 (Unpublished film script courtesy of Bruce Berman, Universal Studios), Reel One, p. 3. (This and all subsequent script dialogue appearing in this book has been carefully compared with the soundtracks of the films themselves. Script dialogue which was not in the films' soundtracks has been deleted to give the present reading audience a similar experience with the movie audience of the 1940s.)

4. Ibid., p. 5.

5. *The Man Who Knew Too Much* (1934), *The Thirty-nine Steps* (1935), *Young and Innocent* (1937), and *North by Northwest* (1959).

6. Hans L. Trefousse, "Failure of German Intelligence in the United States, 1935–1945," *The Mississippi Valley Historical Review* XLII, no. 1 (June 1955), pp. 84–85.

7. Ladislas Farago, *War of Wits* (New York: Funk & Wagnalls, 1954), p. 239.

8. Ibid., pp. 243–244.

9. Ladislas Farago, *The Game of the Foxes* (New York: David McKay, 1971), p. 37.

10. Charles Wighton and Peis Gunter, *Hitler's Spies and Saboteurs* (New York: Henry Holt and Company, 1958), pp. 30–31.

11. Curt Riess, *Total Espionage* (New York: G. P. Putnam's Sons, 1941), p. 87.

12. Ibid., p. 122.

13. Farago, *Foxes*, pp. 315–316.

14. Ibid., p. 431.

15. Ibid., p. 432.

16. *Saboteur*, Reel Two, p. 7.

17. Ibid., p. 10.

18. Ibid., pp. 10–11.

19. Ibid., p. 11.

20. Ibid., Reel Three, p. 3.

21. Ibid., p. 4.

22. Truffaut, *Hitchcock*, p. 105.

23. *Saboteur*, Reel Three, p. 14.

24. Morella, Epstein and Griggs, *Films of World War II*, p. 68.

25. *Saboteur*, Reel Four, pp. 10–11.

26. Ibid., p. 23.

27. *Saboteur*, Reel Five, pp. 13–17.

28. Brigitte Granzow, *A Mirror of Nazism* (n.p., Victor Gollancz Ltd., 1964), pp. 231–232.

29. *Saboteur*, Reel Six, pp. 1–2.

30. Farago, *Foxes*, p. 433.

31. Wighton and Gunter, *Hitler's Spies*, p. 46.

32. Cabell Phillips, *The 1940s: Decade of Triumph and Trouble* (New York: MacMillan Publishing Co., Inc., 1975), p. 129.

33. Wighton and Gunter, *Hitler's Spies*, pp. 55–56.

34. Ibid.

35. *Saboteur*, Reel Seven, p. 7.

36. Richard A. Koenigsberg, *Hitler's Ideology* (New York: The Library of Social Science, 1975), p. 57.

37. Ibid., pp. 56–57.

38. Ibid. p. 57.

39. *Saboteur*, Reel Eight, pp. 8–11.

40. *Saboteur*, Reel Nine, pp. 5–7.

41. Morella, Epstein and Griggs, *Films of World War II*, p. 67.

42. Alton Frye, *Nazi Germany and the American Hemisphere* (New Haven: Yale University Press, 1967), p. 173.

43. Murphy, Stevens, Thuers and Roland, *National Socialism*, p. 10.

44. The story was an original by Hitchcock himself, for which the producers, Frank Lloyd and Jack Skirball, paid $70,000 on condition that he direct it himself. George Perry, *Hitchcock* (London: MacMillan London Limited, 1975), p. 58.

45. Wighton and Gunter, *Hitler's Spies*, p. 65.

46. Ibid., p. 132.

47. Ibid., p. 74.

48. Herbert A. Lightman, "The Subjective Camera," *The Movies as Medium*, ed. Lewis Jacobs (New York: Farrar, Straus & Giroux, 1970), p. 62.

49. *Saboteur*, Reel Ten, p. 7.

50. *Saboteur*, Reel Eleven, p. 6.

51. Bogdanovich, *The Cinema of Alfred Hitchcock*, p. 23.

52. Spoto, *Art*, pp. 126–127.

53. Schickel, *The Men Who Made the Movies*, p. 302.

54. British Film Institute Fiche, *Saboteur*, News Headline.

55. Ibid.

56. Andrew Tudor, *Image and Influence* (London: George Allen and Unwin, 1974), p. 166.

57. Z. A. B. Zeman, *Nazi Propaganda* (London: Oxford University Press, 1964), pp. 47–48.

58. Joseph Bornstein and Paul R. Milton, *Action Against the Enemy's Mind* (New York: Bobbs-Merrill, 1942), p. 21.

59. George R. Poage, ''Age of the Aryan: A Study of Political Religion'' (Ann Arbor: University Microfilms International, 1954), p. 172.

60. Phillips, *The 1940s*, pp. 133–134.

61. Charles Higham and Joel Greenberg, ''Alfred Hitchcock,'' *The Celluloid Muse: Hollywood Directors Speak* (London: Angus & Robertson, 1969), p. 90.

Chapter 4

1. Truffaut, *Hitchcock*, p. 249.

2. Ibid., p. 113.

3. Jo Swerling, *Lifeboat*, Production: Kenneth McGowan, Twentieth Century-Fox, 1944 (Unpublished Film Script courtesy of Jim Kottman, Twentieth Century-Fox), p. 1.

4. Cobbett Steinberg, *Reel Facts: The Movie Book of Records* (New York: Vintage Books, 1978), p. 131.

5. Harris and Lasky, *The Films of Alfred Hitchcock*, p. 120.

6. Higham and Greenberg, ''Alfred Hitchcock,'' p. 91.

7. Truffaut, *Hitchcock*, p. 113.

8. Nicholas Pronay, ''The Newsreel: The Illusion of Actuality,'' *The Historian and Film*, ed. Paul Smith (Cambridge: Cambridge University Press, 1976), p. 81.

9. *Lifeboat*, pp. 6–8.

10. Bogdanovich, *The Cinema of Alfred Hitchcock*, p. 25.

11. Norris McWhirter, editor, *Guinness Book of World Records* (New York: Sterling Publishing Co., 1980), pp. 394–395.

12. *Lifeboat*, p. 10.

13. Henry H. Adams, *1942: The Year That Doomed the Axis* (New York: David McKay Company, 1967), p. 474.

14. Anthony Cave Brown, *Bodyguard of Lies* (New York: Harper & Row, 1975), p. 254.

15. Ibid., p. 257.

16. *Lifeboat*, pp. 14–15.

17. *Lifeboat*, pp. 22–26.

18. *Lifeboat*, pp. 26–29.

19. Brown, *Bodyguard*, p. 387.

20. Sander A. Diamond, *The Nazi Movement in the United States (1924–1941)* (Ithaca, N.Y.: Cornell University Press, 1974), p. 250.

21. Peter Viereck, *Metapolitics: The Roots of the Nazi Mind* (New York: Capricorn Books, 1965), p. 288.

22. George L. Mosse, *Nazism: An Interview with Michael A. Ledeen* (New Brunswick, N.J.: Transaction Books, 1978), p. 37.

23. *Lifeboat*, p. 31.

24. Viereck, *Metapolitics*, p. 288.

25. Mosse, *Ledeen*, p. 37.

26. George R. Poage, "Age of the Aryan", pp. 212–212a.

27. Paul Sothe Holbo, *Isolationism and Interventionism, 1932–1941* (Chicago: Rand McNally & Company, 1967), pp. 57–58.

28. Zevedei Barbu, *Democracy and Dictatorship* (New York: Grove Press, 1956), p. 126.

29. *Lifeboat*, p. 45.

30. Julius W. Pratt, *A History of the United States Foreign Policy* (Englewood Cliffs, N.J.: Prentice-Hall, 1915, 2nd ed.), p. 415.

31. *Lifeboat*, pp. 52–53.

32. Pratt, *Foreign Policy*, p. 415.

33. Ibid.

34. *Lifeboat*, pp. 53–54.

35. David Culbert, "Our Awkward Ally: *Mission to Moscow* (1943)," *American History/ American Film: Interpreting the Hollywood Image*, eds. John E. O'Connor and Martin A. Jackson (New York: Frederick Ungar, 1979), p. 122.

36. Ibid.

37. Ibid.

38. Ibid., p. xviii.

39. Ibid., p. 134.

40. Ibid.

41. John Robert Bengston, *Nazi War Aims* (Rock Island, Ill.: Augustana College Library, 1962), p. 81.

42. Klaus Hildebrand, *The Foreign Policy of the Third Reich* (Berkeley: University of California Press, 1970), p. 135.

43. Bornstein and Milton, *Enemy's Mind*, p. 247.

44. Ibid., p. 248.

45. Anthony Cave Brown, *Bodyguard*, p. 15.

46. Ibid., pp. 20–21.

47. Ibid., pp. 5–6.

48. Ibid., p. 17.

49. Ibid., p. 18.

50. Ibid., p. 22.

51. Ibid., pp. 23–24.

52. *Lifeboat*, pp. 105–106.

53. James A. Gould and Willis H. Truitt, *Political Ideologies* (New York: MacMillan, 1973), p. 1.

54. *Lifeboat*, pp. 119–122.

55. Bornstein and Milton, *Enemy's Mind*, pp. 257–258.

56. *Lifeboat*, pp. 126–128.

57. John S. Gibson, *Ideology and World Affairs* (Boston: Houghton-Mifflin, 1967, rev. ed.), p. 22.

58. Robert E. Sherwood, *Roosevelt and Hopkins* (New York: Harper & Brothers, 1950), pp. 138–139.

59. *Lifeboat*, p. 136.

60. Ibid., pp. 136–139.

61. Brown, *Bodyguard*, pp. 258–259.

62. *Lifeboat*, pp. 145–146.

63. Manfred Jonas, ed., *American Foreign Relations in the Twentieth Century* (New York: Thomas Y. Crowell, 1967), p. 129.

64. *Lifeboat*, p. 151.

65. *Lifeboat*, pp. 160–162.

66. British Film Institute microfiche.

67. Eric Rohmer and Claude Chabrol, *Hitchcock: The First Forty-four Films* (New York: Frederick Ungar Publishing Co., 1979), p. 74.

68. Bosley Crowther, "*Lifeboat*, A Film Picturization of Shipwrecked Survivors, With Tallulah Bankhead, Opens at the Astor Theatre," *The New York Times Film Reviews,* Vol. 3 (New York: The New York Times and Arno Press, 1970), p. 1981.

69. David Lardner, *The New Yorker*, XIX, no. 51 (Feb. 5, 1944), p. 57.

70. Richard Winnington, "Lifeboat," *News Chronicle*, March 19, 1944. (British Film Institute Microfiche).

71. Harris and Lasky, *Films of Alfred Hitchcock*, p. 119.

72. Jon Tuska, "Alfred Hitchcock," *Close-up: The Hollywood Director*, eds. Jon Tuska, Vicki Piekarski, and David Wilson (Metuchen, New Jersey: Scarecrow Press, 1978), p. 395.

73. George Perry, *Hitchcock* (London: MacMillan London Limited, 1975), p. 82.

74. Tuska, *Hollywood Director*, p. 378.

75. Plato, *The Dialogues of Plato*, trans. B. Jowett, 3rd ed., vol. 3 (New York: Oxford University Press, 1892), p. 83.

Chapter 5

1. Truffaut, *Hitchcock*, p. 249.

2. Martin, "Pete Martin Calls on Hitchcock," p. 133.

3. Ibid.

4. Higham and Greenberg, "Alfred Hitchcock," p. 93.

5. Truffaut, *Hitchcock*, p. 121.

6. William L. Laurence, *Dawn Over Zero* (New York: Alfred A. Knopf, 1953), p. 182.

7. Schickel, *The Men Who Made the Movies*, pp. 288–289. [The macguffin is the thing that the spies are after, but the audience doesn't care. It could be the plans of a fort, the secret plans of an airplane engine. It's called a macguffin because, as the story goes, two men are in an English train and one says across to the other, "Excuse me, sir, what is that strange-looking package above your head?" "Oh, that's a macguffin." "What's that for?" "That's for trapping lions in the Scottish highland." "But there's no lions in the Scottish highlands." "Then that's no macguffin." And macguffin doesn't matter at all. You have to have it because the spies must be after something.]

8. Taylor, *Hitch*, p. 200.

9. Bosley Crowther, "*Notorious*, Hitchcock Thriller," *New York Times Film Reviews*, 1939–1948. Vol. 3. (New York: The New York Times and Arno Press, 1970), pp. 2132–2133.

10. Ben Hecht, *Notorious*, Production: Alfred Hitchcock, RKO Pictures, 1946 (Unpublished cutting continuity script courtesy of ABC Television and RKO Pictures, Inc.), p. 86.

11. Ibid., p. 3.

12. Ibid., p. 4.

13. Ibid., pp. 13–14.

14. Ibid., p. 16

15. Thomas Gallagher, *Assault in Norway: Sabotaging the Nazi Nuclear Bomb* (New York: Harcourt Brace Jovanovich, 1975), p. 3.

16. Ibid.

17. Ibid., p. 7.

18. Ibid., pp. 8–9.

19. *Notorious*, p. 18.

20. Ibid., p. 19.

21. Ibid., p. 21.

22. Ibid., p. 20.

23. Ibid., pp. 20–21.

24. Alton Frye, *Nazi Germany and the American Hemisphere* (New Haven: Yale University Press, 1967), p. 67.

25. Thomas C. Sorensen, *The World War* (New York: Harper & Row, 1968), p. 9.

26. Ladislas Farago, *Burn After Reading* (New York: Walker and Co., 1961), p. 202.

27. "Holocaust Victims Still Remembered," *Provo Herald*, 19 October 1981, p. 8.

28. *Notorious*, pp. 24–25.

29. Ibid., p. 26.

30. Gallagher, *Assault*, p. 57.

31. Laurence, *Dawn Over Zero*, p. 78.

32. Gallagher, *Assault*, p. 58.

33. Ibid., pp. 60–61.

34. Stephane Groueff, *Manhattan Project* (Boston: Little, Brown and Company, 1967), p. 89.

35. Robin Wood, *Hitchcock's Films* (New York: A. S. Barnes and Co., 1977), p. 22.

36. Phillips, *The 1940s*, p. 123.

37. Brown, *Bodyguard*, p. 371.

38. Ibid., p. 372.

39. *Notorious*, p. 33.

40. Ibid., p. 34.

41. Samuels, *Encountering Directors,* p. 233.

42. *Notorious*, p. 35.

43. Ibid., p. 36.

44. Murphy, Stevens, Thuers and Roland, *National Socialism*, p. 50.

45. *Notorious*, p. 37.

46. Ibid., pp. 39–40.

47. Ibid., p. 18.

48. Ibid., p. 41.

49. Ibid., p. 43.

50. Ibid., p. 41.

51. Brown, *Bodyguard*, p. 373.

52. Ibid., p. 375.

53. *Notorious*, p. 45.

54. Kimball Young, "What is to be Learned from this Survey?", *German Psychological Warfare*, ed. Ladislas Farago (New York: G. P. Putnam's Sons, 1942), pp. xvi–xvii.

55. Frye, *Hemisphere*, p. 173.

56. *Notorious*, p. 52.

57. Ibid., p. 53.

58. Ibid., p. 56.

59. Ibid., p. 59.

60. Ibid., p. 60.

61. Brown, *Bodyguard*, p. 376.

62. Ibid.

63. *Notorious*, p. 65.

64. Sam P. Simone, "Oral History: Rolland Perry" (Provo, Department of Archives and Manuscripts at Brigham Young University, 1981), p. 22.

65. *Notorious*, p. 71.

66. Ibid., p. 79.

67. Ibid., pp. 81–86.

68. Leslie R. Groves, *Now It Can Be Told* (New York: Harper & Row, 1962), p. 360.

69. Groueff, *Manhattan*, p. 348.

70. Groves, *Told*, p. 322.

71. Ibid.

72. Laurence, *Zero*, p. 221.

73. Simone, *Perry*, p. 25.

74. Crowther, "*Notorious*, Hitchcock Thriller," pp. 2132–2133.

75. James Agee, "Notorious," in *Focus in Hotchcock*, ed. Albert LaValley (Englewood Cliffs, N.J.: Prentice-Hall, 1972), pp. 98–99.

76. Harris and Lasky, *Films of Alfred Hitchcock*, p. 129.

77. Robin Wood, *Hitchcock's Films* (New York: A. S. Barnes and Co., 1977), pp. 46–47.

78. Spoto, *Art*, p. 161.

79. Robert Sklar, *Movie-Made America* (New York: Random House, 1975), p. 279.

Chapter 6

1. Zeman, *Nazi Propaganda*, p. 69.

2. Murphy, Stevens, Thuers and Roland, *National Socialism*, p. 64.

3. Bengston, *Nazi War Aims*, p. 20.

Bibliography

Books

Adams, Henry H. *1942: The Year That Doomed the Axis*. New York: David McKay Company, 1967.

Agee, James. "Notorious." In *Focus on Hitchcock*. Edited by Albert LaValley. Englewood Cliffs, New Jersey: Prentice-Hall, Inc., 1972.

Allen, Carleton Kemp. *Democracy and the Individual*. New York: Books for Libraries Press, 1972.

Barbu, Zevedei. *Democracy and Dictatorship*. New York: Grove Press, 1956.

Behlmer, Rudy, ed. *Memo from David O. Selznick*. New York: The Viking Press, 1972.

Bengston, John Robert. *Nazi War Aims*. Rock Island, Illinois: Augustana College Library, 1962.

Bogdanovich, Peter. *The Cinema of Alfred Hitchcock*. New York: The Museum of Modern Art, 1963.

Bornstein, Joseph, and Paul R. Milton. *Action Against the Enemy's Mind*. New York: Bobbs-Merrill, 1942.

Brown, Anthony Cave. *Bodyguard of Lies*. New York: Harper & Row, 1975.

Buckle, Fort Gerard. *The Mind and the Film*. New York: Arno Press & The New York Times, 1970.

Cameron, Ian. "Suspense and Meaning." In *Movie Reader*, edited by Ian Cameron. New York: Praeger Publishers, 1972.

Cross, Colin. *Adolf Hitler*. London: Hodder and Stoughton, 1973.

Crowther, Bosley. "*Notorious*, Hitchcock Thriller." *New York Times Film Reviews, 1939–1948*, Vol. 3. New York: The New York Times and Arno Press, 1970.

_____. "Lifeboat." *The New York Times Film Reviews, 1939–1948*, Vol. 3. New York: The New York Times and Arno Press, 1970.

Culbert, David. "Our Awkward Ally: *Mission to Moscow* (1943)." In *American History/American Film: Interpreting the Hollywood Image*, edited by John E. O'Connor and Martin A. Jackson. New York: Frederick Ungar Publishing Co., 1979.

Diamond, Sander A. *The Nazi Movement in the United States, 1924–1941*. Ithaca, N.Y.: Cornell University Press, 1974.

Dynia, Philip. "Alfred Hitchcock and the Ghost of Thomas Hobbes." *Cinema Journal* 15, no. 2 (Spring 1976), pp. 27–41.

Eisinger, Chester E., ed. *The 1940s: Profile of a Nation in Crisis*. New York: Doubleday & Company, 1969.

Farago, Ladislas. *Burn After Reading*. New York: Walker and Co., 1961.

_____. *The Game of the Foxes*. New York: David McKay Company, 1971.

_____. *War of Wits*. New York: Funk & Wagnalls Company, 1954

Frye, Alton. *Nazi Germany and the American Hemisphere*. New Haven: Yale University Press, 1967.

Furhammar, Leif, and Folke Isaksson. *Politics and Film*. Translated by Kersti French. New York: Praeger Publishers, 1971.

Gallagher, Thomas. *Assault in Norway: Sabotaging the Nazi Nuclear Bomb*. New York: Harcourt Brace Jovanovich, 1975.

Gibson, John S. *Ideology and World Affairs*. Revised edition. Boston: Houghton-Mifflin Company, 1967.

Gould, James A., and Willis H. Truitt. *Political Ideologies*. New York: The MacMillan Company, 1973.

Gow, Gordon. *Suspense in the Cinema*. London: A. Swemmer, 1968.

Granzow, Brigitte. *A Mirror of Nazism*. Victor Gollancz, 1964. n.p.

Groueff, Stephane. *Manhattan Project*. Boston: Little, Brown and Company, 1967.

Groves, Leslie R. *Now It Can Be Told*. New York: Harper & Row, 1962.

Hammond, Lawrence. *Thriller Movies*. London: Octopus Books Limited, 1974.

Harris, Robert A., and Michael S. Lasky. *The Films of Alfred Hitchcock*. Secaucus, N.J.: The Citadel Press, 1977.

Higham, Charles, and Joel Greenberg. "Alfred Hitchcock." In *The Celluloid Muse: Hollywood Directors Speak*. London: Angus & Robertson, 1969.

Hitchcock, Alfred. "Directing." In *Focus on Hitchcock*. Edited by Albert J. LaValley. Englewood Cliffs, New Jersey: Prentice-Hall, 1972.

Hildebrand, Klaus. *The Foreign Policy of the Third Reich*. Translated by Anthony Fothergill. Berkeley and Los Angeles: University of California Press, 1970.

Holbo, Paul Sothe. *Isolationism and Interventionism, 1937–1941*. Chicago: Rand McNally and Company, 1967.

Jefferson, Thomas. *Democracy*. Selected and arranged with an introduction by Saul K. Padover. New York: Greenwood Press Publishers, 1939.

Johnson, Walter. *The Battle Against Isolation*. Chicago: University of Chicago Press, 1944.

Jonas, Manfred, ed. "President Franklin D. Roosevelt Aligns America with Britain." In *American Foreign Relations in the Twentieth Century*. New York: Thomas J. Crowell Company, 1967.

————. *Isolationism in America, 1935–1941*. New York: Cornell University Press, 1966.

Jones, Ken D., and Arthur F. McClure. *Hollywood at War*. New Jersey: A. S. Barnes and Co., 1973.

Koenigsberg, Richard A. *Hitler's Ideology*. New York: The Library of Social Science, 1975.

Kracauer, Siegfried. *From Caligari to Hitler*. Princeton: Princeton University Press, 1947.

Laurence, William L. *Dawn Over Zero*. New York: Alfred A. Knopf, 1953.

Leish, Kenneth W. *Cinema*. New York: Newsweek Books, 1974.

Lightman, Herbert A. "The Subjective Camera." In *The Movies as Medium*. Edited by Lewis Jacobs. New York: Farrar, Straus & Giroux, 1970.

McGrath, Edward G. *Is American Democracy Exportable?* Beverley Hills: The Glencoe Press, 1968.

McWhirter, Norris, ed. *Guinness Book of World Records*. New York: Sterling Publishing Co., 1980.

Manvell, Roger. *Films and the Second World War*. New York: A. S. Barnes and Company, 1974.

Marquess of Lothian. "Text of Address of the Marquess of Lothian, December 11, 1940." In *International Conciliation: Documents for the Year 1941*. New York: Carnegie Endowment of Intercourse and Education, no date given.

Martin, Pete. "Alfred Hitchcock: Pete Martin Calls on Hitchcock." In *Film Makers on Film Making*. Edited by Harry M. Geduld. Bloomington & London: Indiana University Press, 1967.

Morella, Joe, Edward Z. Epstein and John Griggs. *The Films of World War II*. Foreword by Judith Crist. Secaucus, N.J.: The Citadel Press, 1973.

Mosse, George L. *Nazism: An Interview with Michael A. Ledeen*. New Brunswick, N.J.: Transaction Books, 1978.

Murphy, Raymond E., Francis B. Stevens, Howard Thuers and Joseph M. Roland. *National Socialism*. Washington: United States Printing Office, 1943.

Nolte, Ernst. *Three Faces of Fascism*. Translated by Leila Vennewitz. New York: The New American Library, 1965.

Pechter, William S. *Twenty-four Times A Second*. New York: Harper & Row, 1971.

Perkins, Dexter. *A History of the Monroe Doctrine*. Boston: Little, Brown and Company, 1963.

Perry, George. *Hitchcock*. London: MacMillan London Limited, 1975.

Phillips, Cabell. *The 1940s: Decade of Triumph and Trouble*. New York: MacMillan Publishing Co., 1975.

Plato, *The Dialogues of Plato*, Translated by B. Jowett. 3rd ed., vol. 3. New York: Oxford University Press, 1892.

Poage, George R. "The Age of the Aryan: A Study of Political Religion." Ann Arbor: University Microfilms International, 1954.

Pratt, Julius W. *A History of the United States Foreign Policy*. 2nd ed. Englewood Cliffs, N.J.: Prentice-Hall, Inc., 1965.

Pronay, Nicholas. "The Newsreel: The Illusion of Actuality." In *The Historian and Film*. Edited by Paul Smith. Cambridge: Cambridge University Press, 1976.

Rieselbach, Leroy N. *The Roots of Isolationism*. New York: Bobbs-Merrill Company, 1966.

Riess, Curt. *Total Espionage*. New York: G. P. Putnam's Sons, 1941.

Rohmer, Eric, and Claude Chabrol. *Hitchcock: The First Forty-four Films*. Translated by Stanley Hochman. New York: Frederick Ungar Publishing Co., 1979.

Rosten, Leo. "Movies and Propaganda." In *Film and Society*. Edited by Richard Dyer MacCann. New York: Charles Scribner's Sons, 1964.

Root, Wells. *Writing the Script*. New York: Holt, Rinehart, and Winston, 1979.

Samuels, Charles Thomas. *Encountering Directors*. New York: G. P. Putnam's Sons, 1972.

Schickel, Richard. *The Men Who Made The Movies*. New York: Atheneum, 1975.

Sherwood, Robert E. *Roosevelt and Hopkins*. New York: Harper & Brothers, 1950.

Simon, Rita James. *Public Opinion in America: 1936–1970*. Chicago: Rand McNally College Publishing Company, 1974.

Simone, Sam P. "Oral History Interview: Dr. Rolland Perry." Brigham Young University, Provo, Utah, 1981.

Sklar, Robert. *Movie-Made America*. New York: Random House: 1975.

Sorensen, Thomas C. *The World War*. New York: Harper & Row, 1968.

Spoto, Donald. *The Art of Alfred Hitchcock*. New York: Hopkinson and Blake, 1941 [sic].

Steinberg, Cobbett. *Reel Facts: The Movie Book of Records*. New York: Vintage Books, 1978.

Taylor, John Russell. *Hitch: The Life and Work of Alfred Hitchcock*. Boston: Faber and Faber Limited, 1978.

Thalberg, Irving. "The Modern Photoplay (1929)." In *Film and Society*. Edited by Richard Dyer MacCann. New York: Charles Scribner's Sons, 1964.

Thomas, Bob. *Directors in Action*. New York: Bobbs-Merrill Company, 1973.

Thorp, Margaret. *America at the Movies*. New Haven: Yale University Press, 1939.

Truffaut, François. *Hitchcock*. New York: Simon and Schuster, 1967.

Tudor, Andrew. *Image and Influence: Studies in the Sociology of Film*. London: George Allen & Unwin, 1974.

Tuska, Jon. "Alfred Hitchcock." In *Close-up: The Hollywood Director*. Edited by Jon Tuska, Vicki Piekarski, and David Wilson. Metuchen, N.J.: The Scarecrow Press, 1978.

Congress, Senate, Committees on Interstate Commerce. *A Resolution Authorizing an Investigation of War Propaganda Disseminated by the Motion-Picture Industry and of any Monopoly in the Production, Distribution, or Exhibition of Motion Pictures*. 77th Congress, 1st Session, 1941.

Viereck, Peter. *Metapolitics: The Roots of the Nazi Mind*. New York: Capricorn Books, 1965.

Wighton, Charles and Peis Gunter. *Hitler's Spies and Saboteurs*. New York: Henry Holt and Company, 1958.

Wood, Robin. *Hitchcock's Films*. New York: A. S. Barnes and Co., 1977.

Yacowar, Maurice. *Hitchcock's British Films*. Hamden, Connecticut: Archon Books, 1977.

Young, Kimball. "What is to be Learned from this Survey?" In *German Psychological Warfare*. Edited by Ladislas Farago. New York: G. P. Putnam's Sons, 1942.

Zeman, Z. A. B. *Nazi Propaganda*. London: Oxford University Press, 1964.

Periodicals

BFI Microfiche. "Production Dates Show Magnitude of 'Saboteur.'" News headline.

Hitchcock, Alfred. *The Times*, 23–6–69. BFI Microfiche.

———. "'Stodgy' British Pictures," *Film Weekly*. BFI, Slide 1, Column 2, 14.

"Holocaust Victims Still Remembered." *Herald Entertainer, Provo Herald*, 19 October 1981.

Jacobs, Arthur. "Foreign Policy and Cinema." *Sight and Sound* 15, no. 59, 102–105.

Lambert, Gavin. "Hitchcock and the Art of Suspense." *American Film* 1, no. 4 (Jan–Feb 1976), 16–23.

Lardner, David. *The New Yorker* XIX, no. 51 (Feb 5, 1944), 57.

Monaco, James. "The Cinema and its Double: Alfred Hitchcock." *The Canadian Film Magazine* 5, no. 2, (1976), 6–8.

Pratley, Gerald. "Alfred Hitchcock's Working Credo." *Films in Review* 3, no. 10 (Dec. 1952), 500–503.

Trefousse, Hans L. "Failure of German Intelligence in the United States, 1935–1945." *The Mississippi Valley Historical Review* XCII, no. 1 (June 1955), 84–100.

Wheldon, Huw. "Alfred Hitchcock on His Films." *The Listener* (Aug. 6, 1964), 189–190 (BFI Slide 2, Column 3).

Winnington, Richard. "Lifeboat." *News Chronicle* (March 19, 1944) (British Film Institute).

Films

Bennett, Charles. *The Secret Agent*. Production: Michael Balcon and Ivor Montagu, Gaumont British, 1936.

———. *Sabotage*. Production: Michael Balcon and Ivor Montagu; Shepherd, Gaumont-British Pictures, 1936.

———, Joan Harrison, James Hilton and Robert Benchley. *Foreign Correspondent*. Production: Walter Wanger, United Artists (film soundtrack), 1940.

——— and Alma Reville. *The Thirty-nine Steps*. Production: Michael Balcon, Gaumont British (film soundtrack), 1935.

Gilliatt, Sydney, Frank Launder and Alma Reville. *The Lady Vanishes*. Production: Edward Black, Gainsborough Pictures (film soundtrack), 1938.

Hecht, Ben. *Notorious*. Production: Alfred Hitchcock, RKO Pictures (unpublished cutting continuity script courtesy of ABC Television and RKO Pictures, Inc.), 1946.

Hitchcock, Alfred and Eliot Stannard. *The Lodger*. Production: Michael Balcon, Gainsborough, 1926.

Hitchcock, Alfred. *The Farmer's Wife*. Production: John Maxwell, British International Pictures, 1928, G. B.

Hitchcock, Alfred, Benn W. Levy and Charles Bennett. *Blackmail*. Production: John Maxwell, British International Pictures, 1929, G. B.

Rawlinson, A.R., Charles Bennett, D. B. Wyndham Lewis, Edwin Greenwood. *The Man Who Knew Too Much*. Production: Michael Balcon, Gaumont British Pictures, Great Britain, 1934.

Reville, Alma and Guy Bolton, *Waltzes from Vienna*. Production: Gaumont British, by G.F.D., 1933.

Sherwood, Robert E. and Joan Harrison. *Rebecca*. Production: David O. Selznick, U.S.A., 1940.

Stannard, Eliot. *The Pleasure Garden*. Production: Michael Balcon (Gainsborough,) Eric Pommer (Emelka—G.B.A.), 1925.

———. *The Mountain Eagle*. Production: Michael Balcon, Gainsborough, Emelka, 1926.

Swerling, Jo. *Lifeboat*. Production: Kenneth MacGowan, Twentieth-Century Fox (unpublished film script courtesy of Jim Kottman, Twentieth-Century Fox), 1944.

Viertel, Peter, Joan Harrison and Dorothy Parker. *Saboteur*. Production: Frank Lloyd and Jack H. Skirball, Universal (unpublished film script courtesy of Bruce Berman, Universal Studios), 1942.

Index